DISCOURSES AND ESSAYS.

BY

WILLIAM G. T. SHEDD.

ANDOVER:
WARREN F. DRAPER,
MAIN STREET.
1870.

STEREOTYPED AND PRINTED BY
W. F. DRAPER, ANDOVER.

ADVERTISEMENT TO THE SECOND EDITION.

These Discourses and Essays were collected in a volume in 1856, and have met with an encouraging reception, considering the metaphysical character of most of them. On issuing a new edition, the author has availed himself of the opportunity to make some corrections, and to add an Essay upon the Doctrine of Atonement, which he has frequently been urged to republish. That the volume may contribute to the spread of just views in philosophy and theology, is the sincere desire of the writer.

Andover, March 27, 1861.

CONTENTS.

"There is one department of knowledge, which like an ample palace contains within itself mansions for every other knowledge; which deepens and extends the interest of every other, gives it new charms and additional purpose; the study of which, rightly and liberally pursued, is beyond any other entertaining, beyond all others tends at once to tranquillize and enliven, to keep the mind elevated and steadfast, the heart humble and tender: it is *biblical theology* — the philosophy of religion, and the religion of philosophy." — COLERIDGE.

THE METHOD, AND INFLUENCE, OF THEOLOGICAL STUDIES.

A DISCOURSE DELIVERED BEFORE THE LITERARY SOCIETIES OF THE UNIVERSITY OF VERMONT, AUGUST 5, 1845.

GENTLEMEN OF THE SOCIETIES:

THE subject to which I invite your attention is: *The method, and influence, of Theological Studies.*

Theology more than any other science, suffers from false views of its scope and contents. In the opinion of many, it is supposed to have little or no connection with other sciences, and to exert but a very small and unimportant influence upon other departments of human knowledge. Its contents are supposed to be summed up in the truths of *natural* theology. It is thought to be that isolated and lifeless science which looks merely at the *natural* attributes of God and man, and which consequently brings to view no higher relations, and no deeper knowledge, than those of mere nature. Of course, for such minds theology must be a very unimportant and simple science, treating merely of those superficial qualities which do not reach into the depths of God and man, and of those merely secondary and temporal relationships that rest upon them. Said a member of the Directory appointed by France during its Revolution to remodel Christianity, "I want a simple religion: one with a couple of doctrines." Theology, as understood by many, is the science of the French Director's religion.

But such is not the scope, or the character, of that "sacred and inspired divinity" which Lord Bacon asserts to be "the sabbath and port of men's labors and peregrinations." Nature; the natural attributes of God and man, and the natural laws and relations of creation; forms but a minor and insignificant part of its subject matter. This lower region of being is but the suburb. The metropolis and royal seat of theology is the *supernatural* world; a region full of *moral* being, sustaining most profound and solemn relations to reason and law.

Before proceeding, then, to speak of the true method of theological study, and of its great and noble influences, it will be needful to discuss more at large the real spirit and character of the science itself; and for this somewhat abstract discussion, I bespeak your forbearing and patient attention. It is needed in order to a clear apprehension of the enlarging and elevating influence of the science. Far am I from recommending to the educated man, the pursuit of those seemingly religious studies which never carry him out of the sphere of natural theology, and which cannot awaken enthusiasm of feeling or produce profundity of thought. I am pleading for those really theological studies, which by means of their *supernatural* element and character give nerve to the intellect and life to the heart.

Theology is the science of the supernatural. That we may obtain a clear knowledge of its essential character, let us for a moment consider the distinction between the natural and the supernatural.

That which makes these different from each other in kind, so that the line which divides them divides the universe into two distinct worlds, is this fact:—the natural has no *religious* element in it, while the supernatural is entirely composed of this element. There is and there can be in mere nature nothing religious. There is and there can be in that which is supernatural nothing that is not religious.* When we have said this, we have given the essential difference between the natural and supernatural.

The common notion that by the natural is meant the material and visible, and by the supernatural, the immaterial and invisible, is false. Nature may be as invisible and immaterial as is spirit. Who ever saw or ever will see the natural forces of gravitation, electricity, and magnetism? Who ever saw or ever will see that natural principle of life, of which all outward and material nature is but the manifestation? Back of this world of nature which we apprehend by the five senses, there is an invisible world which is nature still; which is not supernatural; neither the object of supernatural science nor of supernatural interests, because there is no moral element in it. When we have stripped the world of its materiality, and have dissolved all that is visible into unseen forces and vital laws, we have not reached any higher region than that of nature. We have not yet entered the supernatural and religious world. He who worships the vital principle or adores the force of gravity; nay, he who has no higher emotions than those of the natural religionist, which are called forth by the beauty

* Religion is from *religo:*—natural laws have no *religious*, or *binding* force, and in the sphere of nature there can be no such things as *duty*, *guilt*, or *praiseworthiness*.

and glory of visible nature, or by the cloudy and mystic awfulness of invisible nature, is as really an idolater, as is the most debased heathen who bows down before a visible and material idol. And that system of thought which never rises into the world of moral or supernatural reality, is as truly material (whatever may be its professions to the contrary), as is the most open and avowed materialism.

It seems like stating truisms to make such statements as these; and yet some of the most seductive and far-reaching errors in philosophy and theology have arisen from the non-recognition, or the denial, of any thing higher than invisible nature. Ideal Pantheism, a system received by minds of a really profound order, and which boasts of its spirituality, results from the error in question. Hence, although it admits of, and produces, a mystic adoration and a vague dreamy awe, it is utterly incompatible with really spiritual feeling and truly moral emotion.

But the reality, and nature, of the distinction between the natural and supernatural, is still more clearly seen by a contemplation of the Divine attributes; partly because at this point the distinction itself is more marked and plain, and partly because from this point the vital errors in theological and philosophical science take their start.

Although, at first sight, it may appear bold and irreverent, yet a thorough investigation will show that it results in the only true fear and adoration of God, to say that his natural attributes considered by themselves are of no importance at all for a moral being. Taken by themselves, they have no religious quality, and therefore, as such, cannot be the ground of theological science or religious feeling. Considered apart from his supernatural attributes, what meaning have the omnipresence, the omnipotence, and even the adaptive intelligence, of the Deity, for me as a religious being? Of what interest, is the possessor of these merely natural attributes, to me as a rational and moral being, until I know the *supernatural character and person* which reside in them, and make them the vehicle of their operations? I may see the exhibitions of Infinite Power in the heavens above me, and on the earth around me; I may detect the work of an Infinite Intelligence in this world of matchless design and order; but what are these isolated qualities to me as one who possesses *moral* reason and sustains *supernatural* relations? Let that Infinite Power thunder and flash through the skies, and let that Infinite Intelligence clothe the world in beauty and glory; these merely natural attributes are nothing to me, in a religious point of view, until I know *who* wields them, and what *supernatural* and *holy* attributes make them their bearer and agent. Then will I fear spiritually, and then will I adore morally.

This fundamental distinction between the natural and the supernatural is of vital importance to theological science. If not clearly seen and rigidly recognized in theology, this science comes to be nothing more than an investigation of the *natural* attributes of the Deity, and treats merely of those relations of man to the Creator, which the vilest reptile that crawls has in common with him. For if we set aside the supernatural attributes of God, man sustains only the same relations to him that the brute does. He, in common with the brutes that perish, is the creature of the Divine Power, and in common with them is sustained by the Divine Intelligence; that attribute which causes merely natural wants to be supplied by their correlative objects. The mere supervention of consciousness will make no difference between man and brute in relation to the Deity, unless consciousness bring with it the knowledge of his higher *supernatural* attributes. If we set aside his relations to the Wisdom, Holiness, Justice and Mercy of God, we find man on a level with brute existence in all respects. He comes into being, reaches his maturity, declines, and dies, as they do, by the operation of the natural attributes of the Creator manifesting themselves in natural laws, and this is all that can be said of him in reference to his Maker.

The more we contemplate the Divine Being, the more clearly do we see that his supernatural are his constituting attributes; the very Divinity of the Deity. If they are denied, the Creator is immediately confounded with the creature; for his natural attributes, without his moral ones, become the soul of the world, its blind, though unerring principle of life. Or if they are misapprehended, and the difference between the two classes is supposed to be only one of degree, and consequently that there is no essential distinction between nature and spirit, fatal errors will inevitably be the result. There will be no sharply and firmly drawn line between the natural and spiritual worlds, natural and spiritual laws, and natural and spiritual relationships. A mere naturalism must run through theology, philosophy, science, literature and art, depriving each and all of them of their noblest characteristics.

The reality and importance of this distinction between the natural and the supernatural, are to be seen in a less abstract and more interesting manner in the actual life of men. Man is by creation a religious being; and even in his religion we discover his proneness to deny or misapprehend the distinction in question. The religion of the natural man is strictly *natural* religion. It refers solely to the *natural* attributes of God. There is no man who is not pleasurably affected by the manifestation of the Power and intelligent Design of the Deity, as seen in the natural world; and all men who have not been taught experimentally, that there are higher attributes than these, and a higher religion than this, are content with such religion. "As is the earthy, such are they that are earthy." They are strictly natural men, and seek that in God which corresponds to their character. The spirit, or the supernatural part of man, has not yet been renewed and vivified by a supernatural influence, and therefore there is no search after the spiritual attributes of God. The moment that the *supernatural* dawns upon such men, and the *moral* attributes of God appear in their awful and solemn relations to law, guilt, and atonement, they are troubled; and unless mercifully prevented, descend into the low regions of nature, to escape from a light and a purity which they cannot endure.

It will be evident even from this brief discussion that the distinction between the natural and the supernatural is a valid and fundamental one; that the natural world is essentially different from the supernatural, and that theology, as the science of the supernatural, possesses a scope, contents, and influence, as vast and solemn as the field of its inquiry.

And think for a moment what this field is! It is not the earth we tread upon, nor the heavens that are bent over it, all beautiful and glorious as they are. It is not that unseen world of living forces and active laws which lies under the visible universe, giving it existence and causing its manifold motions and changes. This is indeed a deeply mysterious realm, and is a step nearer the Eternal than all that we see with the eye or touch with the hand is; but it is not the proper home of theological inquiry.

Above the kingdoms of visible and invisible nature, there is a world which is the residence of a personal God, with supernatural attributes, and the seat of spiritual ideas, laws, and relations. It is, to use the language of Plato, "that super-celestial place which no one of the poets has hitherto worthily sung, or ever will," where righteousness itself, true wisdom and knowledge, are to be seen in their very essence.* This is the proper field of theological inquiry, and as the mind ranges through it, it comes in sight of all that invests man's spirit with infinite responsibilities, and renders human existence one of awful interest.

But what is the proper method of theological studies? If what has been said relative to the two great kingdoms into which the universe is divided, be true, it is plain that theological studies must commence in that supernatural world whose realities form its subject matter, and that the true method is to descend from spirit to nature, in our investigations. The contrary process has been in vogue for the last century and a half, and the saying "from nature we ascend to nature's God," has come to be received as an axiom in theological science.

If this assertion means anything, it means that by a careful observation of all that we can apprehend by the five senses, in space, we shall obtain a correct and full knowledge of God. The *spirit* of the assertion is this: Nature is first in the order of investigation, because its teachings are more surely correct, and its proofs are

* Phædrus. Opera viii. p. 30. See the whole of the beautiful description of this *ὑπερουράνιος τόπος*: a passage vividly reminding of 1 Cor. ii.

more to be relied on, than those of the supernatural. Let us test it by rigidly applying it to the investigation of the being and character of God. What is there in nature which teaches, or proves, the existence of t· Holiness of God; or his Justice; or his Mercy? What is there in the world in which we live as beings of nature and sense, which necessarily compels us to assume the personality of God? It is true that we are taught by all that exists in "the mighty world of eye and ear," that there are power and adaptive intelligence *somewhere*, but whether they are seated in a self-conscious and personal being, or are only the eternal procession of a blind and unconscious life, we cannot know anything that nature teaches. You see a movement in the natural world: say the growth of a plant or the blowing of a flower. What does that natural movement teach (considered simply by itself, and with no reference to a higher knowledge from another source,) and what have you a right to infer from it? Simply this: that there is a *merely natural* power adequate to its production; but whether that power has any connection with the *moral character of a spiritual person*, you cannot know from anything you see in the natural phenomenon. Now extend this through infinite space, and will the closest examination of all the physical movements occurring in this vast domain, *taken by itself*, lead up to a personal and holy God? What is there in the law of gravity which has the least tendency to lead to the recognition of the law of holiness? Is there any similarity between the two in kind? What can the motions of the sun and stars, the unvarying return of the seasons, the birth, growth, and death, of animated existence, *taken by themselves*, teach regarding the supernatural attributes of God? Take away from man the knowledge of God which is contained in the human spirit and in the written word, and leave him to find his way up to a personal and spiritual Deity by the light of nature alone, and he will grope in eternal darkness, if for no other reason, because he cannot even get the idea of such a Being.

For the truth is, that between the two kingdoms of nature and spirit a great gulf is fixed, and the passage from one to the other is not by degrees, but by a leap; and this leap is not up, but down. There is one theory which assumes that the universe is but the development of one only substance; and if this is a correct theory, then it is true that we can "ascend from nature up to nature's God." For all is continuous development, with no chasm intervening, and the height may consequently be reached from the bottom by a patient ascent. There is another and the true theory, which rejects this doctrine of development, and substitutes in its place that of creation, whereby nature is not an emanation, but springs forth into existence for the first time, at the fiat of the Creator, who is now distinct from the work of his hands. Nature is now, in a certain sense, separate from God, and instead of being able to prove his moral existence, or to manifest his supernatural and constituting attributes, requires a previous knowledge of the Creator, from another source, in order to its own true apprehension.*

Now the true method of obtaining a correct knowledge of an object, is to follow the method of its origin, and therefore true theological science follows the footsteps of

* Whether the absolute is the *ground* or the *cause* is the question which has ever divided philosophers. That it is the *ground* but not the *cause* is the assertion of Naturalism; that it is the *cause* and not the *ground* is the assertion of Theism. Jacobi. Von den Gött. Dingen. Werke. iii. 404, together with the references.

God. It *starts* with the assumption of his existence, and the knowledge of his character derived from a higher source than that of mere nature, that it may find in the works of his hands the illustration of his already known attributes, and the manifestation of his already believed being. True theology descends from God to nature, and rectifies and interprets all that it finds in this complicated and perplexing domain, by what it knows of its Maker from other and higher sources.

Take away from the human spirit that knowledge of the moral attributes of God which it has from its constitution, and from revelation, and compel it to deduce the character of the Supreme Being from what it sees in the natural world, and will it not inevitably become skeptical? As the thoughtful heathen looked abroad over a world of pain and death, was he not forced resolutely to reject the natural inference to be drawn from this sight, and to cling with desperate faith to the dictum of a voice speaking from another quarter, saying: "see what thou mayest in nature apparently to the contrary, He *is* Just; He *is* Holy; He *is* Good."

This false method of theological study proceeds from a belief common to man, resulting partly from his corruption and partly from his present existence in a world of sense. It is the common belief of man that reality in the strictest sense of the term is to be predicated of material things, and in his ordinary thought and feeling, that which is spiritual is unreal. The solid earth which the "swain treads upon with his clouted shoon" has substantial existence, and its material objects are real, but if we watch the common human feeling regarding such objects as the soul and God, we detect (not necessarily a known and determined infidelity, but) an inability to make them as real and substantial as the sun in the heavens, or the earth under foot. Lord Bacon in describing the idols of the tribe; the false notions which are inherent in human nature; says, that "man's sense is falsely asserted to be the standard of things." * It is, however, under the influence of the notion that it is, that man goes to the investigation of truth, and especially of theological truth. Every thing is determined by a material standard, and established from the position of materialism. It is assumed that nature is more real than spirit; that its instructions and evidences are more to be relied on than those of spirit; and that from it, as from the only sure foothold for investigation, we are to make hurried and timid excursions into that dim undiscovered realm of the supernatural which is airy and unreal, and filled with airy and unreal objects.

This is a low and mean idol, and if the inquirer after spiritual truth bows down to it he shall never enter the holy of holies. Spirit is more real than matter, for God is a spirit. Supernatural laws and relations are more real than those of nature, for they shall exist when nature, even to its elements, shall be melted with fervent heat.

Why then should we, as did the pagan mythology, make earth and the earth-born Atlas support the old everlasting heavens? They are self-supported and embosom and illumine all things else. Why should we attempt to rest spiritual science upon natural science; the eternal upon the temporal; the absolute upon the empirical; the certain upon the uncertain? Is all that is invisible unreal, and must a thing become the object of the five senses, before we can be certain of its reality? Not to go out of the natural world; by what in this do-

* Novum Organum, Aph. 41.

main are we most vividly impressed with the conception of reality, and how is the notion of *power* awakened? Not by anything we see with the eye or touch with the hand, but by the knowledge of that *unseen* force and law which causes the motions of the heavens, and makes the "crystal spheres ring out their silver chimes." Not by an examination of the phenomena of the mineral, vegetable, and animal kingdoms, but by the idea of that one vast *invisible* life manifesting itself in them. Even here, upon a thoughtful reflection, that which is unseen shows itself to be the true reality. And to go up higher into the sphere of human existence: where is the substantial reality of man's being? In that path which, in the language of Job, "no fowl knoweth, and which the vulture's eye hath not seen." In that unseen world where human thought ranges, where human feelings swell into a vastness not to be contained by the great globe itself, and where human affections soar away into eternity. No! reality in the high sense of the term belongs to the invisible, and in the very highest sense, to the invisible things of the supernatural world. There is more of reality in the feeblest finite spirit than in all the material universe, for it will survive "the wreck of matter and the crash of worlds." The supernatural is a firmer foundation upon which to establish science than is the natural; its data are more certain, and its testimony more sure than those of nature. None but an open ear, it is true, can hear the voices and the dicta that come from this highest world, but he who has once heard never again doubts regarding them. He *cannot* doubt, if he would. He has heard the tones, and they will continue to sound through his soul, with louder and louder reverberations, through its whole immortality.

Perhaps it will be objected that, granting spiritual

things to be the true realities, yet the mind cannot see them except through a medium, and cannot be certain of their existence except by means of deductions from a palpable and tangible reality like that of the material world. But is it so? Does the spirit need a medium through which to behold the idea and law of Right, for example; and must it build up a series of conclusions based upon deductions drawn from the world of sense, before it can be certain that there is any such reality? — Does not the human spirit see the idea of Right as directly and plainly as the material eye sees the sun at high noon; and when it sees it, is it not as certain of its existence as we are of that of the sun? If man does not see this spiritual entity, this supernatural idea, directly and without a medium, he will never see it, and if it does not of itself convey the evidence of its reality, it can be drawn from no other quarter.

The same may be said of all spiritual entities whatever; of all the objects of the supernatural world. The rational spirit may and must behold them by direct intuition in their own pure white light. It has the organ for doing this. Not more certainly is the material eye designed for the vision of the sun, than the rational spirit is designed for the vision of God. The former is expressly constructed to behold matter, and the latter is just as expressly constructed to behold spirit. Nor let it be supposed that the term "behold" is used literally in reference to the act of the material eye, and merely metaphorically in reference to the act of the spirit. The term is no more the exclusive property of one organ than of the other. Or if it is to belong to one exclusively let us rather appropriate it to that organ which sees eternal distinctions. If the term "sight" is ever metaphorical, surely it is not so when applied to the vision of immutable truths and everlasting realities.

Man, both by nature and by the circumstances in which he is placed, finds it difficult thus to contemplate abstract ideal truth, and when it eludes his imperfect vision he charges the difficulty upon the truth and not upon himself. But for all this the ideal is real, and man is capable of this abstract vision. Upon his ability to free himself from the disturbing influences of sense, to be independent of the physical senses in the investigation of spiritual things, and to see them in their own light by their correlative organ, depends his true knowledge of the supernatural. It is on this ground that Plato asserts it to be the true mark of a philosophic mind to desire to die, because the mind is thereby withdrawn from the distraction of sense, and in the spiritual world beholds the Beautiful, the True, and the Good, in their essence.—Hence with great force he represents those spirits which have not been entirely freed from the crass and sensuous nature of the body, as being afraid of the purely spiritual world and its supernatural objects, and as returning into the world of matter to wander as ghosts among tombs and graves, loving their old material dwelling more than the spirit-land.*

The knowledge which comes from a direct vision of spiritual objects is sure, and needs no evidence of its truth from a lower domain. He who has once in spirit obtained a distinct sight of such realities as the Good, the Beautiful, the True, and their contraries, will never again be in doubt of their existence, or as to their natures. These are entities which once seen compel an everlasting belief. These are objects

* Phædon, Opera I. pp. 115 116, 139.

* * * * * that wake
To perish never;
Which neither listlessness nor mad endeavor,
Nor man nor boy,
Nor all that is at enmity with joy,
Can utterly abolish or destroy.

The true method then of theological studies is to commence in and with the supernatural and to work outward and downward to the natural. The theologian must study his own spirit by the aid of the written word. He will ever find the two in perfect harmony and mutually confirming each other. The supernatural doctrines of theology must be seen in their own light; must bring their own evidence with them, and theology must be a self-supported science.

Whatever may be said in opposition to this method by those who magnify natural theology to the injury of spiritual religion, it has always been the method of inquiry employed by the profoundest and most accurate theologians. Augustine lived at a period when natural science was but little cultivated and advanced, but even if he had possessed all the physical knowledge of the present day, that inward experience with its throes, agonies, and joys, so vividly portrayed in his "Confessions," would still have kept his eye turned inward. The power of Luther and Calvin lies in their realizing views of supernatural objects seen by their own light; and nothing but an absolutely abstract and direct beholding of supernatural realities could have produced the calm assurance and profound theology of that loftiest of human spirits, John Howe.

But what has been the result of the contrary method? Have not those who commenced with the study of natural theology, and who made this the foundation of their inquiries into the nature and mutual relations of

God and man, always remained on the spot where they first stationed themselves? Did they, by logically following their assumed method, ever rise above the sphere of merely natural religion into that of supernatural, and obtain just views either of the Infinite Spirit as personal and therefore tri-une; or of the Finite Spirit as free, responsible and guilty? Did they ever acquire rational views of holy and just law; of law as strictly *supernatural;* and so of its relations to guilt and expiation?

An undue study of natural science inevitably leads to wrong theological opinions. Unless it be pursued in the light which spirit casts upon nature, the student will misapprehend both nature and spirit. Who can doubt that if Priestley had devoted less time to the phenomena of the natural world, and far more to those of the supernatural; less attention to physical laws as seen in the operations of acids and alkalies, and far more attention to the operation of a spiritual law as revealed in a guilty conscience; he would have left a theology far more nearly conformed to the word of God and the structure of the human spirit.

I have been thus particular in speaking of the supernatural element in theological studies, for the purpose of showing where their power lies, and whence their influence comes. I turn now to consider the influence of these studies as they have been characterized, upon education and the educated class in the state.

Genuine education is immediately concerned with the essence of the mind itself, and its power and work appear in the very substance of the understanding. It starts into exercise deeper powers than the memory, and it does more for the mind than merely to fill it. It enters rather into its constituent and controlling principles; rouses and develops them, and thus establishes a basis for the mind's perpetual motion and progress. Whether there be much or little acquired information is of small importance, comparatively, if the mind has that which is the secret of mental superiority, the power of originating knowledge upon a given subject for itself, and can fall back upon its own native energies for information. That process whereby a mind acquires the ability to fasten itself with absorbing intensity upon any legitimate object of human inquiry, and to originate profound thought and clear conceptions regarding it, is education.

The truth of this assertion will be apparent if we bear in mind that knowledge, in the high sense of the term, is not the remembrance of facts, but the intuition of principles. Facts are that through which principles manifest themselves, and by which they are illustrated, but to take them for the essence of knowledge is to mistake the body for the soul. The true knowledge of nature, art, philosophy, and religion, is an insight into their constituent principles, of which facts and phenomena are but the raiment; the "white and glistering" raiment in which the essence is transfigured and through which it shines.

Now, principles are entities that do not exist either in space or time. They cannot be apprehended by any organ of sense, and therefore they are not in space. — They cannot in a literal sense be said to be old or new. Principles are eternal and therefore they are not in time. Where then are they? In the intellectual world: — a world that is not measured by space or limited by periods of time, but which has, nevertheless, as real an existence as this globe. In the world of mind, all those principles which *constitute* knowledge are to be sought for. They lie in the structure of mind, and therefore the development of the mind is but the discovery of principles, and education is the *origination* of substantial knowledge out of the very being who is to be educated.*

Thus, by this brief examination of the true nature of knowledge, do we come round in a full circle to the spot whence we started, and see that he alone is in the process of true education who is continually looking within, and by the gradual *evolution* of his own mind is continually unfolding those principles of knowledge that lie imbedded in it. Such an one may not have amassed great erudition, but he possesses a working intellect which, unencumbered by amassed materials, overflows all the more freely with original principles. We *feel* that such a mind is educated, for its products, are alive and communicate life. From a living impulse it originates a knowledge, regarding any particular subject to which it directs itself, that commends itself to us as truth, by its congeniality and affinity with our own mind, and by its kindling influence upon it.

Accustomed, from the domination of a mental philosophy which rejects the doctrine of innate ideas, to consider learning as something carried into the mind instead of something drawn out of it, it sounds strangely to speak of *originating* knowledge. But who are the really learned statesmen, philosophers, and divines? Not those who merely commit to memory the results of past inquiry, but those in whom after deep reflection the principles of government, philosophy, and religion, rise into sight, with the freshness, inspiration, and splendor, of a new discovery. In asserting however that learning is the product of the mind itself, I mean that it is relatively so.

* This is Plato's meaning when he asserts that learning is recollection:—the reminding of the human spirit of those great principles which are born with it, and which constitute its rationality.—Phædon Opera I. p. 125, et seq. Cudworth's Im. Mor. Book iii, Chap. 3.

It is not asserted that every truly learned mind discovers *absolutely* new principles, and consequently that the future is to bring to light a great amount of knowledge unknown to the past. Far from it. The sum of human knowledge, with the exception of that part relating to the domain of natural science, is undoubtedly complete, and we are not to expect the discovery of any new fundamental principles in the sphere of the supernatural.— But it is asserted with confidence that these old principles must be discovered afresh *for himself*, by every one who would be truly educated. " He who has been born," says an eloquent writer, " has been a first man, and has had the world lying around him as fresh and fair as it lay before the eyes of Adam himself." In like manner, he who has been created a rational spirit, has a world of rational principles encircling him, which is as new and undiscovered for him as it was for the first man. In the hemisphere of his own self-reflection and self-consciousness, the sun must rise for the first time, and the stars must send down their very freshest influences, their very first and purest gleam.

For education, in the eminent sense of the term, is dynamic and not atomic. It does not lie in the mind in the form of congregated atoms, but of living, salient, energies. It is not therefore poured in from without, but springs up from within. The power of pure thought is education. Indeed the more we consider the nature of mental education, the more clearly do we see that it consists in the power of pure, practical reflection; the ability so to absorb the mind that it shall sink down into itself, until it reaches those ultimate principles, bedded in its essence, by which facts and all acquired and remembered information are illuminated and vivified. It cannot be that he who remembers the most, is the most thoroughly educated man, or that the age which is in possession of the greatest amount of books and recorded information, is the most learned. No! learning is the product of a powerful mind, which, by self-reflection and absorption in pure, practical thought, goes down into those depths of the intellectual world, where, as in the world of matter, the gems and gold, the seeds, and germs, and roots, are to be found. It is related that Socrates could remain a whole day utterly lost in profound reflection.* This was the education in that age of no books, to which, through his scholar Plato, himself educated in the same way, is owing a system of philosophy, substantial with the very essence of learning; a system which for insight into ultimate principles is at the head of all human knowledge.

Such being the nature of education, it is evident that theological studies are better fitted than any others, to educe a rational mind. For they bring it into immediate communication with those supernatural realities and truths which are appropriate to it, and which possess a strong power of development. There is in the human mind a vast amount of latent energy forming the basis for an endless progress, and this will lie latent and dormant unless the forces of the supernatural world evolve it. The world of nature unfolds merely the superficies of man, leaving the hidden depths of his being unstirred, and only when the windows of heaven are opened are the fountains of this great deep broken up. For proof of this assertion, consider the influence which the theological doctrine of the soul's immortality exerts upon the spirit. When man realizes that he is immortal he is supernaturally roused. Depths are revealed in his being which he did not dream of, down into which he looks with solemn awe, and energies which had hitherto slum

* Convivium. Platonis Opera vii. p. 278.

bered from his creation are now set into a play at which he stands aghast. Never do the tides of that shoreless ocean, the human soul, heave and swell as they do when it feels what the scripture calls "the power of an endless life." The same remark holds true of all properly theological doctrines. An unequalled developing influence rains down from this great constellation.

And the intellect as well as the heart of man feels the influence. Hence that period in a man's life which is marked by a realizing and practical apprehension of the doctrines of spiritual religion is also marked by a great increase of intellectual power. A manlier and more substantial cultivation begins, because the being has become conscious of his high origin and the awfulness of his destiny, and a stronger play of intellectual power is evoked, because the stream of supernatural influence flows through the whole man, and both head and heart feel its vivification. The value of theological studies, in an intellectual point of view, does not consist so much in the amount of information as in the amount of energy imparted by them. The doctrines of theology, like the solar centres, are comparatively few in number, and while the demand they make upon the memory is small, the demand they make upon the power of reflection is infinite and unending. For this reason, theological studies are in the highest degree fitted to originate and carry on a true education. There is an invigorating virtue in them which strengthens while it unfolds the mental powers, and therefore the more absorbing the intensity with which the mind dwells upon them, the more it is endued with power.

This truth is very plainly written in literary history. If we would see that period when the mind of a nation was most full of original power, we must contemplate its theological age. We ever find that the national intellect is most energetically educed in that period when the attention of educated men is directed with great earnestness to theological studies, while that period which is characterized by a false study, or a general neglect, of them, is one of very shallow education. Compare the education of the English mind during the sixteenth and seventeenth centuries, with its education in the eighteenth. The great difference between the two, is owing to the serious and profound reflection upon strictly theological subjects that prevailed in the first period, and to the absence of such reflection in the second. The former was a theological age in the strict sense of the term; a period when the educated class felt very powerfully the vigor proceeding from purely supernatural themes. The latter was a period when, through the influence of a system of philosophy which teaches that every thing must be learned through the five senses, a mere naturalism took the place of supernaturalism, and when, as a matter of course, the mind of the literary class was not the subject of those developing and energizing influences which proceed only from supernatural truths.

Again, that we may still more clearly see the vigorous character imparted to education by purely theological studies, let us consider two individuals who stand at the head of two different classes of literary men, and afford two different specimens of intellectual culture: — Lord Chancellor Bacon and Lord Chancellor Brougham.

The education of Bacon is the result, in no small degree, of the influence of the truths of supernatural science. There was no naturalism in the age of Bacon; there was none in his culture; and there is none in his writings. He lived at a period when the English mind was stirred very deeply by religious doctrines, and when the truths of the supernatural world were very absorbing topics of thought and discussion, not only for divines, but for statesmen. We of this enlightened nineteenth century, are in the habit of calling those centuries of reformation, dark, in comparison with our own; but with all the darkness on some subjects, it may be fearlessly asserted that since the first two centuries of the history of Christianity, there has never been a period when so large a portion of the race have been so *deeply* and *anxiously* interested in the truths pertaining to another world, as in those two centuries of reformation; the sixteenth and seventeenth. With all the lack of modern improvements and civilization, there was everywhere a firm belief in the supernatural, and a sacred reverence for religion. Even the very keenness and acrimony of the theological disputations of that period prove that men believed, as they do not in an indifferent age, that religious doctrines are matters of vital interest.

Bacon lived in this age; in its first years, and felt the first and freshest influences of the great awakening. His intellect felt them, and hence its masculine development and vigor. The products of his intellect felt them, and hence the solid substance, strong sinew, and warm blood, of which they are made.

The education of Brougham has been obtained in a very different age from that of Bacon: an age when the faith and interest which the learned class once felt in the realities of another world, have transferred themselves to the realities of this. It has also been the result, in no small degree, of the belief and the study of the half-truths of natural theology. While then the recorded learning of Bacon bears the stamp of originality, is drenched and saturated with the choicest intellectual spirit and energy, makes an epoch in literary history, and sends forth through all time an enlivening power, the recorded learning of Brougham is destitute of fresh life, being the result of a diligent acquisition, and not of profound contemplation, gives off little invigorating influence, and cannot form a marked period in the history of literature.

Thus far we have considered the developing and energizing influence of theological studies; but if we should stop here, we should be very far from discovering their full worth. There is a merely *speculative* development and energy of the mind which is heaven-wide from genuine education, and really prevents growth in true knowledge.

There have ever been, and, so long as man shall continue to be a fallen spirit, there ever will be, two kinds of thought. The one speculative and hollow; the other practical and substantial. The one wasting itself upon the factitious products of its own energy; the other expending itself upon those great realities which are veritable, and have an existence independent of the finite mind. The natural tendency of the intellect, *when not actuated by a rational and holy will*, is to produce purely speculative thought, and in this direction do we see all intellect going which does not feel the influence of moral and spiritual truth. The speculative reason is a wonderful mechanism, and if kept within its proper domain, and applied to its correlative objects, is an important instrument in the attainment of truth and culture, but if suffered to pass over its appointed limits, and to occupy itself with the investigation of subjects to which it is not adapted, it brings in error rapidly and *ad infinitum*, preventing the true progress and repose of the spirit. There is no end to the manufactures of the speculative faculty, or to the productive energy of its life, when once the process of speculation is begun. Nay, it is the express doctrine of Fichte (the most intensely and purely speculative intellect the world has yet seen) that the finite mind having the principle of its own movement within itself, by working in accordance with its own indwelling laws, is able to *create*, and actually *does create the grea universe itself!* The history of philosophy disclose much of such speculative thought, and hence the dissatisfaction of philosophy with what it has hitherto done, and its striving after a substantial and genuine knowledge. Man as a moral being cannot be content with these hollow speculations, for spirit as well as nature abhors a vacuum. Thought must be filled up with substantial verity, and knowledge must become practical, in order to the repose and true education of the mind.

Yet notwithstanding the unsatisfying nature of speculative thinking, an intellectual life and enthusiasm are generated by it which invest it with a charming facination for the mind that is led on by a merely speculative interest. What though the thinker is bewildered and lost in the mazes of speculation; he is bewildered and lost in wonderful regions, the astounding nature of whose objects represses, for a time, the feelings of doubt and dissatisfaction. He is like the pilgrim lost in "the gorgeous East," who is *delightedly* lost amid the luxuriant entanglements and wild enchantments of the oriental jungle. In this exciting world of speculation, the energies of the intellect are in full action, the thirst and curiosity for knowledge are keen, and under the impulse of these the thinker says with Jacobi; "though I know the insufficiency of my philosophizing, still I can only philosophize right on." *

* Jacobi, quoted by Tholuck. Vermischte Schriften. ii. 427; and see a similar remark by Kant, Kritik der reinen Vernunft. p. 196. The philoso-

It is possible to evoke intellectual energy so powerfully and habitually that the action shall become organic, and the intellect shall be instinctively busy with the production and reproduction of speculations; and though the thinker gets no repose of soul by it, yet he is so much under the power of the intellectual appetite that he will not cease to gratify it. There is no more mournful chapter in the history of literary men than that which records their unending speculative struggles; their efforts to find peace of mind and true education in the application of merely speculative energy to the solution of the great problems of moral existence. The process of speculation continually becomes more and more impeded, as at every advance still more mysterious problems come into sight, not soluble by this method; the over-tasked intellect at length gives out, and its gifted possessor falls into the abyss of unbelief like an archangel.

It is not enough therefore that the latent power of the mind is developed merely; it must be developed by some substantial objects, and it must be expended upon some veritable realities. In other words, the thought of man must be called forth by the ideas and principles of the supernatural world, and the mind of man must find repose and education in moral truth.

pher, (says Chalybäus in the conclusion of his lecture upon Jacobi, Vorlesungen p. 77.) as well as the poet, can say of himself:—

Ich halte diesen Drang vergebens auf,
Der Tag und Nacht in meinem Busen wechselt,
Wenn ich nicht sinnen oder dichten soll,
So ist das Leben mir kein Leben mehr!
Verbiete du dem Seidenwurm, zu spinnen—
Wenn er sich schon dem Tode näher spinnt,
Das köstlichste Geweb' entwickelt er
Aus seinem Innersten, und läszt nicht ab
Bis er in seinen Sarg sich eingeschlossen.

The reader of Plato is struck with the earnestness with which this truly philosophic and educated mind insists upon knowing *that which really is*, as the end of philosophy. It matters not how consecutive and consistent with itself a system of thought may be, if it has no correspondent in the world of being, and does not find a confirmation in the world of absolute reality. The form may be distinct, and the proportions symmetrical, but the thing is spectral and unsubstantial, and though it be dignified with the name of philosophy, it is nevertheless a pure figment. Though not the product of the fancy but of a far higher faculty, a merely speculative philosophical system is but a *product;* a creation of the brain, to which there is, objectively, nothing correspondent. As an instance of such philosophizing, take the system of Spinoza. No one can deny that as a merely speculative unity, it is perfect, and perfectly satisfies the wants of that part of the human understanding which looks for nothing but a theoretical whole. All its parts are in most perfect harmony with each other, and with the whole. This system is conceived and executed in a most systematic spirit, and if man had no moral reason which seeks for something more than a merely speculative unity, it would be for him the true theory of the universe. But why is it not, and why cannot the human mind be content with it? Because a rational spirit cannot *rest* in it. There is in this system, great and architectural as it is, no repose or home for a moral being, and therefore it is not truth; for absolute truth is infallibly known by the absolute and everlasting satisfaction it affords to the moral spirit.

Another great aim of education, therefore, is the calm repose of the mind; its settlement in indisputable truth. This can proceed only from the study of the purely spiritual truths of theology, because such is their nature that there can be no real dispute regarding them, whereas merely speculative dogmas are susceptible of, and awaken, an endless ratiocination. There has always been, for example, even among thoughtful men a keen dispute regarding some points in the mode of the Divine existence, but none at all regarding the Divine character. The doctrine of the subsistence of creation in the creator has ever awakened honest disputations among sincere disputants, but the doctrine that God is holy has never been doubted by a conscientious thinker. This holds true of all speculative and practical doctrines. Within the sphere of theory and speculation there is room for endless wanderings, and no foundation upon which the spirit can stand still and firm. Within the sphere of practice and morality there need be no doubt nor error, and the sincere mind, by a direct vision of the truths of this practical domain of knowledge, may enter at once and forever into rest.

The influence of purely theological studies, in producing an education that ministers repose and harmony to the mind, is great and valuable. The intellectual energy is not awakened by abstractions, nor is it expended upon them, but upon those supernatural realities which are the appropriate objects of a rational contemplation, and which completely satisfy the wants of an immortal being. For that which imparts substantiality to thought, is religion, and all reflection which does not in the end refer to the moral and supernatural relations of man, is worthless. Though a fallen spirit, man still bears about with him the great idea of his origin and destiny. This allows him no real peace or satisfaction but in religious truth, and there are moments, consequently, in the life of the educated man, when he feels with deep despondency the need of the purer culture, and the more satisfactory reflection, of better studies. If any, short of strictly theological studies, can give repose of mind, they would have given it to the poet Goethe. Yet that mind, singularly symmetrical and singularly calm by nature, after ranging for half a century through all regions save that strictly supernatural world of which we have spoken, and after obtaining what of culture and intellectual satisfaction is to be found short of spiritual truths; that mind, so richly and variously gifted, at the close of its existence on earth confessed that it had never experienced a moment of genuine repose.

The German poet is not the only one whose education did not contribute to repose and peace of mind. The literary life has not hitherto been calm and satisfied. From all times, and from all classes of educated minds, there comes the mournful confession that "he that increaseth knowledge increaseth sorrow," and that all learning which does not go beyond the consciousness of the natural man and have for its object the Good, the True, and the Divine, cannot satisfy the demands of man's ideal state. From Philosophy, from Poetry, and from Art, is heard the acknowledgment that there is no repose for the rational spirit but in moral truth. The testimony that the whole creation groaneth and travaileth in pain, together, is as loud and convincing from the domain of letters, as it is from the cursed and thistle-bearing ground. From the immortal longing and dissatisfaction of Plato, down to the wild and passionate restlessness of Byron and Shelley, the evidence is decisive that a spiritual and religious element must enter into the education of man in order to inward harmony and rest.

Time forbids a longer discussion of this part of the

subject. It may be said as a result of the whole, that a thorough study of theology as the science of the supernatural, results in a profundity and harmony of education which can be obtained in no other way, and if the culture which comes from poetry and fine literature generally be also mingled with it, a truly beautiful as well as profound education will be the result of the alchemy.

I turn now to consider the influence of theological studies upon Literature. And let me again remind you that I am speaking of *purely* theological studies, as they have been defined. There is an influence proceeding from so-called theological studies, which deprives literature of its depth, power, beauty, and glory; the *quasi* religious influence of naturalism, of which the poetry of Pope, the philosophy of Locke, the divinity of Priestley, and the morality of Paley, are the legitimate and necessary results.

The fact strikes us in the outset, that the noblest and loftiest literature has always appeared in those periods of a nation's existence, when its literary men were most under the influence of theological science. Whether we look at Pagan or Christian literature, we find this assertion verified. The mythology and theology of Greece exerted their greatest influence upon Homer, the three dramatists, and Plato; and these are the great names in Grecian literature. If Cicero is ever vigorous and original he is in his ethical and theological writings. The beautiful flower of Italian literature is the "unfathomable song" of the religious Dante. The beauty and strength of English literature are the fruit of those two pre-eminently theological centuries: — the sixteenth and seventeenth. The originality and life which for the last century has given German literature the superiority over other literatures of this period, must be referred mainly to the tendency of the German mind toward theological truth. And judging *a priori*, we should conclude that such would be the fact. We might safely expect that the human mind would produce its most perfect results, when most under the influences that come from its birth-place. We might know beforehand, that truth and beauty would flow most freely into the creations of man's mind, when he himself is in most intimate communication with that world where these qualities have their eternal fountain.

1. The first and best fruit of the influence of theology upon literature is *profundity*. This characteristic of the best literature of a nation is immediately noticed by the scholar, so that its decrease or absence is, for him, the chief sign of deterioration. In that glorious age of a nation when the solemn spirit of religion informs everything; when, compared with after ages, the nation seems to be very near the supernatural world in feeling and sentiment; when prophet, poet, and priest, are synonymes; then arises its most profound literature.

By a profound literature, is meant one that addresses itself to the most profound faculties of the human soul. The so-called polite literature, is the lightest and most unessential product of the human mind. It is the work of the inferior part of the understanding, deriving little life or vigor from its deepest powers, and having no immediate connection with its highest cultivation. It occupies the attention of man in his youthful days, affording an ample field in which the fancy may rove and revel, and starting some of the superficial life of the intellect; but in the mature and meditative part of his existence, when the great questions relating to his origin and destiny are raised, he leaves these gay and pleasant studies for that more profound literature which comes home to deeper faculties and wants.

A survey of literature generally, at once shows that but a very small portion of it is worthy to be called profound. How very little of the vast amount which has been composed by the literary class, addresses itself to the primitive faculties of the human soul! The greater part merely stimulates curiosity, exercises the fancy, and perhaps loads the memory. Another portion externally polishes and adorns the mind. It is only a very small portion, which by speaking to the Reason and the rational and creative Imagination, and rousing into full play of life those profound powers, ministers strength, true beauty, and true culture to the soul.

Consider for a moment the character of the English literature of the present day. I do not now refer to the dregs and off-scourings which are doing so much to debauch the English mind, but to the bloom and flower. And I ask if it does anything more for the scholar than to externally adorn and embellish his education? Has it the power to educate? Does it have a strong tendency to *develop* a historical, a philosophical, a poetical, or artistic capability if it lie in the student? Must not a more profound literature be called upon to do this, and must not the scholar who would truly develop what is in him, go back to the study of Homer and Plato; of Dante; of Shakspeare, Bacon, and Milton? If he contents himself with the study of the best current literature, will he do anything more than produce a refinement destitute of life; a culture without vigor; and will he himself in his best estate be anything more than an intellectual voluptuary, utterly impotent and without vivifying influence upon letters?

There is then a profound portion of literature speaking to the deeper part of man, from which he is to derive a profound literary cultivation. A brief examination will show that its chief characteristics arise from its being impregnated by theology; not necessarily by the formal doctrines of theology, but by its finer essence and spirit. Theology, it has been said, is the science of the supernatural and therefore of the strictly mysterious. The idea of God, which constitutes and animates the science, is a true mystery. But that which is truly mysterious is truly profound, and deepens everything coming under its influence. Indeed mystery, in the philosophical sense of the term, is the author of all great qualities. Sublimity, Profundity, Grandeur, Magnificence, Beauty, cannot exist without it. Like night, it induces a high and solemn mood, and is the parent and nurse of profound and noble thought. That literature which is pervaded by it, becomes deep-toned, and speaks with emphasis to the deeper powers of man. Even when there is but an imperfect permeation by this influence; when mystery is not fully apprehended, and the mind is not completely under its power; even when the Poet feels

"What he can ne'er express, yet cannot all conceal,"

there is a noble inspiration in his lines, which, with all its vagueness, deepens the feelings and elevates the conceptions. It is related of Fichte, that in very early childhood he would stand motionless for hours, gazing into the distant ether.* As such he is a symbol of the soul which is but imperfectly possessed by that mystery which surrounds every rational being. Those vague yearnings and obscure stirrings of the boy's spirit, as with strained eye he strove to penetrate the dark depths of infinite space, typify the workings of that soul which in only an imperfect degree partakes of this "vision and

* Fichte's Leben. I. 7.

faculty divine." And as those motions in this youthful spirit awaken interest in the observer, betokening as they do no common mood and tendency, so even the vague and shadowy musings of the mind which is but feebly under the influence of mystery: — a Novalis, or a Shelley,— are not without their interest and elevation.

But when a genius appears in the history of a nation's literature, who sees the great import and feels the full power of those true mysteries which are the subject matter of theological science, then creations appear which exert an inspiring influence upon all after ages, and by their profundity and power betoken that they are composed of no volatile essence, and produced by no superficial mental energy. They are not to be comprehended or admired at a glance, it is true, and therefore are not the favorites of the falsely educated class, but ever remain the peculiar property and delight of that inner circle of literary men in whom culture reaches its height of excellence.

It may appear strange to attribute the noblest characteristics of literature to the mysteries of theology, but a philosophical study of literature convincingly shows that from this dark unsightly root grows "the bright consummate flower." It is the spirit of this solemn and dark domain, which, by connecting literature with the moral and mysterious world, and by giving it a direct or indirect reference to the deepest and most serious relations of the human spirit, renders it profound, and raises it infinitely above the mass of common light literature.

2. This same influence of theology imparts that *earnest and lofty purpose* which resides in the best literature. The chief reason why the largest portion of the productions of the literary class contributes nothing to true cul-

tivation, and is destitute of the highest excellence, is the fact that it is not animated by a purpose. The poet composes a poem with no specific and lofty *intention* in his eye, but merely to give vent to a series of personal states and feelings. He writes for his own relief and gratification, not realizing, as Milton did, that "poetic abilities, wheresoever they be found, are the inspired gift of God, rarely bestowed; and are of power *beside the office of a pulpit*, to imbreed and cherish in a great people the seeds of virtue and public civility," and should be used for this noble purpose. The literary man generally, does not even dream that he is obligated to work with a good and elevated object in his eye, but is exempt from the universal law of creation, which obligates every finite spirit to live and labor for truth and God.

But sin always takes vengeance, and all literature which is purposeless, and does not breathe an earnest spirit, is destitute of the highest excellence. It will want the solemnity, the enthusiasm, the glow, the grandeur, and the depth, which proceeds only from a lofty and serious intention in the mind of the author. And this purpose can dwell only in the mind which is haunted by the higher ideas and truths of supernaturalism. It is in vain for the literary man to seek his inspiration in the earthly, or the intellectual, world. He must derive it from the heaven of heavens.

Both in heathen and in Christian literature, we find the noblest productions to be but the embodiment of a purpose; and the purpose is always intimately connected with the moral world. The Iliad proposes to exhibit the battle of heaven and earth, of gods and men, united in defence of the rights of injured hospitality. This proposition pervades the poem, and greatly contributes to invest it with the highest attributes of literature. The Grecian drama is serious and awful with the spirit of law and vengeance. Its high *motive*, is to teach all those solemn and fearful truths regarding justice and injustice which constitute the law written on the heart, and are the substance of the universally accusing and condemning conscience of man. Pagan though the Greek drama be, yet when we consider the loftiness and fixedness of its intention to bring before the mind all that it can know of the supernatural short of revelation, we hesitate not to say that it is immeasurably ahead of much of so-called Christian literature, in its doctrine and influence, as well as in its literary characteristics. As the scholar contemplates the elevated moral character running through this portion of Grecian literature, and contrasts it with much of that which is called Christian in distinction from heathen, he is led to take up that indignant exclamation of Wordsworth uttered in another connection,

> * * * * * * I'd rather be
> A Pagan, suckled in a creed outworn.

Of all literary men who have written since the promulgation of the Christian religion, Milton seems to have most strongly felt the influences of theology, and he more than all others was animated and strengthened by a high moral aim. In his literary works he distinctly and intentionally has in view the advancement of truth and the glory of God. These were "his matins duly, and his even-song." And to this noble purpose, as much as to his magnificent intellectual powers, are owing the profundity, loftiness, grandeur, truth, and beauty, which, in the literary heavens make his works like his soul, "a star that dwells apart."

We live in an age when theology has become entirely

dissevered from literature, and when supernatural science forms no part of the studies of the cultivated class. There was a period when literary men devoted the best of their time to the high themes of religion, and when literature took a deep hue and tincture from theology. There was a period when such a man as Bacon wrote theological tracts and indited most solemn and earnest prayers; when such a man as Raleigh composed devotional hymns; when such a man as Spenser sung of the virtues and the vices; when such a man as Shakspeare expended the best of his poetic and dramatic power in exhibiting the working of the moral passions; and when such a man as Milton made the fall of the human soul the "great argument" of poetry. There was a time when literature was in a very great degree impregnated by theology. But that time has gone by, and the productions of later ages show, by their ephemeral and inefficient character, that they have not that truly spiritual element which makes literature ever fresh and invigorating. Whatever may be the embellishment, the charm, and the fascination, of modern literature, for the student in certain stages of his growth, it does not permanently rouse and enliven like the old. It may satisfy the wants of the educated man for a time, but there does come a period in the history of every mind that is truly progressive in its character, when it will not satisfy, and the student must "provide a manlier diet." The mind when in the process of true unfolding cannot be ultimately cheated. Wants, which in the first stages of its development were dormant, while more shallow cravings were being met by a weak aliment, eventually make themselves felt, and send the subject of them after more substantial food. The favorite authors of the earlier periods of education are thrown aside as the taste becomes more severe, the sympathies more refined, and profounder feelings are awakened; the circle diminishes, until the scholar finally rests content with those few writers in every literature, who speak to the deeper spirit, because full of the vigor and power of the higher world.

The student while in the enjoyment of it may not distinctly know whence comes the charm and abiding spell of the older literature; but let him transfer himself into periods of national existence when faith in the supernatural had become unbelief, and when literary men had lost the solemn and earnest spirit of their predecessors, and he will know that religion is the life of literature, as it is of all things else. He will discover that the absence of an enlarging and elevating influence in letters, is to be attributed to the absence of that theological element with which the human mind, notwithstanding the corruption of the human spirit, has a quick and deep affinity.

I have thus, gentlemen of the societies, spoken of the true method of Theological Studies, and of their great and noble influences upon education and literature. If I have spoken with more of a theological tone than is usually heard upon a literary festival like the present occasion, I might excuse myself by simply saying, in the language of Bacon, that every man is a debtor to his profession. But I confess to a most sincere and earnest desire of awakening in the minds of those who are soon to become a part of the educated class of the land, an interest and love for that noblest and most neglected of the sciences: — theology. This science has come to be the study of one profession alone, and of one that unhappily includes but a very small portion of the educated class. And yet in the depth and breadth of its relations, as well as in the importance of its matter, it is the science of the sciences. God is the God of every man, and the science which treats of Him and his ways deeply concerns every man, and especially every one who in any degree is raised above the common level, by the opportunity and effort to cultivate himself. It is a great error to suppose that theological studies should be the exclusive pursuit of the clergy, and that the remainder of the literary class in the state should feel none of the enlargement and elevation of soul arising from them. — When the idea of a perfect commonwealth shall be fully realized — if it ever shall be on earth — theology will be the light and life of all the culture and knowledge contained in it. Its invigorating and purifying energy will be diffused through the whole class of literary men, and through them will be felt to the uttermost extremities of the body politic. All other sciences will be illuminated and vivified by it, and will then reach that point of perfection which has ever been in the eye of their most genial and profound votaries.

For a knowledge of the aims of the most gifted and enthusiastic students of science, discovers the need of the influence of theology, in order to the perfection of science, as well as of letters. That which makes Burke one of the few great names in political science, is the solemn and awful view he had of law as strictly supernatural in its essence; of law, in his own language, as "prior to all our devices, and prior to all our contrivances, paramount to all our ideas, and all our sensations, antecedent to our very existence, by which we are knit and connected in the eternal frame of the universe, out of which we cannot stir." * It was his high aim therefore to render political science religious in its character, and to found government upon a sacred and reverential sentiment towards law, in the breasts of the governed. Politics in his eye,

* Speech in the impeachment of Hastings. Works, iii, p. 327.

and government in his view, are essentially different from the same things, as viewed by that large class of political men who do not appear to dream, even, that there is a supernatural world, or that there are supernatural sanctions and supports to government. But the speculative views regarding politics advanced by Burke will never be practically realized among the nations, until the influence of the high themes of spiritual theology is felt among them, and political science will not be a perfect scheme, until constructed in the light and by the aid of theological doctrine. The sanction, the sacredness, the authority, and the binding power, of law, as the foundation of government and political science, for which Burke plead so eloquently, come from the supernatural world, and are not apprehensible except in the light of that science which treats of that world. The fine visions and lofty aspirations of Burke, relative to government and political science, depend therefore upon the practical and theoretical influence of theology for their full realization.

Let me briefly refer to another instance, in which we see that the high aims of a most profound and genial student will be attained only under the influence of the science of the supernatural. It has been the high endeavor of Schelling to spiritualize natural science; to strip nature of its hard forms, and by piercing beneath the material, to behold it as immaterial ideas, laws, and forces.* This is not only a beautiful, but it is the true, idea of nature and natural science. Schelling however has failed to realize it *in a perfect manner.* However great may be his merit in infusing life into this domain

* System des transcend. Idealismus, p. 5. For a full exhibition of this method of natural science, see Carus's Physiologie, Erster Theil.

of knowledge, and in overthrowing the mechanical view of nature, he has not constructed his system so as to maintain a pure theism, and therefore when viewed in connection with the true system of the universe, with which every individual science must harmonize, its falsity, in the great whole of knowledge, is apparent. And the imperfection of this system is owing, first, to the absence of a sharp and firm line of distinction between the natural and the supernatural, and secondly, to the want of that protection from pantheism, which a truly profound philosopher can find only in the purely supernatural doctrines of theology.

It is not true then that the theologian by profession is alone concerned with theology. He who would obtain correct views in political or natural science, as well as he who would be a mind of power and depth in the sphere of literature; in short, *the student generally;* has a vital interest in the truths of supernatural science.— And it is this conviction, gentlemen, which I would fix and deepen in your minds. Your attention might have been directed to some more popular theme; to some one of the aspects of polite literature, present or hoped for; but I preferred to direct your thoughts to a range of neglected but noble studies, confident that if any permanent interest should be thereby awakened in your minds towards them, a substantial benefit would be conferred upon you. I would then, not with the feigned earnestness which too generally characterizes appeals upon such an occasion as the present, but with all the solemn earnestness of the Sabbath, urge you to the serious pursuit of theological studies. It matters not, which may be the particular field in which you are to labor as educated men; the influence of these studies is elevating and enlarging in any field, and upon all the public professions.

If the Law is to be the special object of your future study, your idea of human law will be purified and corrected by your study of the divine law, and the general spirit and bearing of your practice will be elevated by those high studies which, more than any others, generate high principles of action.

Should you enter the arena of Political life, the influence of these studies will be most salutary. In this sphere, a man at the present day needs a double portion of pure and lofty principle, and should anxiously place himself under the most select influences. If the *serious* political spirit of Washington, and Jay, and Madison, is ever again to actuate our politics, it will be only through the return of that reverence for law, as flowing from a higher reality than the naturally corrupt will of man, and that faith in government as having its ground and sanctions in the supernatural and religious world, which characterized them. If politics is ever to cease to be a game, and is ever again to be considered as one of the solemn interests pertaining to human existence, it will be only when our young men enter this field under the influence of studies, and a discipline, that purge away low and sordid views, and induce a serious integrity and a self-sacrificing patriotism. If then you would sustain a relation to the government of your country, honorable to yourselves, and beneficial to it, imbue your minds and baptize your views and opinions with the theological spirit. Then you will be a statesman in the old and best sense of the word; not a mere office holder or seeker of office; but one in whom the great idea of the state resides and lives, and who by its indwelling power is full of the patriotic sentiment, and inspired by the noble spirit of allegiance to government and country.*

Finally, if you are to be one of the ministers and interpreters of Nature, or one who devotes himself to the cultivation of Fine Letters, the influence of these studies will be great and valuable. In the light of the supernatural, you will best interpret nature, and under the power of theology, you will be best enabled to contribute a profound and lofty addition to literature.

No one who watches the signs of the times, and especially the rapid and dangerous change now going on in the public sentiment of our country relative to the foundations of religion, government, and society, can help feeling that under Providence, very much is depending upon the principles and spirit which the educated young men take out with them into active life. Bacon, long ago, said that the principles of the young men of a nation decided its destiny, and the course of human events since his day has verified his assertion. It is certainly true in its fullest sense of this nation and its young men. Unless an upbuilding and establishing influence proceeds from the educated class, the disorganizing elements which are already in a furious fermentation in society will eventually dissolve all that is solid and fixed in it; and unless this class feel some stronger and purer influence than that of this world; unless it feels the power of the objects and principles of the other world; it will hasten rather than counteract the coming dissolution. Merely human culture, and merely natural

* Das Wort Staatsmann ist hier in dem Sinn des antiken πολιτικὸς genommen, und es soll dabei weniger daran gedacht werden, dasz einer etwas bestimmtes im Staat zu verrichten hat, was völlig zufällig ist, als dasz einer vorzugsweise in der Idee des Staats lebt. Schleiermacher. Reden. p. 28.

science, cannot educe that moral weight and force in the cultivated class, without which the state cannot long hold together. These must come from the general influence of theological science upon the minds of the educated; from the infusion into culture of that reverence for God, and that purifying insight into supernatural truth, without which culture becomes skeptical and shallow, powerless for good and all-powerful for evil.

In closing, permit me to remind you that you need the influence of these studies personally, without reference to your relations to the world at large. You need them in order to attain the true end of your own existence. However sedulously you may cultivate yourselves in other respects, you will not be cultivated for eternity, without the study and vital knowledge of theology. It has been foreign to the main drift of my discourse, and to the occasion, to speak of that deepest, that saving, knowledge of supernatural religion which proceeds from being taught by the Eternal Spirit. I have spoken only of the general and common influence of the doctrines of purely supernatural, in distinction from those of merely natural, theology. They have a great power in themselves, apart from their special vivification by the Divine Spirit. This is worthy of being sought after, and to this I have urged you. But if you would feel the full power of theology; if you would secure the freest, fairest, and holiest development of your spirits; if you would accomplish the very utmost of which you are capable, for your country and for man, in the sphere in which you shall be called to labor; if you would secure a strength which you will soon find you need in the struggle into which you are about to enter: — the struggle with the real world, and the still fiercer struggle with your real selves; then study theology experimentally. The discipline to which you have been subjected in the course of your training in this University, so far as human influence can do so, leads and urges you in this direction; for it is the plan and work of one of those elect and superior spirits (few and rare in our earthly race) who have an instinctive and irresistible tendency to the Supernatural.* This has been the tendency of your training, and if you will only surrender yourselves to this tendency, heightened and made effectual by special divine influences, as it will be for every scholar who seeks them with a solemn spirit, you will fully realize the idea of a perfect education.

* The allusion is to the late President Marsh.

THE TRUE NATURE OF THE BEAUTIFUL, AND ITS RELATION TO CULTURE.

A DISCOURSE DELIVERED BEFORE THE LITERARY SOCIETIES OF AMHERST COLLEGE, AUGUST 13, 1851.

GENTLEMEN OF THE LITERARY SOCIETIES: —

COMING as I do in the most beautiful season of the year, into the midst of some of the most beautiful scenery on the continent, and from the midst of scenery differently but equally beautiful; coming in mid-summer into the valley of the River from the valley of the Lake; you will not be surprised that my subject has connections with the environment in which I wrote and in which I speak. Surrounded, both while thinking and while giving utterance to my thoughts, by Beauty; composing and speaking in the midst of a material nature saturated and suffused with this element; it will not appear forced or unnatural if I find in it, the theme of our reflections at this hour.

It is not my purpose however to surrender myself, or to lead others to surrender themselves, to the extreme influence and impression of this quality, and to fall into a vague and rhapsodic train of thought or feeling. On the contrary my aim will be purely and perhaps intensely practical, and I hope with the aid of your own afterthought to make the particular aspect of the general subject of Aesthetics, that will be exhibited, contribute to scholarship, culture, and character.

The specific theme then, to which I would invite your attention, is: *The true theory and relative position of the Beautiful, with reference more particularly to culture and to character.* In investigating this subject, I think we shall find it one for the times, and the class of men addressed. If I am not mistaken we shall find, in a false theory of Beauty, and, as a consequence, in the false position which it holds as a source and instrument of culture, the root of some of the radical defects, and false tendencies, of the educated class. For if this class need any one thing more than another, it is a rational, sober, and severe, estimate of the *essential* nature of the Beautiful, and especially of the relation which it sustains to the True and the Good. In our age there is danger that culture will go the way that Grecian and Roman culture went, and from the same cause; an undue cultivation of the aesthetic nature, to the neglect of the intellectual and moral. There is always danger lest the most influential class in society, the literary and cultivated portion, form and shape themselves by Beauty more than by Truth, by Art more than by Philosophy and Religion.

If we accept the Platonic classification, all things in the universe arrange themselves under these three terms: the Beautiful, the True, and the Good. These three ideas cover and include all that can possibly come before the human mind as a worthy object of thought and action. On them, as a foundation, the human mind has built up its most permanent and grandest structures, and with them, in some one or other of their manifold aspects the human mind is constantly occupied. The idea of the Good lies at the bottom of all religion, and of all inquiries connected with this chief concern of man. The idea of the True lies at the bottom of all science, and of the scientific tendency in individuals and nations. The idea of the Beautiful underlies all those products and agencies of the human soul that address the imagination; all art, and all literature in the stricter signification of the term, as the antithesis of science. This classification, the work of the most philosophic brain of antiquity, at once so simple and so comprehensive, may therefore well stand as the condensation and epitome of all thought, and the key to all the varieties in human culture and national character.

But what is the order in which these ideas stand? — Which is first and which is last in importance? Which is most necessary and absolute in its nature? Which is the substance, and which is the accident? The answer to these questions, the theory upon this point, according as it shall be, is either vital or fatal. It will determine the whole style and character of human culture, both individual and national. If Beauty is placed first, in speculation and in life, and Truth and Goodness are regarded as subordinate, a corresponding style of education will follow. If the True and the Good are recognized as the substance, and the Beautiful as the property and shadow, another and entirely different style will result. Here, therefore, the inquirer stands at the point of divergence between the two principal species of civilization and culture of which human history is made up; that of luxury, enervation, decline, and fall, on the one hand, and that of severity, strength, growth, and grandeur, on the other. At this point, also, he stands upon the line which divides the lower from the higher forms of literature; the lower from the higher products of art itself; the more shallow and erroneous, from the more profound and correct, systems of philosophy and religion. Here is the summit-level and ridge whence the streams flow due east and due west, never to mingle in a common ocean. For if history teaches anything, it teaches that according as a nation and a national mind starts from the one or the other of these ideas, as a point of departure and as the guiding thought in its career, will be its style of development.

The true theory of Beauty subordinates it to the True and the Good. Any estimate of it, that sets it above these two eternal and necessary ideas, is both incorrect and unphilosophical. The closer we think, and the nearer we get to the essence of these three conceptions, the more clearly shall we perceive that while Truth and Goodness appear more and more absolute and necessary, Beauty, *in comparison with them*, appears more and more relative and contingent. The human mind can never, in its own thinking, annihilate the True and the Good, i. e. it cannot conceive of their non-existence. It cannot abstract them from the Divine nature and from the created universe, and have anything substantial left.— These *must* be.

> * * * * if *these* fail,
> The pillared firmament is rottenness
> And earth's base built on stubble.

But not so with Beauty. The mind can abstract it from the nature of God, and if Truth and Goodness still remain, there is still something august, something awe-inspiring, something sublime, left. The mind can think it away from the universe of God, but if that universe is still filled with the manifestations of wisdom and excellence, it is still worthy of its architect. It is indeed true that Beauty has a real and immanent existence, both in the being of God and in creation; but the point we are urging is, that it is there as *subordinate* to these moral elements, and these higher ideas. It is indeed true that from eternity to eternity Beauty is a quality in the nature of the First Perfect and the First Fair, and from this fountain has welled up and poured over into the whole creation of God like sunset into the hemisphere, but it has been only as the accompaniment and adornment of higher and more august qualities. The Beautiful is not, as some teach, either the True or the Good; neither is it more absolute and perfect than these. These are the substance, the eternal essence, and it, *in relation to them*, is the accident. The Beautiful indeed inheres in the True and the Good, and it forever accompanies them, even as light, according to the fine saying of Plato, is the shadow of God; but it is not therefore to be regarded as the highest of all ideas, or as the crowning element in the universe.

For where does Beauty reside? Where is its seat? Always in the *form*, as distinguished from the substance. When the human soul swells with the feeling, it is impressed not by the truth and substantial reality of an object, but by something that in comparison with this is secondary and accidental. When, for example, the sense for Beauty is completely filled and deluged by a sun-set or a sun-rise, the essential meaning of this scene is not necessarily in the soul. That which this scene is for Science, its truth for the pure intellect, is most certainly not in the mind; for the poetic vision and the scientific vision are contraries. And that which it is for Religion may be, and too often is, alien to the soul; for this feeling for the Beauty that is in the sun-rise, is by no means identical with the feeling for the Goodness that is there. In every instance it is the form and not the substance, it is the beauty and not the truth, that addresses the aesthetic nature, while in every instance it is the substance and not the form, it is the true and not the beautiful, that addresses the intellectual and moral natures.

And why should it not be so? If, as we have seen, the Beautiful is a subordinate quality; if it is only the glittering garment of the universe; to what part of man's nature should it appeal, but to that luxury rather than necessity of the human soul, the aesthetic sense. And so it is. Over against that Beauty which the Creator has poured with lavish, I had almost said indifferent, hand, over his creation, he has set a portion of man's nature, whose function it is to drink it in, and as He never intended that this mere decoration of his works should engross the soul to the exclusion of the wisdom and goodness displayed in them, so He never intended that the sense for the Beautiful should absorb and destroy the sense for the True and the Good.

We shall see still more clearly the correctness of this theory of the Beautiful, by considering for a moment the nature and influence of that department which is based upon this idea, viz: Fine Art. The aim and end of Art is fine form, and nothing but fine form. I do not forget that in every work of Art there is a truth at the bottom, and that the power of a painting or a statue is dependent upon the *meaning* everywhere present in it. Still this significant thought at the base, this intellectual expression in the product, is not that which *constitutes it a work of Art.* It is the beauty of this thought, the fine form of this idea, which is the end of Art, and which renders its products different from those of Science. For if Art were merely and purely an expression of truth, how would it differ from Science, and why would not every subject that had meaning in it be a fit one for the artist?

Art, it is true, has a significance, and it is high and ideal in proportion to the depth and fulness of the idea it embodies, yet it differs from Science and Religion by employing both the True and the Good *as means only.* Its own sole *end* is Beauty, to which it subordinates all else. It embodies Truth and Virtue only that it may exhibit the beauty in them, and addresses the intellect and heart only that it may reach the imagination. After all its connection with the substance, Art is still formal. And this is no disparagement to it. It is no undervaluation to draw sharp lines about a department of human effort, and strip off what does not essentially belong to it. Fine Art has its own proper and important vocation, and Science and Religion have theirs, and each is honored by being strictly defined, and rigorously confined to its own aim, end, and limits.

Now such being the nature of Fine Art, considered as a department of human effort and an instrument to be employed in educating the human mind, what must be its influence if left to itself; if unbalanced and uncompleted by other departments? What style of culture will the idea of the Beautiful originate in the individual and national mind, when severed from the ideas of the True and the Good? The answer to this question is to be found in history. One of the great historical races, in the plan of Providence, received its training and development under the excessive and exorbitant influence of Beauty, and for a moment I invite your attention to an examination of the results.

The Greek mind was eminently aesthetic, and the Greek nature was controlled by a too strong and intense tendency to the Beautiful. If the human mind is truthful and solemn anywhere, it is so within the sphere of religion; but we may say of the Greek, as was said of one of the most genial of modern errorists by one of the most profound of modern thinkers, that he was more in love with the beauty of religion than its truth. The Greek religion was the worship of Beauty, and the whole life of the people; private and public, literary and political; was formed by this idea to an extent and thoroughness never witnessed before or since. But the Greek mind, with all the charm and influence it has exerted upon the modern mind, and will continue to exert till the last syllable of recorded time, had one great and radical defect. The True and the Holy did not interest it sufficiently. These ideas did not mould it and form it from the centre. Hence the Greek nature was not a deep and solemn one. It never felt, unless we except the heroic period in its history; a period that is hardly historic; the influence of that which is higher than Beauty, and which has an affinity with a more profound part of the human constitution than the aesthetic sense.

The truth is, that as the intellectual and moral nature of man is his highest endowment, so the True and the Good, as the highest ideas, are its proper correspondent. When, therefore, as in the case of the Greek, a relatively inferior portion of the soul became superior, and a relatively inferior idea became ultimate and engrossing, it was not possible that the highest development of human nature should take place, or the highest style of culture should be originated. The influence which the Greek mind has exerted upon the modern world, great as it has been, and beneficial as it has been, has nevertheless not been of the absolutely highest order, unless we set the aesthetic above the intellectual and moral, Art before Science and Religion, and the culture springing from the form above that springing from the substance.

Far be it from me, on such an occasion and before

such an audience, to undervalue classical education. I have not the slightest sympathy with that Jacobinism in literature, which would throw aside the study of the ancient classics and shut out the modern mind from the beauty, and symmetry, and cultivating influence, of Greek and Roman letters. Still it should be remembered that no single literature can do everything for the human intellect. On the contrary, each and every literature that is historic has one particular function to perform. In the education of the modern mind, classical literature has its own peculiar office to discharge, and this is, to infuse that beauty and symmetry which it possesses in so high degree into modern thought; to furnish a fine Form for the modern Idea. For it must not for a moment be supposed that the modern mind is to go back to the ancient for the substance of literature. The Christian world cannot go back into the Pagan world in search for the True and the Good, but it ever must go back there for the Beautiful. For the sphere of knowing, and consequently of reflection and feeling, in which the ancient mind moved, was narrow and contracted, compared with the "infinite and sea-like arena" on which the modern careers. Not that minds may not be found in the ancient world of equal depth, grasp, and power, with any that have adorned modern literature, but the materials on which they were compelled to labor fell far short of that which is the subject of modern effort, in depth, richness, and compass. The range of thought and feeling, in which the ancient mind moved, in respect to the great subjects pertaining to man's origin and destiny, was "cabined, cribbed and confined," compared with that vast expanse in which it is the privilege of the modern to think and feel. The Christian Revelation, while it imparted more determinateness and significance to those doctrines of natural religion upon which Plato and Aristotle had reflected with such truthfulness and profundity, at the same time lodged in the mind of the modern world an amount of new truth, that widened infinitely the field of human vision, and the scope of human reflection. We have but to compare Homer, Aeschylus, and Virgil, with Dante, Shakspeare, and Milton, to see how immensely the range of the human mind was augmented by a Divine Revelation. In these latter instances, it moves in a region large enough for it, and feels the influence of those "truths deep as the centre" with which it is connected by origin and destiny; while in the former instances, though the vague yearnings, and obscure anticipations, and unsatisfied longings, evidence the heaven-born nature of the human spirit, yet they serve only to reveal still more clearly the helplessness of its bondage, and the closeness of its confinement to this "bank and shoal of time." *

But although the Christian Religion so widened the sphere of human thought and feeling, and so deepened and spiritualized the processes of the human mind, and so enriched it in the material for literature, it indirectly diminished its artistic ability, and rendered it less able to embody its conceptions. This very opulence in the material, and this very elevation of the theme, embarrassed the mind. For in proportion to the richness and intrinsic excellence of the thought, does the difficulty increase,

* Hence that undertone of melancholy in the more serious portions of classical literature, (as the Histories of Tacitus, and the Morals of Plutarch) unrelieved by any notes of hope or triumph struck out by the knowledge, and the prospect, of the final consummation. The gloom of Dante is far different from the gloom of Aeschylus; for while, like his, it springs from the consciousness of the life-long conflict between good and evil, it is illumined by the knowledge of the final issue. In the case of the Pagan, he gloom is made thicker by the total ignorance of the great hereafter.

of putting it into a form worthy of it. The problem of Art, in every instance, is to attain an exact correspondence between the matter and the form; to embody the idea in just the right amount of material, so that the idea shall not overflow and drown the form, nor the form overlay and crush the idea. Hence, among other qualities, the *cleanness*, the *niceness*, of a successful work of Art. But this problem, it is plain, becomes more difficult, in proportion as the idea, or guiding thought, is more profound or significant in its nature. For by reason of its depth and expanse it becomes vastly more comprehensive and pregnant, and less capable of being brought within the limitation of Art, within the bounds of a form. The nearer the subject-matter approaches the infinite; the more vast and unlimited the idea in the mind; the greater the difficulty of exhibiting it in the finite shapings of Art.

Now the ancient mind had these advantages. In the first place the material, the truth, upon which it labored, was far more wieldy and compassable than that which is presented to the modern mind, and in the second place it was (especially in the instance of the Greek) a much more artistic mind, in and of itself. The result, consequently, was a far closer correspondence between the substance and the form, and hence a much more successful solution of the problem of Fine Art, than has ever been attained by any other people.

The modern mind therefore, the Christian world, while it cannot go back into the Pagan world for the substance of literature, for the True and the Good, must ever go back there for the form, for the Beautiful. And it was precisely because the European mind, in the fifteenth century, felt the need of this aesthetic element in culture, which it was conscious of not possessing, that it betook itself to classical literature. At that period, when the human mind was waking up from the dormancy of the middle ages, and was beginning to feel the fresh impulses of the Christian Religion, it was filled, to overflowing, with ideas and principles, thoughts and feelings. Its powers and energies were being almost preternaturally roused by this influx of new truth, the natural tendency of which is to stir the human soul, preconformed as it is to its influence, to its inmost centre. But this season of mental fermentation was no time for serene contemplation, and beautiful construction. The whole *materiel* for a new literature was originated; but originated in a mind agitated to its lowest depths by the energy and force that was pouring through it, and which for this very reason was not master of itself, or of the material with which it was laboring. *Form;* rounded, symmetrical, finished, *Form;* was needed for this Matter, and hence the modern betook himself to the study of that literature preeminent above all others for its artistic perfection. The study of the serene and beautiful models in which Grecian thought embodied itself, tamed the wildly-working mind of the Goth, and imparted to it that calm, artistic, *formative*, power by which the intellectual chaos was to become cosmos.*

* It is indeed true, that in the higher forms of Greek literature there is a remarkable depth and seriousness of sentiment which seems to militate against the position taken. Here the Beautiful is more in the back-ground, and the True mainly in the fore-ground. But it should be remembered that the real nature and tendency of the Greek appears far more in the lighter forms of the literature, and especially in that wilderness of works of Art that covered all Greece, than in the deep-toned poetry of Homer and Aeschylus, or the profound sentiment of Plato and Thucydides. This portion of Greek literature derived its tone and matter from that elder period; that heroic age; when the national mind was impressed, as the elder mind always has been, more by the essential than the formal, more by Truth than by Beauty.

But if the literature of the Greeks is predominantly aesthetic, and performs this aesthetic function in the system of modern education, the national character was still more so. The student of Grecian history, especially of the internal history of the Greeks, is struck with the disparity between the national character and the national literature; between the products of the Greek mind, or rather of a few choice Greek minds, and the Greek himself. The more the student becomes acquainted with that extremely imaginative and extremely tasteful, but too lively and too volatile, race of men, the more does he wonder that so much depth and truth of sentiment should be found in the literature that sprang up among them; the more does he wonder that the native bent and tendency of the national mind did not overrule, and suppress, all these higher elements. It is only on the supposition that the great men of Greece were above their race, and breathed in a more solemn and meditative atmosphere than that sunny air in which the Athenian populace lived, that he can account for the remarkable difference between the profound, severe, and moral, spirit of the Greek tragedy, and the fickle, gay, and altogether trifling, temper of the Ionic race.

Whatever this excessive tendency to the Beautiful may have wrought out of the Greeks, in some respects, it is certain that it contributed to the enervation and destruction of all strong character in the nation. That Ionic race, instead of following indulgently and extravagantly, as they did, their native bias, ought to have subjected it to the most severe education and restraint. Those two other ideas which dawned in such solemnity and power upon the intellect of their greatest philosopher, ought to have rained down influence upon them. Those more serious and awe-inspiring objects of reflection, the True and the Good, ought to have dawned upon the popular mind in a clearer light and with a more overcoming power. How different, so far as all the grand and heroic elements of national character are concerned, were the Greeks of that golden age of ancient Art, the age of Pericles, from the Romans of the days of Numa! We grant that there is but little outward beauty, in that naked and austere period in Roman history, but there is to be found in that *character*, as it comes down to us in the legends of Livy and has been reconstructed in the pages of Niebuhr, the strongest, and soundest, and grandest, and sublimest, nationality in the Pagan world. And this was owing to the fact that the early Roman was intellectual and moral, rather than aesthetic. I am speaking, it will be remembered, of a Pagan character, and my remarks must be taken in a comparative sense. Bearing this in mind, we may say that the strength and grandeur of the national character of the first Romans, sprang from the fact that it was moulded and shaped mainly by the ideas of Truth and Virtue. The aesthetic nature was repressed, and, if you please, almost entirely suppressed, but the intellect and the moral sense were developed all the more. Hence those high qualities in their national character; courage, energy, firmness, probity, patriotism, reverence for the gods and the oath; qualities that were hardly more visible in the ancient, than they are in the modern, Greek.

And this brings us to the more distinct consideration of what we suppose to be the influence of Fine Art, when it becomes the leading department of effort, and the chief instrument and end of culture, for the individual or the nation. The effect of the Beautiful upon the human soul, when unmixed, uncounteracted, and exorbitant, is enervation. And this, from the very nature of the element itself. We have seen that it cannot be placed upon an equality with the other two elements that enter into the constitution of the universe. It cannot be regarded as so substantial and so necessary in its nature, as the True and the Holy. It is only the property and decoration of that which is essential and absolute. It is only the form. It consequently does not address the highest faculties of the human soul, and if it did, could not waken or generate power in them. When, therefore, it is made to do the work of the higher ideas; when it is compelled to go beyond its own proper sphere, the aesthetic nature, and to furnish aliment for the intellectual and moral nature; it is set at a work it can never do. The intellect and moral sense demand their own appropriate objects ; they require their correlatives, the True and the Good; they cry out for the substance and cannot be satisfied with the form, however beautiful. When therefore Beauty is selected as the great idea, by which the individual or national mind is to be moulded, the result is of necessity mental enervation. The human intellect cannot, any more than the human heart, be content with mere form. Like the heart, it cries out, in its own way, for the living God; for Truth and Goodness, the most essential qualities in the Divine nature; for Wisdom and Virtue, the most essential elements in the moral universe He has made. And what is there in the very process of Art itself, when it is isolated from the other and higher departments of human effort, that goes to render man more intellectual? The very vocation of Art is to sensualize; using the term technically and in no bad sense. Its processes, so far as they are merely artistic, are not spiritualizing, but the contrary. The vocation of Art is to bring down an idea of the human mind; a purely intellectual, purely immaterial, entity; into the sphere of sense, and there materialize it into colors, and lines, and outlines, and proportions, for the sense. The very calling of Art, as a department of effort, is to render sensuous the spiritual. And the fact that it does this, in the case of all high Art, in an ideal manner; that in the genuine product, the idea shines out everywhere through the beautiful form; does not conflict with the position. If, therefore, in a general way and for the purpose of characterizing the departments, we may say that in Science and Religion the mental process is spiritualizing, we may affirm that in Art the process is sensualizing. If in the analysis and synthesis of the True and the Good, the mind passes through an increasingly intellectual process, in the embodiment of the merely Beautiful, it passes through an exactly opposite one. If Philosophy and Religion tend to render the mind more intellectual, Fine Art tends to render it more material and sensuous by fixing the eye on the form.

Now such an influence as this upon the human mind and character, if unbalanced and uncounteracted, is enervating. There may be, and generally has been, great outward refinement and a most luxurious elegance thrown over the culture that originates under such influences, but it is too generally at the expense of strength and virtue and heroism of character. However high the aims of the individual or the nation may have been in the outset, history shows too plainly, that the nerve was soon relaxed and the mind slackened all away, at first, into a too luxurious, and finally, into a voluptuous culture. When the Artist, by the very theory and metaphysical nature of his vocation, is compelled to keep his eye on Beauty, on Fine Form, on the sensuously Agreeable, he must be a strong and virtuous nature that is not mastered by his calling. If he can preserve an austere tone; if he can even keep himself up on the high ground of an abstract and ideal Art, and not sink into a too ornate and licentious style; we may be certain that there was great moral stamina at bottom.

But speculation aside, let us appeal to history again. What does the story of Art in modern times teach in relation to the position that the unmixed, unbalanced, effect of the Beautiful, is mental enervation? The most wonderful age of Art was that of Leo X. The long slumber of the aesthetic nature of man, during the barbarism and warfare of those five centuries between the dismemberment of the Roman empire and the establishment of the principal nations and nationalities of modern Europe, was broken by an outburst of Beauty and Beautiful Art, as sudden, rapid, and powerful, as the bloom and blossom of spring in the arctic zone. Such a multitude of artists and such an opulence of artistic talent, will probably never be witnessed again in one age or nation. But did a grand, did even a respectable, national character spring into existence along with this bloom of Art, this shower of Beauty? We know that there were other influences at work, and among others a religious system whose very nature it is to carnalize and stifle all that is distinctively spiritual in the human soul; but no one can study the history of the period, without being convinced that this excessive and all-absorbing tendency of the general mind of Italy towards Beauty and Fine Art, contributed greatly to the general enervation of soul. Most certainly it did not work counter to it. Read the memoirs of a man like Benvenuto Cellini; an inferior man it is true, but an artist and reflecting the general features of his time; and see how utterly unfit both the individual and national culture of that period was for any lofty, high-minded, truly historic, achievement. The solemn truths of Religion, and the lofty truths of Philosophy, exerted little or no influence upon that group of Italian artists, so drunken with Beauty. They possessed little of that intellectual severity which enters into every great character; little of that strung muscle and hard nerve which should support the intellect as well as the will.— And therefore it is that we cannot find in the Italian history of those ages, any more than in the Italian character of the present day, any of that high emprise and grand achievement which crowds the history of the Teutonic races, less art-loving, but more intellectual and moral.— These races and their descendants have sometimes been charged with a destitution of the aesthetic sense, and the inferiority of their Art, compared with that of Italy, has been cited as proof of their inferiority as a race of men; but it is enough to say in reply, that these Goths, educating themselves mainly by the ideas of the True and the Good, have given origin to all the literatures, philosophies, and systems of government and religion, that constitute the crowning glory of the modern world. The Italian intellect was enfeebled and exhausted by that unnatural birth of Beauty upon Beauty. Ever since the fourteenth century, it has been wandering about in that world of fine forms, like Spenser's knight in the Bower of Bliss, until all power of intellect is gone.

Every truly great and grand character, be it individual or national, is more or less a severe one; a character which, comparatively, is more intellectual and moral, than aesthetic.* This position merits a moment's examin-

* According to the etymology of the old Grammarians, favored by Doederlein, the severe is the *intensely true.* Doederlein i. 76, præferendum censet vett. Gramm. sententiam qua *severus* cognationem habeat cum *verus* * * * ita ut *se*, ex more Gr. α priv., intensivam vim contineat. —*Facciolati's Lexicon in loc.*

ation. And in the first place, look into political history and see what traits lie at the bottom of all the best periods in national development. Out of what type of mind and style of life has the venerable, the *heroic*, age always sprung? Are men enervate or are they austere, are they aesthetic or are they intellectual and moral in culture, during that period when the national virtue is formed and the historic renown of the people is acquired?

The heroic age of Greece, as it comes down to us in the Homeric poems, was a period of simplicity and strictness. The Greeks of that early time were intellectual men, moral men, compared with the Greeks of the days of Alcibiades. Turn to the pages of Athenæus, and get a view of the in-door life and every-day character of a still later period in Grecian history, and then turn to the corresponding picture of the heroic period contained in the Odyssey, mark the difference in the impression made upon you by each representation, and know from your own feelings, that all that is strong, and heroic, and simple, and grand, in national character springs from a severe mind and a predominantly moral culture, and all that is feeble, and supine, and inefficient, and despicable, in national character, springs from a luxurious mind and a predominantly aesthetic culture.

And how stands the case with Rome? Which is the venerable period in her history? Is it to be sought for in the luxurious and (so far as Rome ever had it) the aesthetic civilization of the empire, or in the intellectual and moral civilization of the monarchy and republic? All the strength and grandeur of the Roman character and of the Roman nationality lies back of the third Punic war. Nay, if Rome had been conquered by Carthage, and had gone out of political existence, its real glory, its proper historic renown, would have been greater than it is. If in the idea called up by the word Rome, there were wanting, there could be eliminated, the physical corruption and the luxurious but merely outward refinement of the empire, and there were left only the severe virtue, the sublime endurance, and the moral grandeur, of the monarchy and republic, the idea would be more sublime in history and more impressive in contemplation. And whence originated that Sabine element, that tough core, that hard kernel, in the Roman character, that lay at the centre and kept Rome up, during her long agony of intestine and external conflict? It had its origin among the mountains, amid the great features of nature, and it was purified by the privation and hardship of a severe life in the forests of central Italy, on that spine of the Ausonian peninsula, until it became as sound, sweet, and hard, as the chestnuts of the Appenines upon which it was fed. Intellectual and moral elements, and not an aesthetic element, were the hardy root of all the political power and prosperity of Rome.

There is no need, even if there were time, to cite instances corroborating the view presented, from modern political history. The Puritanism of Old England and of New England will readily suggest itself, to every one, as the one eminently severe national character, with which the power and glory of the English and Anglo-American races, and the highest hopes of the modern world, are vitally connected. It will be sufficient to say, that the more profound is our acquaintance with political history, the more clearly shall we see that all that is powerful, and permanent, and impressive, in the nations, nationalities, and governments of the world, sprang directly or indirectly from a nature in which the aesthetic was subordinate to the intellectual and moral, and for which the True and the Good were more supreme ideas than the Beautiful.

Furthermore, the position taken holds true in the sphere of literature also. The great works in every instance are the productions of a severe strength; of "the Herculeses and not the Adonises of literature," to use a phrase of Bacon. When the aesthetical prevails over the intellectual and moral, the prime qualities, the depth, the originality, and the power, die out of letters, and the mediocrity that ensues is but poorly concealed by the elegance and polish thrown over it. Even when there is much genius and much originality, an excess of Art, a too deep suffusion of Beauty, a too fine flush of color, is often the cause of a radical defect. Suppose that the poetry of Spenser had more of that passion in it which Milton mentions as the third of the three main qualities of poetry; suppose (without however wishing to deny the great excellence of the Fairy Queen in regard to intellectual and moral elements) that the proportion of the aesthetic had been somewhat less, would it not have been more powerful and higher poetry? Suppose that the mind and the culture of Wieland and Goethe had been vastly more under the influence of Truth, and vastly less under that of Beauty; that the substance instead of the form, had been the mould in which these men were moulded and fitted as intellectual workmen; might not the first have come nearer to our Spenser, and might not the latter have produced some works that would perhaps begin to justify his ardent but ignorant admirers in placing him in the same class with Shakspeare and Milton; a position to which, as it is, he has not the slightest claim?

As a crowning and conclusive proof of the correctness of the view presented, I will refer you to only one mind.

I refer you to John Milton, one of those two minds which tower high above all others in the sphere of modern literature. If there ever was a man in whom the aesthetic was in complete subjection to the intellectual and moral, without being in the least suppressed or mutilated by them, that man was Milton. If there ever was a human intellect so entirely master of itself, of such a severe type, that all its processes seem to have been the pure issue of discipline and law, it was the intellect of Milton. In contemplating the grandeur of the products of his mind, we are apt to lose sight of his mind itself, and of his intellectual character. If we rightly consider it, the discipline to which he subjected himself, and the austere style of intellect and of Art in which it resulted, are as worthy of the reverence and admiration of the scholar as the Paradise Lost. We have unfortunately no minute and detailed account of his every-day life, but from all that we do know, and from all that we can infer from the lofty, colossal, culture and character in which he comes down to us, it is safe to say that Milton must have subjected his intellect to a restraint, and rigid dealing with its luxurious tendencies, as strict as that to which Simon Stylites or St. Francis of Assisi subjected their bodies. We can trace the process, the defecating purifying process, that went on in his intellect, through his entire productions. The longer he lived and the more he composed, the severer became his taste, and the more *grandly* and *serenely* beautiful became his works. It is true that the theory of Art, and of culture, opposed to that which we are recommending, may complain of the occasional absence of Beauty, and may charge as a fault an undue nakedness and austerity of form. But one thing is certain and must be granted by the candid ritic, that whenever the element of Beauty *is* found in

Milton, it is found in absolute purity. That severe refining process, that test of light and of fire, to which all his materials were subjected, left no residuum that was not perfectly pure. And therefore it is, that throughout universal literature, a more absolute Beauty and a more delicate aerial grace, are not to be found than appear in the Comus and the fourth book of Paradise Lost.

But we are not anxious on this point of Beauty, especially in connection with the name of Milton. Sublimity is a higher quality, and so are Strength and Grandeur; and if Beauty does not come *in the train*, and *as the mere ornament*, of these, it is not worth while to seek it by itself and for its own sake. And much will be gained when education, and culture, and authorship, shall dare to take this high stand which Milton took; shall dare to pass by Beauty, in the start, and to aim at higher elements and severer qualities, in the train, and as the ornament of which, a real Beauty and an absolute Grace shall follow of themselves.

Returning then to the intellectual character of Milton, let me advise you to study that character until you see that the strict, and philosophically severe, theory of the Beautiful and of Art lies under the whole of it. Milton had no affinities for excessive sensuous Beauty. He was no voluptuary in any sense. So far as the sense was concerned he was abstemious as an ascetic, and so far as the soul was concerned he knew no such thing as luxury. He devoted himself to poetry, an Art which, glorious as it is, yet has tendencies that need counteraction, which tempts to Arcadian and indulgent views of human life and human character, and which, as literary history shows, has too often been the medium through which dreamy and uncontrolled natures have communicated themselves to the world. But as a poet, he constructed with all the severity of Science and all the purity of Religion. The poetic Art, as it appears in Milton, is spiritual and spiritualizing.*

If this element of severity is entirely wanting in a man; if he is entirely destitute of austerity; if his nature is wholly and merely aesthetic, constantly melting and dissolving in an atmosphere of Beauty; whatever else may be attributed to him, strength and grandeur cannot be. We do not deny that there is a sort of interest in such natures, but we deny that it is of the highest sort. If a man is born with a beautiful soul, and it is his tendency (to use a Shaksperean phrase) "to wallow in the lily beds;" to revel in luxurious sensations, be they wakened by material or immaterial Beauty; unless he subject his mind to the training of higher ideas, and of a higher department than that of Fine Art, his career will end in the total enervation of his being. This tendency ought in every instance to be disciplined. The individual in whom it exists, ought to superinduce upon it a strictness and austerity that will check its luxuriance, and bring it within the limits of a severer and therefore purer taste.

The least injurious and safest form which an undue aesthetic tendency can take on, is a quick sense for the Beautiful in nature. But even here, an unbalanced, uneducated, tendency is enervating That dreamy mood of young poets, that dissolving of the soul in "the light of setting suns," must be educated and sobered by a severe discipline of the head and heart, or no poetry will

* We may say of Milton, in reference to the severe ideal character of his Art, as Fuseli has said of the same feature in Michael Angelo; "he is the salt of Art." He *saves* it from its inherent tendency to corruption, by a larger infusion of intellectual and moral elements, than exists in the average productions of the department.

be produced that will go down through all ages. It is not so much a deep tendency as a transient mood of the soul, and needs the infusion of intellectual and moral elements, in order that it may become "the vision and faculty divine." Turn to a great collection, like Chalmers' British Poets, and observe how large a portion of this mass of poetry is destitute of the power of producing a *permanent* impression upon the human imagination; how little out of this great bulk is selected to be read by the successive generations of English students; how small a portion of it, compared with the whole amount, is profoundly and genuinely poetic; and at the same time notice how very much of it was evidently composed under the influence which the Beautiful in nature exerts upon an undisciplined, and uneducated, aesthetic sense, and you will have the strongest possible proof of the enervating, enfeebling, influence of this quality when isolated from the intellectual and moral.—The mind needed a severer culture, and a discipline wrought out for it by higher ideas, that could *use* and *elaborate* these obscure feelings, these dim dreams, this blind sense, for the purposes of a higher and more genuine Art. It is often said, we know, that science is the death of poetry; that the study of the Kantean philosophy injured the poetry of Schiller, and the study of all philosophies the poetry of Coleridge; that the charm, and the glow, and the flush, and the fulness, and the luxuriance, and the gorgeousness, were all destroyed by the acid and blight of science. But we do not believe this. These poets might have written more had their imagination not been passed through these severe processes of the intellect, they might have been more fluent, but that they would have written more that will have a *lasting* poetic interest remains to be seen. Their Art is all the higher, for the check and restraint imposed upon their poetic nature. And who will not say, to take a plain example, that if the young soul of Keats could have been corded with a stronger muscle, and overshaded with a severer tone of feeling and sentiment; that if a more masculine culture could have been married with that genuinely feminine soul; a higher poetry and a still purer Beauty would have been the offspring of this hymeneal union? *

And this brings us to the more positive side of the subject. Thus far we have spoken in a negative way of what the Beautiful is not, and of what it cannot do for the human soul and human culture. We now affirm that only on the theory which subordinates Beauty to Truth can the highest style of Beauty itself be originated, and that only when the department of Aesthetics is subordinate to those of Philosophy and Religion, does a genuinely beautiful culture, either individual or national, spring into existence. Without this check and subordination, the aesthetic quality will destroy itself by becoming excessive. The more staple elements that must enter into and substantiate it, will all evaporate; as if the warm organic flesh should all turn into the fine flush of the complexion; as if the air and the light and the foliage and the waters, all the *material*, all the *solidity*, of a beautiful landscape, should vanish away into mere crimson and vermilion. For, as we have already observed, true Beauty in a work of Art, is conditioned upon the presence in it of some intelligible idea. There must be some truth and some expression, in order to the existence of the pure quality itself. Beauty cannot stand alone. There must be a meaning underneath of which

* If the school of Tennyson needs any one thing, it is an austerer culture.

it is the clothing. There must be an intellectual conception within the product, to which it can cling for support, and from which it derives all its growing, lasting, highest, charm for a cultivated taste. Hence it is, that as we go up the scale, Beauty actually becomes more ideal, more and more intellectual and moral. It undergoes a refining process, as it rises in grade, whereby the sensuous element, so predominant in the lower products of Art, is volatilized. There is more appeal to the soul and less to the sense, as we go up from the more florid and showy schools of painting, e. g., to the more severe and spiritual. The same is true of the Beautiful in nature. As we ascend from the inferior to the higher vegetation, we find not only a more delicate organization, but a more delicate Beauty. The gaudy and coarse coloring gives place to more exquisite hues, in proportion as *mind;* in proportion as the *presiding intelligence* of the Creator; comes more palpably into view. In the words of Milton, all things are

> * * more refined, more spirituous, and pure,
> As nearer to Him placed, or nearer tending,
> Till body up to spirit work.
> * * * * * * So from the root
> Springs *lighter* the green stalk; from thence the leaves
> More *aery;* last the bright consummate flower
> *Spirits odorous* breathes; flowers and their fruit,
> Man's nourishment, by gradual scale sublimed
> To *vital spirits* aspire, to *animal,*
> To *intellectual.**

And all things grow more highly beautiful as we keep pace with this upward step in nature, until we pass over into the distinctively spiritual sphere, and reach the

* Par. Lost. v. 475.

crown and completion of all Beauty; the beauty of character, or the "beauty of holiness." Observe that all along this limitless line we find a growing severity; that is, an increase of the intellectual or moral element. Sensuous beauty is displaced, or rather absorbed and transfigured, by intellectual beauty; the ideas of the True and the Good more and more assert their supremacy, by employing the Beautiful as the mere medium through which *they* become visible, even as light, after traversing the illimitable fields of ether without either color or form, on coming into an atmosphere, into a medium, thickens into a solid blue vault.

A reference to the actual history of Fine Art will also verify the position here taken. As matter of fact, we find this spiritualizing process; this advance of the substance and this retreat of the form; going on in every school of Art that grew more purely and highly beautiful, and in the soul of every artist who went up the scale of artists. That school which did not grow more ideal, invariably grew more sensuous and less beautiful, and that artist who did not by study and discipline become more severe and studied in style, invariably sunk down into the lower grade. All the works of Art that go down through succeeding ages with an ever-growing beauty as well as an ever-towering sublimity; all the great models and master-pieces; owe their origin to a most severe taste and a most spiritual idea. The study of the great models in every department of Art, be it painting, or sculpture, or poetry, will convince any one that the imagination, the artist's faculty, when originating its greatest works imposes restraints upon itself; in reality is severe with itself. If the artist allows his imagination to revel amid all the possible forms that will throng, and press, through this wonderfully luxuriant and productive power; if he suffers it to waste its energy in an idle play with its thick-coming fancies; if, in short, he does not preserve it a *rational* imagination, and regulate it by the deeper element and severer principle inherent in it, his productions will necessarily be in the lower style. It is for this reason that the artist betakes himself to study. He would break up this revelry of a lawless, uneducated, imagination. He would set limits to a vague and aimless energy. He would wield a productive talent that lies lower down; that works more calmly and grandly; more according to reason and a profounder Art. The educating process, in the case of the artist, is intended to repress a cloying luxuriance and to superinduce a beautiful austerity; to substitute an ideal for a material beauty. Hence we see that the artist, as he grows in power and high excellence, grows in strictness of theory and severity of taste. His products are marked by a graver beauty, and the presence of a purer ideal, as he goes up the scale of artists.

As an example, we may cite the instance of Michael Angelo. For grandeur, sublimity, and power of permanent impression, he confessedly stands at the head of his Art, and although in regard to beauty, Raphael may dispute the palm with him, and by some may be thought his superior, yet no one can deny that (as in the case of Milton) whenever this element does appear in "the mighty Tuscan," it is of the most absolute and perfect species.*

* Winckelmann, looking from his point of view, which was that of classic Art merely, has expressed a disparaging opinion in regard to Angelo, so far as the Beautiful is concerned, and seems to have laid the foundation for the superficial and too general opinion, that in respect to this quality he was by nature greatly inferior to Raphael. But the able editors of his works justly call attention to the fact, that Winckelmann is wrong in judging of modern Art in this servile way, and allude to a scarce and but little known poem of Angelo's, in which a most delicate and feminine appreciation of beauty

Yet all his productions are characterized by an austere manner. The form is always subservient, and perhaps sometimes somewhat sacrificed, to the idea. And, at any rate, the man himself, compared with the Italian artists generally, compared with Raphael especially, was a spiritual man both in culture and character. We confess that we look with a veneration bordering upon awe upon that grand nature, severe, abstract, and ideal, in an age that was totally sensuous in head and heart, and in a profession whose most seductive and dangerous tendency is to soften and enervate. By the force of a strong heroic character, as well as a hard and persevering study both of Art and of Nature, he counteracted that tendency to a sensuous and a sensualizing beauty, which we have noticed as the bane of Art, and in that nerveless age, so destitute of lofty virtue and stern heroism, stands out like the Memnon's head on the dead level of

is apparent. "In this poem," say they, "the great Michael Angelo reveals himself in a manner that appears striking and wonderful to such as have known him only from his paintings and statues. Heartfelt admiration for beauty, love too deep to be disclosed to its object, a gentle touching sadness wakened by the sense of an existence that cannot satisfy an infinite affection, and a melancholy longing, growing out of this, for dissolution and freedom from the bonds of earth, form the ground-tone of this warmly-glowing poem, in which Angelo gives an expression of the feminine element in his great and mighty nature, that is all the more lovely from the fact that the masculine principle is the prevailing and predominant one in his works of Art."—*Winckelmann's Werke von Meyer und Schulze*, iv. 43, *and Anmerk.* p. 262.

Consonant with this are the following remarks of Lanzi. "We may here observe that when Michael Angelo was so inclined, he could obtain distinction for those endowments in which others excelled. It is a vulgar error to suppose that he had no idea of grace and beauty; the Eve of the Sistine Chapel turns to thank her Maker, on her creation, with an attitude so fine and lovely, that it would do honor to Raphael"

History of Painting, (*Roscoe's Trans.*) i. 176.

the Nile, grand and lonely, yet with "elysian beauty and melancholy grace."

And, in this connection, I cannot refrain from calling your attention to that greatest of American artists, who is at once a proof and illustration of the truth of the general theory advanced. No man will suspect Allston of an underestimate of the Beautiful. In the whole catalogue of ancient and modern artists, there is not to be found a single one in whose mind this element existed in more unmixed and absolute purity: — beauty

> * * * chaste as the icicle
> That's curded by the frost from purest snow,
> And hangs on Dian's temple.

But this spirituality was the fruit not only of a pure nature, but of a high theory. He recognized and felt the supremacy of the True and the Good, over the Beautiful. The reader of his lectures on Art, is struck with the religious carefulness with which he insists upon the superior claims of Truth over those of mere Art, and the earnestness with which he seeks to elevate and spiritualize the profession which he honored and loved, by making it the organ and proclamation of Truth and Holiness. By this, we think the fact can be explained that he produced so little, compared with the exhaustless fertility of the Italian artists. His ideal was so high; the Beautiful was so *spiritually* beautiful for him; that color and form failed to embody his conceptions. His uniform refusal to attempt the representation of Christ; a far too common attempt in Italian Art; undoubtedly rested upon this fact. It was not because his intensely spiritual mind had a less adequate idea of the Divine-Man, than that which floated before the Catholic imagination, but because there beamed upon his ethereal vision, a FORM of such high and awful beauty as could not be put upon a material canvas. It was because he saw so much that he did so little.

But, Gentlemen, there is a still more practical and important side to this whole subject. The department of Art sustains a relation to the growth and development of the human mind, and human society. Like all other departments of human effort, it should therefore be subservient to the great moral end of human existence, and if there were no other alternative, it would be better that the aesthetic nature, and the whole department of Art, and the whole wide realm of the Beautiful, should be annihilated, than that they should continue to exist at the expense of the intellectual and moral, of the True and the Good. We are not at all driven to the alternative, if there be truth in the general theory that has been presented, but if we were, we acknowledge boldly that we would side with the Puritan iconoclast and dash into atoms the Apollo Belvidere itself. Rather than that the department of Art should annihilate Philosophy and Religion; rather than that an enervate beauty should eat out manly strength and severe virtue from character; rather than that a sensualizing process should be introduced into the very heart of society, though it were as beautiful as an opium dream; we would see the element struck out of existence, and man and the universe be left as bald and bare as granite. We honor therefore, that trait in our ancestors, (so often charged upon them as a radical defect in nature, and so often tacitly admitted as such even by some of their descendants), which made them afraid of Fine Art; afraid of music and painting and sculpture and poetry. They dreaded the form, but had no dread of the substance, and therefore were the most philosophic of men. They dreaded the material, but had no dread of the ideal, and therefore were the most intellectual of men. They dreaded the sensuous, but had no dread of the spiritual, and therefore were the most religious of men. The Puritan nature owed but little, comparatively speaking, to aesthetic culture. It was not drawn upon and drawn out, as some natures have been, by Literature and Art, for in the plan of Providence its mission was active rather than contemplative; but we do not hesitate to say, that the contents and genius were there, and that even on the side of the imagination, that nature, had it been unfolded in this direction, would have left a school and a style of Art, using the term in its widest acceptation, second to none. And as it is, we see its legitimate tendency and influence in the poetry of Milton. The Miltonic style of Art is essentially the Puritan Art; beautiful only as it is severe and grand; the Beautiful superinduced upon the True and the Holy.

Gentlemen: —

In the opening of my discourse, I alluded to the fact, that the style of civilization and culture peculiar to the individual or the nation, is determined by the theory, which is consciously or unconsciously assumed, of the nature and relative position of the Beautiful: and at the close of it, I would call your attention to it again. My aim is not iconoclastic. My aim, in all that I have said, has been, not to destroy or in the least to disparage the department of Aesthetics, but to establish and recommend a high and strict and philosophic theory of it, for the purpose of putting it in its right place in the encyclopædia, and thus of promoting its own true growth, and what is of still more importance, the growth of the human mind. Called upon to address scholars, I desire to do something that will contribute to high-toned culture, high-toned thinking, and high-toned character. And I know of no better way, on such an occasion as the present, than to bring out distinctly before the youthful and recipient student, a philosophic, severe, and lofty, theory in regard to that whole department of Art, so fascinating to the young mind and so liable to be employed to excess by it. Depend upon it, Gentlemen, the older you grow and the riper scholars you become, the more severe will be your tastes and the more austere will be your literary sympathies. You will come to see more and more clearly, that neither music, nor painting, nor sculpture, nor architecture, nor poetry, can properly be made the main instrument of human development; that the human intellect and heart demand ultimately a "manlier diet;" that you must become powerful minds and powerful men, mainly through the culture that comes from Science and Religion. You will never, indeed, lose your relish for the Beautiful; on the contrary, you will have a keener and a nicer sense for it, and for all that is based upon it; but you will find a declining interest in its lower forms.—Schools of Poetry and of Art that once pleased you, will become insipid, and perhaps offensive, to your severer taste, your more purged eye, your more rational imagination. There will be fewer and fewer works in the aesthetic sphere that will throw a spell and work a charm, while the deep and central truths of Philosophy and Religion will draw, ever draw, your whole being to themselves, as the moon draws the sea.

And in this way, you will be fitted to do the proper work of educated men in the midst of society. I have alluded to the downward movement, the uniform decay, of the ancient civilizations. History teaches one plain and mournful lesson; that man cannot safely be left to his luxurious tendencies, be they of the sense or the soul. There must be austerity somewhere. There must be a strong head and a sound heart somewhere. And where ought we to look for these but in the educated class? In whom, if not in these, ought we to find that theory of education, that style of culture, and that tone of intellect, which will right up society when it is sinking down into luxury, or hold it where it is if it is already upright and austere? Educated men, amid the currents and in the general drift of society, ought to discharge the function of a warp and anchor. They, of all men, ought to be characterized by strength. And especially do our own age and country need this style of culture. Exposed as the national mind is to a luxurious civilization; as imminently exposed as Nineveh or Rome ever were; the Beautiful is by no means the main idea by which it should be educated and moulded. As in the Prometheus, none but the demi-gods Strength and Force can chain the Titan. Our task, gentlemen, as men of culture, and as men who are to determine the prevailing type of culture, is both in theory and practice to subject the Form to the Substance; to bring the Beautiful under the problem of the True and the Good. Our task, as descendants of an austere ancestry, as partakers in a severe nationality, is to retain the strict, heroic, intellectual, and religious, spirit of the Puritan and the Pilgrim, in these forms of an advancing civilization. In order to this; in order that the sensuously and luxuriously Beautiful may not be too much for us; strength and reserve are needed in the cultivated classes. They must be reticent and, like the sculptor, chisel and re-chisel, until they cut off and cut down to a simple and severe beauty, in Art and in Literature, in Religion and in Life.

THE CHARACTERISTICS, AND IMPORTANCE, OF A NATURAL RHETORIC.

AN INAUGURAL DISCOURSE DELIVERED IN AUBURN THEOLOGICAL SEMINARY, JUNE 16, 1852.

THERE is no greater or more striking contrast, than exists between a thing that is alive, and a thing that is dead; between a product of nature, and a product of mechanism; between a thing which has a principle within it, and a "thing of shreds and patches." The human mind notices this contrast between the various objects that come before it, the quicker and the more sharply, because it is itself a living thing, and because its own operations are unifying, organizing, and vivifying, in their nature. We sometimes speak of the mechanism of the human understanding, and of a mechanizing process as going on within it. But this language is metaphorical, and employed to denote the uniformity and certainty of intellectual processes, rather than their real nature. Man is a living soul, and there is no action anywhere, or in anything, that is more truly and purely vital, more entirely diverse from and hostile to the mechanical and the dead, than the genuine action of the human mind. Hence it is, that the mind notices this contrary quality and characteristic in an object with the rapidity of instinct, and starts back from it with a sort of organic recoil. Life detects death, and shrinks from death, instantaneously. Nature abhors art and artifice, as decidedly as, according to the old philosophy, it abhors a vacuum.

This distinction between the natural and the artificial, furnishes a clue to the difference which runs through all the productions of man, and reveals the secret of their excellence or their defects. How often and how spontaneously do we sum up our whole admiration of a work by saying, "it is natural," and our whole dislike by the words, "it is artificial?" The naturalness and life-likeness in the one case, are the spring of all that has pleased us; the formality and artifice in the other, are the source of all that has repelled or disgusted us. Even when we go no further in our criticism, this general statement of conformity or oppugnancy to nature, seems to be a sufficient criticism. And with good reason. For, if a production has nature, has life in it, it has real and permanent excellence. It has the germ and root of all excellences. And if it has not nature or life in it; if it is a mechanical, or an artificial, or a formal thing; it has the elements of all defects and all faults in it.

It will be noticed here, that we have used the term Art in its more common and bad sense, of contrariety to Nature, and not in that technical and best signification of the word, which implies the oneness and unison of the two. For, true Art, Fine Art, has Nature in it, and the genuine artist, be he painter, or poet, or orator, is one who paints, or sings, or speaks, with a natural freedom and freshness. Hence it is, that we are impressed by the great productions of Fine Art, in the same way that we are by the works of Nature. A painting, warm from the easel of Claude Lorraine, appeals to what is alive in us,

8*

in the same genial way that a vernal landscape does.— An oration from a clear brain, a beating heart, and a glowing lip, produces effects analogous to those of light, and fire, and the electric currents. In this way, a mysterious union is found to exist between outward nature, and that inward nature in the soul of man which we call genius; and in this way we see that there is no essential difference between Nature and Art.*

But in the other and more common sense of the term Art; and the sense in which we shall employ it at this time; there is no such mystic union and unison between it and Nature. It is its very contrary; so much so, that the one kills and expels the other; so much so, that, as we have said, the one affords a universal test of the faultiness, and the other of the excellence, of the productions of the human mind, in all departments of effort. For the Natural is the true, while the Artificial is the false. *Truth* is the inmost essence of that principle by which a production of the human mind is so organized and vitalized, as to make a fresh and powerful impression.— Whenever in any department of effort, the human mind has reached verity, and is able to give a simple and sincere expression to it, we find the product full of nature, full of life, full of freshness, full of impression. This,

* Nature's own work it seemed, (nature taught art.)
Paradise Regained, ii. 295.

All nature is but art unknown to thee. POPE.

Nature is the art of God. SIR THOMAS BROWNE.

There is a nature in all artificial things, and again, an artifice in all compounded natural things. CUDWORTH.

The art of seeing nature is in reality the great object of the studies of the artist. SIR JOSHUA REYNOLDS.

Art may, in truth, be called the *human world*. ALLSTON.

For a philosophic statement of this theory see Kant's Urtheilskraft §§ 45, 46, and Schelling's discourse upon the relation of Art to Nature.

and this ultimately, is the plain secret of the charm in every work of genius and of power. In every instance, the influence which sways the observer, or the hearer, or the reader, is the influence of the veritable reality, of the real and the simple truth. The Artificial, on the contrary, is the false. Examine any formal production whatever, and we shall be brought back in the end to a pretence, to a falsehood. The mind of the author is not filled with the truth, and yet he pretends to an utterance of the truth. Its working is not genial and spontaneous like that of nature, and yet he must give out that it is. From the beginning to the end of the process, therefore, an artificial production is essentially untrue, unreal, and hence unnatural.

We have thus briefly directed attention to this very common distinction between the Natural and the Artificial, and to the ground of it, for the purpose of introducing the general topic upon which we propose to speak on this occasion: which is,

The Characteristics and importance of a Natural Rhetoric, with special reference to the work of the Preacher.

There is no branch of knowledge so liable to an artificial method, as that of Rhetoric. Strictly defined, it is, indeed, as Milton calls it, an instrumental art, and hence, from its very nature, its appropriate subject-matter is the *form* of a discourse. While Philosophy, and History, and Theology, are properly occupied with the substance of human composition; with truth itself and thought itself; to Rhetoric is left the humbler task of putting this material into a form suited to it. Hence, it is evident, that by the very nature and definition of Rhetoric, this department of knowledge and of discipline is liable to formalism and artificiality. While the mind is carried by the solid, material, branches of education, further and further into the very substance of truth itself; while History, and Philosophy, and Theology, by their very structure and contents, tend to deepen and strengthen the mental processes; Rhetoric, in common with the whole department of Fine Art, seems to induce superficiality and formality. And when a bad tendency seems to receive aid from a legitimate department of human knowledge, it is no wonder that it should gain ground until it convert the whole department into its own nature. Hence, as matter of fact, there is no branch of knowledge, no part of a general system of education, so much infected, in all ages, with the merely formal, the merely hollow, the merely artificial, and the totally lifeless, as Rhetoric. The epigram which Ausonius wrote under the portrait of the Rhetorician Rufus, might, with too much truth, be applied to the Rhetorician generally:

Ipse rhetor, est imago imaginis.*

The need, therefore, of a Rhetoric that educates like nature, and not artificially; a Rhetoric that organizes and vitalizes the material that is made over to it for purposes of form; is apparent at first glance. Without such a method of expression, the influence of the solid branches of education themselves is neutralized. However full of fresh and original thought the mind may be, if it has been trained up to a mode of presenting it, that is in its own nature artificial and destructive of life, the freshness and originality will all disappear in the process of imparting it to another mind. A Rhetoric that is conformed to nature and to truth, is needed, therefore, in order that the department itself may be co-ordinate with those higher departments of knowledge in which the foundation of

* Ausonii Epig. LI.

mental education is laid. Without such a concurrence with the material branches of education, such a merely formal and instrumental branch as that of Rhetoric, is useless, and worse than useless. For it only diverts the mind from the thought to the expression, without any gain to the latter, and to the positive detriment of the former.

1. Rhetoric, therefore, can be a truly educating and influential department, only in proportion as it is *organizing* in its fundamental character. In order to this, it must be grounded first of all in logic, or the laws of thinking, and so become not a mere collection of rules for the structure and decoration of single sentences, but a habit and process of the human mind. The Rhetorician must make his first sacrifice to the austerer muses. In an emblematic series by one of the early Florentine engravers, Rhetoric is represented by a female figure of dignified and commanding deportment, with a helmet surmounted by a regal crown on her head, and a naked sword in her right hand. And so it should be. Softness, and grace, and beauty, must be supported by strength and prowess; the golden and jewelled crown must be defended by the iron helmet, and the steel sword. A rhetorical mind, therefore, in the best and proper sense of the term, is at bottom a constructive mind; a mind capable of methodizing and organizing its acquisitions and reflections into forms of symmetry, and strength, and in a greater or less degree of beauty. It is a mind which, in the effort to express itself, begins from within and works outward, and whose product is, for this reason, characterized by the unity and thorough compactness of a product of Nature. Such, for example, was the mind of Demosthenes, and such a product is the Oration for the Crown. The oratorical power of this great master is

primarily a constructive talent; an ability to methodize and combine. Take away this deeply-running and rigorous force by which the various parts of the discourse, the whole *materiel* of the plan and division, are compelled and compacted together, and this orator falls into the same class with the Gorgiases and the false Rhetoricians of all ages. Take away the *organization* of the Oration for the Crown, and a style and diction a hundred fold more brilliant and gorgeous than that which now clothes it, would not save it from the fate of the false Rhetoric of all ages.

Such again, for example, was the mind of the Apostle Paul, and such was the character of his Rhetoric. Those short epistles, which like godliness are profitable for all things, and ought to be as closely studied by the sermonizer as they are by the theologian, are as jointed and linked in their parts as the human frame itself, and as continuous in the flow of their trains of thought as the current of a river. The mind of this great first preacher to the Gentiles, this great first sermonizer to cultivated and sceptical Paganism, was also an organizing mind. How naturally does Christian doctrine, as it comes forth from this intellect whose native characteristics were not destroyed, but only heightened and purified, by inspiration — how naturally and inevitably does Christian truth take on forms that are fitly joined together, and compacted by that which every joint supplieth; statements that are at once logic and rhetoric, and satisfy both the reason and the feelings. For does not the profoundest theologian study the Epistle to the Romans to find ultimate and absolute statements in sacred science, and does not the most unlettered Christian read and pray over this same epistle, that his devotions may be kindled and his heart made better? Does not, to use the illustration of the Christian Father, does not the lamb find a fording place and the elephant a swimming place in this mighty unremitting stream?

This thoroughness in the elaboration of the principal ideas of a discourse, and this closeness in compacting them into the unity of a plan, is, therefore, a prime quality in eloquence, and it is that which connects Rhetoric with all the other departments of human knowledge, or rather makes it the organ by and through which these find a full and noble expression. For, contemplated from this point of view, what is the orator but a man of culture who is able to *tell* in round and full tones what he knows; and what is oratory but the art whereby the acquisitions and reflections of the general human mind are *communicated* to the present and the future. We cannot, therefore, taking this view of the nature of Rhetoric, as essentially organizing in its character, separate it from the higher departments of History, or Philosophy, or Theology, but must regard it as co-ordinate and concurrent with them. The rhetorical process is to go on in education, along with these other processes of acquisition and information and reflection, so that the final result shall be a mind not only disciplined inwardly but manifested outwardly to other minds; so that there shall be not only an intellect full of thought, and a heart beating with feeling, and an imagination glowing with imagery, but a living expression of them all, in forms of unity and simplicity and beauty and grandeur. In this way Rhetoric really becomes, what it was once claimed to be, the very crown and completion of all culture, and the rhetorical discipline, the last accomplishment in the process of education, when the man becomes prepared to take the stand on the orator's bema before his fellow men, and dares to attempt a transfer of his consciousness into them.

2. The second characteristic of a natural Rhetoric is the *amplifying* power. If Rhetoric should stop with the mere organizing of thought, it might be difficult to distinguish it from logic. But this constructive talent in the Rhetorician, is accompanied by another ability which is more purely oratorical. We mean the ability to dwell amply upon an idea until it has unfolded all its folds, and lays off richly in broad full view. We mean the ability to melt the hard solid ore with so thorough and glowing a heat, that it will run and spread like water. We mean the ability to enlarge and illustrate upon a condensed and cubic idea, until its contents spread out into a wide expanse for the career of the imagination and the play of the feelings.

This union of an organizing with an amplifying power, may be said to be the whole of Rhetoric. He who should combine both in perfect proportions, would be the ideal orator of Cicero. For while the former power presents truth in its clear and connected form for the understanding, the latter transmutes it into its imaginative and impassioned forms, and the product of these two powers, when they are blended in one living energy, is Eloquence. For Eloquence, according to the best definition that has yet been given, is the union of Philosophy and Poetry in order to a practical end.* When, therefore, the logical organization is clothed upon with the imaginative and impassioned amplification, there arises "a combination and a form indeed;" a mental product adapted more than all others to move and influence the human mind.

* Theremin's Rhetoric, Book i. Chapters iii., iv.

But we shall see still more clearly into the essential characteristics of a Natural Rhetoric, by passing, as we now do, after this brief analysis, to the second part of our discourse, which proposes to treat of the worth and importance of such a Rhetoric to the preacher.

1. And in the first place, a natural as distinguished from an artificial Rhetoric, is of the highest worth to the preacher because it is *fruitful.*

The preacher is one who, from the nature of his calling, is obliged to originate a certain amount of thought within a limited period of time, which is constantly and uniformly recurring. One day in every seven, as regularly as the motion of the globe brings it around, he is compelled to address his fellow men upon the very highest themes, in a manner and to an extent that will secure their attention and interest. No profession, consequently, makes such a steady and unintermittent draught upon the resources of the mind as the clerical, and no man so much needs the aid of a fertile and fruitful method of discoursing as the Christian preacher. Besides this great amount of thinking and composition that is required of him, he is moreover shut up to a comparatively small number of topics, and cannot derive that assistance from variety of subjects, and novelty in circumstances, which the secular orator avails himself of so readily. The truths of Christianity are few and simple, and though they are richer and more inexhaustible than all others, they furnish little that is novel or striking. The power that is in them to interest and move men, must be educed from their simple and solid substance, and not from their great number or variety. The preacher may, it is true, be able to maintain a sort of interest in his hearers by the biographical, or geographical, or archaeological, or historical, or literary, accompaniments of the Scriptures, but his permanent influence and power over them as a preacher must come from his ability to develop clearly, profoundly, and freshly, a few simple and unadorned doctrines. Far be it from me to undervalue the importance of that training and study, by which we are introduced into that elder and oriental world in which the Bible had its origin, and with whose scenery, manners and customs, and modes of living and thinking, it will be connected to the end of time. No student of the Scriptures, and especially no sacred orator, can make himself too much at home in the gorgeous East; too familiar with that Hebrew spirit which colors like blood the whole Bible, New Testament as well as Old Testament. But at the same time he should remember that all this knowledge is only a means to an end; that he cannot as a preacher of the Word, rely upon this as the last source whence he is to derive subject matter for his thinking and discourse year after year, but must by it all be carried down to deeper and more perennial fountains, to the few infinite facts and the few infinite truths of Christianity.

The need, therefore, of a Rhetorical method that is in its own nature fertile and fruitful, is plain. And what other ability can succeed but that organizing and amplifying power, which we have seen to be the substance of the Rhetoric of Nature as the contrary of Art. Through the former of these, the preacher's mind is led into the inmost structure and fabric of the individual doctrine, and so of the whole Christian system; and through the latter he is enabled to unroll and display the endless richness of the contents. It is safe to say, that a mind which has once acquired this natural method of developing and presenting Christian truth, cannot be exhausted. No matter how much drain may be made upon it, no matter how often it may be called upon to preach the "things new and old," it cannot be made dry. The more it is drawn from, the more salient and bulging is the fulness with which it wells up and pours over. For this *organic* method is the key and the clue. He who is master of it, he with whom it has become a mental habit and process, will find the treasures of wisdom and knowledge in the Scriptures opening readily and richly to him. He will find his mind habitually in the vein.

2. And this brings us to a second characteristic of a Natural Rhetoric, whereby it is of the greatest worth to the preacher, viz., that it is a *genial* and *invigorating* method. All the discipline of the human mind ought to minister to its enjoyment and its strength. That is a false method of discipline, by which the human mind is made to work by an ungenial effort, much more by spasms and convulsively. It was made to work like nature itself, calmly, continuously, strongly, and happily. When, therefore, we find a system of training, resulting in a labored, anxious, intermittent, and irksome, activity, we may be sure that something is wrong in it. The fruits of all modes of discipline that conform to the nature of the human mind and the nature of truth, are freedom, boldness, continuity, and pleasure, of execution. In this connection weakness and tedium are faults; sickness is sin.

But the mental method for which we are pleading, while making the most severe and constant draft upon the mental faculties, at the same time braces them and inspires them with power. The mind of the orator, in this slow organization and continuous amplification of the materials with which it is laboring, is itself affected by a reflex action. That truth, that divine truth, which the preacher is endeavoring to throw out, that it may renovate and edify the soul of a fellow being, at the same time strikes in, and invigorates his own mind, and swells his own heart with joy.

This feature, this genial vigor, in what we have styled a Natural Rhetoric, acquires additional importance when we recur to the fact that has already been mentioned, viz., that inasmuch as Rhetoric is a formal or instrumental department, its influence is liable to become, and too often has become, debilitating to the human mind. When this branch of discipline becomes artificial and mechanical in its character, by being severed too much from those profounder, and more solid, departments of human knowledge from whose root and fatness it must derive all its nourishment and circulating juices; when Rhetoric degenerates into a mere collection of rules for the structure of sentences and the finish of diction; no studies or training will do more to diminish the resources of the mind, and to benumb and kill the vitality of the soul, than the Rhetorical. The eye is kept upon the form merely, and no mind, individual or national, was ever made strong or fertile by the contemplation of mere form. The mind under such a tutorage works by rote, instead of from an inward influence and an organic law. In reality, its action is a surface-action, which only irritates and tires out its powers. Perhaps the strongest objections that have been advanced against a Rhetorical course of instruction, find their support and force here. Men complain of the dryness, and the want of geniality, of a professed Rhetorician. The common mind is not satisfied with his studious artifice, and his measured movements, but craves something more; it craves a robust and hearty utterance, a hale and lifesome method. Notice that it is not positively displeased with this precision and finish of the Rhetorician, but only with the lack of a genial impulse under it. It is its sins of omission that have brought Rhetoric into disrepute.

But when the training, under consideration, results in a genial and invigorating process, by which the profoundest thinking and the best feeling of the soul are discharged to the utmost, and yet the mind feels the more buoyant for it, and the stronger for it, all such objections vanish. There is, we are confident, there is a method of disciplining the mind in the direction of Rhetoric, and for the purposes of form and style, that does not in the least diminish the vigor and the healthiness of its natural processes. If there is not, then the department should be annihilated. If there can be no Rhetorical training in the schools, but such as is destructive of the freshness, and originality, and geniality, of native impulses and native utterances, then it were far better to leave the mind to its unpruned and tangled luxuriance; to let it wander at its own sweet will, and bear with its tedious windings and its endless eddies. Here and there, at least, there would be an onward movement, and the inspiration of a forward motion. But it is not so. For, says Shakspeare: —

> There is an Art which * * * shares
> With great creating Nature.

There is a close and elaborate discipline which is in harmony with the poetry, and the feeling, and the eloquence, of the human soul, and which, therefore, may be employed to evoke and express it. There is a Rhetoric which, when it has been wrought into the mind, and has become a spontaneous method and an instinctive habit with it, does not in the least impair the elasticity and vigor of nature, because in the phrase of the same great poet and master of form from whom we have just quoted, "It is an Art that Nature makes, or rather an Art which itself is Nature." Such a Rhetoric may, indeed, be defined to be an Art, or discipline, which enables man to be natural; an Art that simply develops the genuine and hearty qualities of the man himself, of the mind itself.—For the purpose of all discipline in this direction, is not to impose upon the mind a style of thought and expression unnatural and alien to it, but simply to aid the mind to be itself, and to show itself out in the most genuine and sincere manner. The Rhetorical Art is to join on upon the nature and constitution of the individual man, so that what is given by creation, and what is acquired by culture, shall be homogeneous, mutually aiding and aided, reciprocally influencing and influenced. And let not this mental veracity, this truthfulness to a man's individuality and mental structure, be thought to be an easy acquisition. It is really the last and highest accomplishment. It is a very difficult thing for a discourser to be *himself*, genuinely and without affectation. It is a still more difficult thing for an orator, a man who has come out before a listening and criticising auditory, to be himself; genuinely, fearlessly and without mannerism, communicating himself to his auditors precisely as he really is. A simple and natural style, says Pascal, always strikes us with a sort of surprise; for while we are on the lookout for an *author*, we find a *man*, while we are expecting a formal *art*, we find a throbbing *heart*. This is really the highest grade of culture, and the point toward which it should always aim, viz: to bring Nature out by means of art; and Rhetorical discipline, instead of leaving the pupil ten-fold more formal and artificial than it found him, ought to send him out among men, the most artless, the most hearty, and the most genuine, man of them all.

Now of what untold worth is such a mental method and habit to the preacher of the Word! On this method, literally and without a metaphor, the more he works the stronger he becomes, the more he toils the happier he is. He finds the invention and composition of discourse a means of self-culture and of self-enjoyment. He finds that that labor to which he has devoted his life, and to which, perhaps, in the outset, he went with something of a hireling's feeling, is no irksome task, but the source of the noblest and most buoyant happiness. That steady unintermittent drain upon his thought and his feeling, which he feared would soon exsiccate his brain and leave his heart dry as powder, he finds is only an outlet for the ever accumulating waters!

This invigorating and genial influence of the Rhetorical method now under consideration, furthermore, is of special worth in the present state of the world. There never was a time when the general mind was so impatient of dulness as now. He who addresses audiences at the present day must be vigorous and invigorating, or he is nothing. Hence the temptation, which is too often yielded to by the sacred orator, to leave the legitimate field of Christian discourse and to range in that border land which skirts it, or perhaps to pass into a region of thought that is really profane and secular. The preacher feels the need of saying something fresh, vigorous, and genial, and not being able to discourse in this style upon the old and standing themes of the Bible, he endeavors to christianize those secular and temporal themes with which the general mind is already too intensely occupied, that he may find in them subjects for entertaining, and, as he thinks, original discourse. But this course on the part of the Christian minister, must always end in the decline of spiritual religion, both in his own heart and in that of the Church. Nothing, in the long run, is truly edifying to the Christian man or the Christian Church, that is not really religious. Nothing can renovate and sanctify the earthly mind, but that which is in its own nature spiritual and supernatural. Not that which resembles Christian truth, or which may be modified or affected by Christian truth, can convict of sin and convert to God, but only the substantial and real Christian truth itself. Nothing but material fire can be relied upon as a central sun, as a radiating centre.

The Christian preacher is thus shut up to the old and uniform system of Christianity in an age when, more than in any other, men are seeking for some new thing; when they are seeking and demanding stimulation, invigoration, animation, and impression. His only true course, therefore, is to find the new in the old; to become so penetrated with the spirit of Christianity, that he shall breathe it out from his own mind and heart, upon his congregation, in as fresh and fiery a tongue of flame as that which rested upon the disciples on the day of Pentecost; to enter so thoroughly into the genius and spirit of the Christian system, that it shall exhibit itself, through him, with an originality and newness kindred to that of its first inspired preachers, and precisely like that which characterizes the sermonizing of the Augustines and the Bernards, the Luthers and the Calvins, the Leightons, the Howes, and the Edwardses, of the Church. What renders the sermons of these men so vivific and so invigorating to those who study them, and to the audiences who heard them? Not the variety or striking character of the topics, but the thoroughness with which the truth was conceived and elaborated in their minds. Not an artificial Rhetoric, polishing and garnishing the outside of a subject in which the mind has no interest, and into the interior of which it has not penetrated; but an organizing Rhetoric, whereby the sermon shot up out of the great Christian system, like a bud out of the side of a great trunk or a great limb, part and particle of the great whole; an amplifying Rhetoric whereby the sermon was the mere evolution of an involution, the swelling, bursting, leafing out, blossoming, and fructuation, of this bud.

3. And this brings us, in the third place, to the worth of this Rhetorical method to the preacher, because it is *closely connected with his theological training and discipline.*

It is plain, from what has been said, that eloquent preaching cannot originate without profound theological knowledge. The eloquent preacher is simply the thorough theologian who has now gone out of his study, and up into the pulpit. In other words, eloquence in this as well as in every other instance is founded in knowledge. Cicero says that Socrates was wont to say that all men are eloquent enough on subjects whereon they have knowledge;* a saying which re-appears in the common and homely rule for eloquence, "*Have* something to say, and then say it."

Hence a Rhetorical training which does not sustain intimate relations to the general culture and discipline of the pupil, is worthless. At no point does an artificial Rhetoric betray itself so quickly and so certainly as here. We feel that it has no intercommunication with the character and acquisitions of the individual. It is a foreign method, which he has adopted by a volition, and

* De Oratore, i. 14.

not a spontaneous one which has sprung up out of his character and culture, and is in perfect sympathy with it. But the Rhetoric of nature has all the theological training of the preacher back of it as its support, beneath it as its soil and nutriment. All that he has become by long years of study and reflection, goes to maintain him as a Rhetorician, so that his oratory is really the full and powerful display of what he is and has become by vigorous professional study. The Rhetoric is the man himself.

In this way, a showy and tawdry manner is inevitably avoided, as it always should be, by the preacher. It cannot be said of him, as it can be of too many, "He is a *mere* Rhetorician." For this professional study, this lofty and calm theological discipline, this solemn care of human souls, this sacred professional character, will all show themselves in his general style and manner, and preclude every thing ostentatious or gaudy, much more every thing scenic or theatrical. The form will correspond to the matter. The matter being the most solemn and most weighty truth of God, the form will be the most chastened, the most symmetrical, and the most commanding, manner of man.

And in this way, again, the rhetorical training of the preacher will exert a reflex influence upon his theological training. A true sacred Rhetoric is a sort of practical theology, and is so styled in some nomenclatures. It is a practical expansion and exhibition of a scientific system for the purpose of influencing the popular mind. When, therefore, it is well conceived and well handled, it exerts a reflex influence upon theological science itself, that is beneficial in the highest degree. It cannot, it is true, change the nature and substance of the truth, but it can bring it out into distinct consciousness. The effort to popularize scientific knowledge, the endeavor to put logic into the form of rhetoric, imparts a clearness to conceptions, and a determination to opinions, that cannot be attained in the closet of the mere speculatist. Not until a man has endeavored to transfer his conceptions; not until he has pushed his way through the confusion and misunderstandings of another man's mind, and has tried to lodge his views in it; does he know the full significance and scope of even his own knowledge.

But especially is this action and re-action between theology and sacred Rhetoric of the highest worth to the preacher, because it results in a due mingling of the theoretic and the practical in his preaching. The desideratum in a sermon is such an exact proportion between doctrine and practice, such thorough fusion of these two elements, that the discourse at once instructs and impels; and he who supplies this desideratum in his sermonizing, is a powerful, influential, and eloquent, preacher. He may lack many other minor things, but he has the main thing; and in time these other minor things shall all be added unto him. In employing a Rhetoric that is at once organizing and amplifying in its nature and influence, the theological discipline and culture of the preacher are kept constantly growing and vigorous. Every sermon that is composed on this method, sets the whole body of his acquisitions into motion, and, like a bucket continually plunged down into a well and continually drawn up full and dripping, aerates a mass that would otherwise grow stagnant and putrid.

4. Fourthly and finally, the worth of a natural, as distinguished from an artificial, Rhetoric, is seen in the fact that it is connected, most intimately, *with the vital religion of the man and the preacher.* For no Rhetoric can

be organizing and vivifying, that is not itself organic and alive. Only that which has in itself a living principle, can communicate life. Only that which is itself vigorous, can invigorate. The inmost essential principle, therefore, of a Rhetoric that is to be employed in the service of religion, must be this very religion itself: deep, vital, piety in the soul of the sacred orator. Even the pagan Cato, and the pagan Quinctilian after him, made goodness, integrity and uprightness of character, the foundation of eloquence in a secular sphere, and for secular purposes. The orator, they said, is an upright man, first of all an *upright man*, who understands speaking. How much more true then is it, that Christian character is the font and origin of all Christian eloquence; that the sacred orator is a holy man, first of all a *holy man*, who understands speaking.

We shall not, surely, be suspected of wishing to undervalue or disparage a department to which we propose to consecrate our whole time and attention, and, therefore, we may with the more boldness say, that we have always cherished a proper respect for that theory which has been more in vogue in some other denominations than in our own, that the preacher is to speak as the spirit moves him. There is a great and solid truth at the bottom of it, and though the theory unquestionably does not need to be held up very particularly before an uneducated ministry, we think there is comparatively little danger in reminding the educated man, the man who has been trained by the rules and maxims of a formal and systematic discipline, that the spring of all his power, as a Christian preacher, is a *living spring*. It is well for the sacred orator, who has passed through a long collegiate and professional training, and has been taught sermonizing as an art, to be reminded that the living principle, which is to render all this culture of use for purposes of practical impression, is vital godliness; that he will be able to assimilate all this material of Christian eloquence, only in proportion as he is a devout and holy man. Without this interior religious life in his soul, all his resources of intellect, of memory, and of imagination, will be unimpressive and ineffectual; the mere iron shields and gold ornaments that crush the powerless Tarpeia.

For the first and indispensable thing in every instance is *power*. Given an inward and living power, and a basis for motion, action, and impression, is given. In every instance we come back to this ultimate point. There is a theory among philosophers, that this hard, material world, over which we stumble, and against which we strike, is at bottom two forces or powers, held in equilibrium; that when we get back to the reality of the hard and dull clod, upon which "the swain treads with clouted shoon," we find it to be just as immaterial, just as mobile, just as nimble, and just as much a living energy, as the soul of man itself. Whether this be truth or not within the sphere of matter, one thing is certain, that within the sphere of mind we are brought back to forces, to fresh and living energies, in every instance in which the human soul makes an eloquent impression, or receives one. Examine an oration, secular or sacred, that actually moved the minds of men, a speech that obtained votes, or a sermon that, as we say, saved souls, and you find the ultimate cause of this eloquence, so far as man is concerned, to be a *vital* power in the orator. The same amount of instruction might have been imparted, the same general style and diction might have been employed in both cases, but if that eloquent *power* in the man had been wanting, there would have been no actuation of the hearer, and consequently no eloquence.

It is, therefore a great and crowning excellence of the Rhetorical method which we have been describing, that its lowest and longest roots strike down into the Christian character itself. It does not propose or expect to render the preacher eloquent without personal religion. It tells him on the contrary, that although God is the creator and sovereign of the human soul, and can therefore render the truth preached by an unregenerate man and in the most unfeeling irreligious manner, effectual to salvation, yet that *the preacher* must expect to see men moved by his discourses, only in proportion as he is himself a spiritually-minded, solemn, and devout man. Here is the *power*, and here is its hiding place, so far as the finite agent is concerned. In that holy love of God and of the human soul, which Christianity enjoins and produces; in that religious affection of the soul which takes its origin in the soul's regeneration; the preacher is to find the source of all his eloquence and impression as an orator, just as much as of his usefulness and happiness as a man and a Christian. Back to this last centre of all, do we trace all that is genuine, and powerful, and influential, in Pulpit Eloquence.

But by this is not meant merely that the preacher must be a man of zealous and fervid emotions. There is a species of eloquence, which springs out of easily excited sensibilities, and which oftentimes produces a great sensation in audiences of peculiar characteristics, and in some particular moods. But this eloquence of the flesh and the blood, without the brain; this eloquence of the animal, without the intellectual, spirits; is very different from that deep-toned, that solemn, that commanding eloquence, which springs from the life of God in the soul of man. We feel the difference, all men feel the difference, between the impression made by an ardent but superficial emotion, and that made by a deep feeling; by the sustained, equable, and strong, pulsation of religious affections, as distinguished from religious sensibilities. When a man of the latter stamp feels, we know that he feels upon good grounds and in reality; that this stir and movement of the affections is central and all-pervading in him; that the eternal truth has taken hold of his emotive nature, moving the *whole* of it, as the trees of the wood are moved with the wind. It is this moral earnestness of a man who habitually feels that religion is the chief concern for mortals here below; it is this profound consciousness of the perfections of God and of the worth of the human soul; which is the inmost principle of sacred eloquence, the *vis vivida vitæ* of the sacred orator.

I have thus, as briefly as possible, exhibited the principal features of what is conceived to be a true method in rhetorical instruction and discipline; not because they are new, or different from the views of the best Rhetoricians of all ages, but merely to indicate the general spirit in which I would hope, by the blessing of God, to conduct the department of instruction committed to my care by the guardians of this Seminary. The department of Sacred Rhetoric and Pastoral Theology is one that, from the nature of the case, is not called upon to impart very much positive information. Its function is rather to induce an intellectual method, to form a mental habit, to communicate a general spirit to the future clergyman. It is, therefore, a department of growing importance in this country, and in the present state of society and the Church. Perhaps the general tone and temper of the clerical profession was never a matter of more importance than now. The world, and this country especially, is guided more and more by the general tendencies of particular classes and professions. In politics, a party or class, that really *has* a tendency, and maintains it persistently for a length of time, is sure in the end to draw large masses after it. In reforms, a class that is pervaded by a distinctive spirit, which it sedulously preserves and maintains, is sure of a wide influence, finally. In literature, or philosophy, or theology, a school that has a marked and determined character of its own, and keeps faith with it, will in the course of time be rewarded for its self-consistency by an increase in numbers and in power. In all these cases, and in all other cases, the steady, continuous stream of a general tendency sucks into its own volume all the float and drift, and carries it along with it. And the eye of the reflecting observer, as it ranges over the ocean of American society, can see these currents and tendencies, as plainly as the eye of the mariner sees the Gulf-stream.

How important, then, is any position which makes the occupant to contribute to the formation of a general spirit and temper, in so influential a class of men as the clerical! Well may such an one say, Who is sufficient for this thing? For myself, I should shrink altogether from this toil, and this responsibility, did I not dare to hope that the providence of that Being, who is the sovereign controller of all tendencies and all movements in the universe, has led me hither. In his strength would I labor, and to Him would I reverently commend myself and this institution.

THE NATURE, AND INFLUENCE, OF THE HISTORIC SPIRIT.

AN INAUGURAL DISCOURSE DELIVERED IN ANDOVER THEOLOGICAL SEMINARY, FEB. 15, 1854.

THE purpose of an Inaugural Discourse is, to give a correct and weighty impression of the importance of some particular department of knowledge. Provided the term be employed in the technical sense of Aristotle and Quinctilian, the Inaugural is a demonstrative oration, the aim of which is to justify the existence of a specific professorship, and to magnify the specific discipline which it imparts. It must, consequently, be the general object of the present discourse to praise the department, and recommend the study, of History.

As we enter upon the field which opens out before us, we are bewildered by its immense expanse. The whole hemisphere overwhelms the eye. The riches of the subject embarrass the discussion. For this science is the most comprehensive of all departments of human knowledge. In its unrestricted and broad signification, it includes all other branches of human inquiry. Everything in existence has a history, though it may not have a philosophy, or a poetry; and, therefore, history covers and pervades and enfolds all things as the atmosphere does the globe. Its subject-matter is all that man has thought, felt, and done, and the line of Schiller is true even if taken in its literal sense: the final judgment is the history of the world.*

If it were desirable to bring the whole encyclopaedia of human knowledge under a single term, certainly history would be chosen as the most comprehensive and elastic of all. And if we consider the mental qualifications required for its production, the department whose nature and claims we are considering, still upholds its superiority, in regard to universality and comprehensiveness. The historic talent is inclusive of all other talents. The depth of the philosopher, the truthfulness and solemnity of the theologian, the dramatic and imaginative power of the poet, are all necessary to the perfect historian, and would be found in him, at their height of excellence, did such a being exist. For it has been truly said, that we shall sooner see a perfect philosophy, or a perfect poem, than a perfect history.

We shall, therefore, best succeed in imparting unity to the discourse of an hour, and in making a single and, therefore, stronger impression, by restraining that career which the mind is tempted to make over the whole of this ocean-like arena, and confining our attention to a single theme.

It will be our purpose, then, to speak,

First, Of that peculiar spirit imparted to the mind of an educated man, by historical studies, which may be denominated the historic spirit; and

Secondly, Of its influence upon the theologian.

The historic spirit may be defined to be: the spirit of

* Resignation.

the race as distinguished from that of the individual, and of all time as distinguished from that of one age.

We here assume that the race is as much a reality as the individual; for this is not the time nor place, even if the ability were possessed, to reopen and reargue that great question which once divided the philosophic world into two grand divisions. We assume the reality of both ideas. We postulate the real and distinct, though undivided, being of the common humanity and the particular individuality. We are unable, with the Nominalist, to regard the former as the mere generalization of the latter. The race is more than an aggregate of separate individualities. History is more than a collection of single biographies, as the national debt is more than the sum of individual liabilities. Side by side, in one and the same subject; in every particular human person; exist the common humanity with its universal instincts and tendencies, and the individuality with its particular interests and feelings. The two often come into conflict with an earnestness, and at times in the epic of history with a terrible grandeur, that indicates that neither of them is an abstraction; that both are solid with the substance of an actual being, and throb with the pulses of an intense vitality.

The difference between history and biography involves the distinct entity and reality of both the race and the individual. Biography is the account of the peculiarities of the single person disconnected from the species, and is properly concerned only with that which is characteristic of him as an isolated individual. But that which is national and philanthropic in his nature; that which is social and political in his conduct and career; all that links him with his species and constitutes a part of the development of man on the globe; all this is historical and not biographic. Speaking generally in order to speak briefly, all that activity which springs up out of the pure individualism of the person, makes up the charm and entertainment of biography, and all that activity which originates in the humanity of the person furnishes the matter and the grandeur of history.

History, then, is the story of the race. It is the exhibition of the common generic nature of man as this is manifested in that great series of individuals which is crowding on, one after another, like the waves of the sea, through the ages and generations of time. The historic muse omits and rejects everything in this march and movement of human beings that is peculiar to them as selfish units; everything that has interest for the man, but none for mankind; and inscribes upon her tablet only that which springs out of the common humanity, and hence has interest for all men and all time.

History, therefore, is *continuous* in its nature. It is so because its subject-matter is a continuity. This common human nature is in the process of continuous evolution, and the wounded snake drags its slow length along down the ages and generations. No single individual; no single age or generation; no single nationality, however rich and capacious; shows the whole of man, and so puts a stop to human development. The time will, indeed, come, and the generation and the single man, will one day be, in whom the entire exhibition will close. The number of individuals in the human race is predetermined and fixed by Him who sees the end from the beginning. But until the end of the series comes, the development must go on continuously, and the history of it, must be continuous also. It must be linked with all that has gone before; it must be linked with all that is yet to come. As it requires the whole series of individuals, in order to a complete manifestation of the species, so it requires the whole series of ages and periods, in order to an entire account of it.

But while history is thus continuous in its nature, paradoxical as it may appear, it is at the same time *complete* in its spirit. Observe that we are speaking of the abstract and ideal character of the science; of that quality by which it differs from other branches of knowledge. We are not speaking of any one particular narrative that has actually been composed, or of all put together. History as actually written is not the account of a completed process, because, as we have just said, the development is still going on. Still, the *tendency* of the department is to a conclusion. History looks to a winding up. We may say of it, as Bacon says of unfulfilled prophecies: "though not fulfilled punctually and at once, it hath a springing and germinant accomplishment through many ages." It contains and defines general tendencies; it intimates, at every point of the line, a final consummation. The historical processes that have actually taken place, all point at, and join on upon, the future processes that are to be homogeneous with them. That very continuity in the nature of this science, of which we have spoken, results in this completeness, or tendency to a conclusion, in its spirit. Like a growing plant, we know what it will come to, though the growth is not ended. For it is characteristic of an evolution, provided it is a genuine one, that seize it when you will, and observe it at any point you please, you virtually seize the whole; you observe it all. Each particular section of a development exhibits the qualities of the whole process, and the organic part contemplated by itself throbs with the general life. Hence it is that each particular history; of a nation, or an age, or a form of government, or a school of philosophy, or a Christian doctrine; when conceived in the spirit of history, wears a finished aspect, and sounds a full and fundamental tone. And hence the proverb: man is the same in all ages, and history is the repetition of the same lessons.

So universal and virtually complete in its spirit is this science, that a distinguished modern philosopher has asserted that it may become a branch of *à priori* knowledge, and that it actually does become such in proportion as it becomes philosophic. Being the account, not of a dislocation, but of a development, and this of *one* race; being the exhibition of the unfolding of one single idea of the Divine mind; the history of the world, he contends, might be written beforehand by any mind that is master of the idea lying at the bottom of it. The whole course and career of the world, is predetermined by its plan, and supposing this to be known, the historian is more than "the prophet looking backward," as Schlegel calls him; he is the literal prophet. He does not merely inferentially foretell, by looking back into the past, but he sees the whole past and future *simultaneously* present in the Divine idea of the world, of which by the hypothesis he is perfectly possessed.

This philosopher believed in the possibility of such an absolutely perfect and *à priori* history, because he taught that the mind of man and the mind of God are one universal mind, and that the entire knowledge of the one may consequently be possessed by the other. While, however, the philosopher erred fatally in supposing that any being but God the Creator, can be thus perfectly possessed of the organic idea of the world, or that man can come into an approximate possession of it except as it is revealed to him by the Supreme mind, in providence and revelation, we must yet admit that the world is constructed according to such an idea or plan, and that for this reason, coherence, completeness, and universality, are the distinguishing characteristics of its development.

While, therefore, we deny that history as actually written, or as it shall be, comes up to this absolute and metaphysical perfection, it would be folly to deny that it has made any approximation towards it, or that it will make still more. So far as the account has been composed under the guiding light of this divine idea, which is manifesting itself in the affairs of men; so far, in other words, as it has been written in the light of providence and revelation; it has been composed with truth, and depth, and power. Historians have been successful in gathering the lessons and solving the problems of their science in proportion as they have recognized a providential plan in the career of the world, and have had some clear apprehension of it. The most successful particular narratives seem to be parts of a greater whole. — They have an easy reference to general history; evidently belong to it; evidently were written in its comprehensive spirit and by its broad lights. So much does this science abhor a scattering, isolating, and fragmentary, method of treating the subject-matter belonging to it, that those histories which have been composed without any historic feeling; with no reference to the Divine plan and no connection with the universe; are the most dry and lifeless productions in literature. Disconnection, and the absence of a unifying principle, are more marked, and more painfully felt, in historical composition, than in any other species of literature. Even when the account is that of a brief period, or mere point, as it were, in universal space, the mind demands that it be rounded and finished in itself; that it exhibit, in little, that same complete and coherent process, which is going on more grandly, on the wider arena of the world at large.

History, then, is the exhibition of the *species.* Its lessons may be relied upon as the conclusions to which the human race have come. In these historic lessons, the narrowness of individual and local opinions has been exchanged for the breadth and compass of public and common sentiments. The errors to which the single mind; the isolated unit, as distinguished from the organic unity; is exposed, are corrected by the sceptical and critical processes of the general mind.

What, for illustration, is its teaching in regard to the presence and relative proportions in a political constitution of the two opposite elements, permanence and progression? Will not the judgment, in regard to this vexed question, that is formed on *historic* grounds, be, to say the least, safer and truer, than that formed upon the scanty experience of an individual man? Will not the decision of one who has made up his mind after a thoughtful study of the ancient tyrannies and republics of Greece and Rome, of the republican states of Italy in the middle ages, of the politics of Europe since the formation of its modern state-system, be nearer the real truth than that of a pledged and zealous partisan, on either side of the question; than that of the ancient Cleon or Coriolanus; than that of the modern Rousseau or Filmer? And why will it be nearer the truth? Not merely because these men were earnest and zealous. Ardor and zeal are well in their place. But because these minds were individual and local; because they were not historic and general in views and opinions.

Take another illustration from the department of philosophy. A great variety of theories have been projected respecting the nature and operations of the human mind, so that it becomes difficult for the bewildered inquirer to know which he shall adopt. But will he run the hazard of fundamental error, if he assumes that that theory is the truth, so far as truth has been reached in this domain, which he finds substantially present in the philosophic mind in all ages? if he concludes that the historic philosophy is the true philosophy? And will it be safe for the individual to set up in this department, or in the still higher one of religion, doctrines which have either never entered the human mind before, or, if they have, have been only transient residents?

The fact is, no one individual mind is capable of accomplishing, alone and by itself, what the *race* is destined to accomplish only in the slow revolution of its cycle of existence. It is not by the thought of any one individual, though he were as profound as Plato and as intuitive as Shakspeare, that truth is to obtain an exhaustive manifestation. The whole race is to try its power, and, in the end, or rather at every point in the endless career, is to acknowledge that the absolute is not yet fully known; that the knowledge of man is still at an infinite distance from that of God. Much has been said, and still is, of the spirit of the age; and extravagant expectations have been formed in regard to its insight into truth and its power of applying it for the progress of the species. But a single age is merely an individual of larger growth. There is always something particular, something local, something temporary, in every age, and we must not look here for the generic and universal any more than in the notions of the individual man. No age is historic, in and by itself. Like the individual, it only contributes its portion of investigation and opinion, to the sum total of material which is to undergo the test, not of an age, but of the ages.

Considerations like these go to show, that there is in that which is properly historic, nothing partial, nothing defective, nothing one-sided. It is the individual which has these characteristics; and only in proportion as the individual man becomes historic in his views, opinions and impressions; only as his culture takes on this large and catholic spirit, does he become truly educated. It is the sentiment of mankind at large, it is the opinion of the race, which is to be accepted as truth. When, therefore, the mind of the student, in the course of its education, is subjected to the full and legitimate influence of historical studies, it is subjected to a rectifying influence. The individual eye is purged, so that it sees through a crystalline medium. That darkening, distorting matter, composing oftentimes the idiosyncracy rather than the individuality of the intellect, is drained off.

Having thus briefly discussed the nature of the historic spirit by a reference to the abstract nature of the science itself, let us now seek to obtain a more concrete and lively knowledge of it, by looking at some of its actual influences upon the student. Let us specify some of the characteristics of the historical mind.

I. In the first place, the historical mind is both reverent and vigilant.

The study of all the past raises the intellect to a loftier eminence than that occupied by the student of the present; the man of the time. The vision of the latter is limited by his own narrow horizon, while that of the former goes round the globe. As a consequence, the historic mind is impressed with the vastness of truth. It knows that it is too vast to be all known by a single mind, or a single age; too immense to be taken in at a single glance, much less to be stated in a single proposition. Historic studies have, moreover, made it aware of the fact that truth is modified by passing through a variety of minds; that each form taken by itself is imperfect, and that, in some instances at least, all forms put together do not constitute a perfect manifestation of the "daughter of time." The posture and bearing of such a mind, therefore, towards all truth, be it human or divine, is at once reverent and vigilant. It is seriously impressed by the immensity of the field of knowledge, and at the same time is adventurous and enterprising in ranging over it. For it was when the human imagination was most impressed by the vastness of the globe, that the spirit of enterprise and adventure was most rife and successful. Before the minds of Columbus and De Gama, before the imagination of the Northmen and the early English navigators, space stretched away westward and southward like the spaces of astronomy, and was invested with the awfulness and grandeur of the spaces of the Miltonic Pandaemonium. Yet this sense of space, this mysterious consciousness of a vaster world, was the very stimulation of the navigator; the direct cause of all modern geographical discovery. The merely individual mind, on the contrary, seeing but one form of truth, or, at most, but one form at a time, is apt to take this meagre exhibition for the full reality, and to suppose that it has reached the summit of knowledge. It is self-satisfied and therefore irreverent. It is disposed to rest in present acquisitions and therefore is neither vigilant nor enterprising.

II. And this naturally suggests the second characteristic of the historical mind: its productiveness and originality.

Such a mind is open to truth. The first condition to the advancement of learning is fulfilled by it; for it is the fine remark of Bacon, that the kingdom of science, like the kingdom of heaven, is open only to the child; only to the reverent, recipient, and docile, understanding. Perhaps nothing contributes more to hinder the progress of truth than self-satisfied ignorance of what the human mind has already achieved. The age that isolates itself from the rest of the race and settles down upon itself, will accomplish but little towards the development of man or of truth. The individual who neglects to make himself acquainted with the history of men and of opinions, though he may be an intense man within a very narrow circumference, will make no real advance and no new discoveries. Even the ardor and zealous energy, often exhibited by such a mind, and, we may say, characteristic of it, contribute rather to its growing ignorance, than its growing enlightenment. For it is the ardor of a mind exclusively occupied with its own peculiar notions. Its zeal is begotten by individual peculiarities, and expended upon them. Having no humble sense of its own limited ability, in comparison with the vastness of truth, or even in comparison with the power of the universal human mind, it closes itself against the great world of the past, and, as a penalty for this, hears but few of the deeper tones of the "many voiced present." In the midst of colors it is blind; in the midst of sounds it is deaf.

That mind, on the contrary, which is imbued with the enterprising spirit of history, contributes to the progress of truth and knowledge among men, by entering into the great process of inquiry and discovery which the race as such has begun and is carrying on. It moves onward with fellow-minds, in the line of a preceding advance, and consequently receives impulse from all the movement and momentum of the past. It joins on upon the truth which has actually been unfolded, and is thereby enabled to make a positive and valuable addition to the existing knowledge of the human race.

For the educated man, above all men, should see and constantly remember, that progress in the intellectual world, does not imply the discovery of truth *absolutely* new; of truth of which the human mind never had even an intimation before, and which came into it by a mortal leap, abrupt and startling, without antecedents and without premonitions. This would be rather of the nature of a Divine revelation than of a human discovery. A revelation from God is different in kind from a discovery of the human reason. It comes down from another sphere, from another mind, than that of man; and, although it is conformed to the wants of the human race, can by no means be regarded as a natural development out of it; as a merely historical process, like the origination of a new form of government, or a new school of philosophy. A discovery of the human mind, on the contrary, is to be regarded as the pure, spontaneous, product of the human mind; as one fold in its unfolding.

It follows, consequently, that progress in human knowledge, progress in the development of human reason, does not imply the origination of truth absolutely and in all respects unknown before. The human mind has presentiments; dim intimations; which thicken all along the track of human history like the hazy belt of the galaxy among the clear, sparkling, mapped, stars. These presentiments are a species and a grade of knowledge.— They are not distinct and stated knowledge, it is true, but they are by no means blank ignorance. The nebulae are *visible*, though not yet resolved. Especially is this true in regard to the mind of the race; the general and historic mind. How often is the general mind restless and uneasy with the dim anticipation of the future discovery? This unrest, with its involved longing, and its potential knowledge, comes to its height, it is true, in the mind of some one individual who is most in possession of the spirit of his time, and who is selected by Providence as the immediate instrument of the actual and stated discovery. But such an one is only the secondary cause of an effect, whose first cause lies lower down and more abroad. There were Reformers before the Reformation. Luther articulated himself upon a process that had already begun in the Christian church, and ministered to a want, and a very intelligent want too, that was already in existence. Columbus shared in the enterprising spirit of his time, and differed in degree, and not in kind, from the bold navigators among whom he was born and bred. That vision of the new world from the shores of old Spain; that presentiment of the existence of another continent beyond the deep; a presentiment so strong as almost to justify the poetic extravagance of Schiller's sonnet,* in which he says, that the boding mind of the mariner would have *created* a continent, if there had been none in the trackless West to meet his anticipation; that prophetic sentiment, Columbus possessed, not as an isolated individual, but as a man who had grown up with his age and into his age; whose teeming mind had been informed by the traditions of history, and whose active imagination had been fired by the strange narratives of anterior and contemporaneous navigation.

Another proof of the position that the individual mind owes much of its inventiveness and originality to its ability to join on upon the invention and origination already in existence, is found in the fact, that some of

* Columbus.

the most marked discoveries in science have occurred simultaneously to different minds. The dispute between the adherents of Newton and Leibnitz respecting priority of discovery in the science of Fluxions, is hardly yet settled; but the candid mind on either side will acknowledge that, be the mere matter of priority of detailed discovery and publication as it may, neither of these great minds was a servile plagiary. The Englishman, in regard to the German, thought alone and by himself; and the German, in regard to the Englishman, thought alone and by himself. But both thought in the light of past discoveries, and of all then existing mathematical knowledge. Both were under the laws and impulse of the general scientific mind, as that mind had manifested itself historically in preceding discoveries, and was now using them *both* as its organ of investigation and medium of distinct announced discovery. The dispute between the English and French chemists, respecting the comparative merits of Black and Lavoisier, is still kept up; but here, too, candor must acknowledge that both were original investigators, and that an earlier death of either would not have prevented the discovery.

Now in both of these instances the minds of individuals had been set upon the trail of the new discovery by history; by a knowledge of the then present state and wants of science. They had kept up with the development of science; they knew what had actually been achieved; they saw what was still needed. They felt the wants of science, and these felt wants were dim anticipations of the supply, and finally led to it. It was because Newton and Leibnitz both labored in a historical line of direction, that they labored in the same line, and came to the same result, each of and by himself. For this historical basis for inquiry and discovery is common to all. And as there is but one truth to be discovered, and but one high and royal road to it, it is not surprising that often several minds should reach the goal simultaneously.

A striking instance of the productive power imparted to the individual mind by its taking the central position of history, is seen in the department of philosophy. In this department it is simply impossible, for the individual thinker to make any advance unless he first make himself acquainted with what the human mind has already accomplished in this sphere of investigation. Without some adequate knowledge of the course which philosophic thought has already taken, the individual inquirer in this oceanic region is all afloat. He does not even know where to begin, because he knows not where others have left off; and the system of such a philosopher, if it contain truth, is most commonly but the dry repetition of some previous system. Originality and true progress here, as elsewhere, are impossible without history. Only when the individual has made his mind historic by working his way into that great main current of philosophic thought, which may be traced from Pythagoras to Plato and Aristotle, from Aristotle to the Schoolmen, and from the Schoolmen to Bacon and Kant, and moving onward with it up to the point where the next stage of true progress and normal development is to join on; only when he has thus found the proper point of departure in the present state of the science, is he prepared to depart, and to move forward on the straight but limitless line of philosophic inquiry. It is for this reason that the speculative systems of Germany exhibit such productiveness and originality. Whatever opinion may be held respecting the correctness of the Germanic mind in this department, no one can deny its fertility. The Teutonic philosopher first prepares for the appearance of his system, by a history of philosophy in the past, and then aims to make his own system the crown and completion of the entire historic process; the last link of the long chain. It is true that, in every instance thus far in the movement of this philosophy, the intended last link has only served as the support of another and still other links, yet only in this way of historic preparation could such a productive method of philosophizing have been attained. Only from the position of history, even though it be falsely conceived, can the speculative reason construct new and original systems.

A good illustration of the defectiveness which must attach to a system of philosophy, when it is not conceived and constructed in the light of the history of philosophy, is seen in the so-called Scotch school. A candid mind must admit that the spirit and general aim of this system was sound and correct. It was a reaction against the sensual school, especially as that system had been run out to its logical extreme in France. It recognized and made much of first truths, and that faculty of the mind which the ablest teacher of this school loosely denominated Common Sense, and still more loosely defined, was unquestionably meant to be a power higher than that which "judges according to sense." But it was not an original system, in the sense of grasping with a stronger and more *scientific* grasp than had ever been done before, upon the standing problems of philosophy. It is true that it addressed itself to the solution of the old problems, in the main, in the right spirit and from a deep interest in the truth, but it did not go low enough down, and did not get near enough to the heart of the difficulty, to constitute it an original and powerful system of speculation. Its greatest defect is the lack of a *scientific* spirit, which is indicated in the fact that, although it has exerted a wide influence upon the popular mind, it has exerted but little influence upon the philosophic mind, either of Great Britain or the Continent.

And this defect is to be traced chiefly to the lack of an extensive and profound knowledge of the history of philosophic speculation. The individual mind, in this instance, attempted a refutation of the acute arguments of scepticism, without much knowledge of the previous developments of the sceptical understanding and the counter-statements of true philosophy. A comprehensive and reproductive study of the ancient Grecian philosophies, together with the more elaborate and profound of the modern systems, would have been a preparatory discipline for the Scottish reason that would have armed it with a far more scientific and original power. Its aim, in the first place, would have been higher, because its sense of the difficulty to be overcome would have been far more just and adequate. With more knowledge of what the human intellect had already accomplished, both on the side of truth and of error, its reflection would have been more profound; its point of view more central; its distinctions and definitions more philosophical and scientific; and its refutations more conclusive and unanswerable.*

* This deficiency in scientific character, in the Scotch philosophy, is felt by its present and ablest defender, Sir William Hamilton. More deeply imbued with the spirit of the department than either Reid or Stewart was, because of a wider and more thorough scholarship than either of them possessed, he has been laboring to give it what it lacks. But it is more than doubtful whether any mind that denies the possibility of metaphysics as distinguished from psychology, will be able to do much towards imparting a *necessary* and *scientific* character either to philosophy generally, or to a system which is popular rather than philosophic, in its foundations and superstructure.

Thus we might examine all the departments of human knowledge, singly by themselves, and we should find that, in regard to each of them, the individual mind is made at once recipient and original by the preparatory discipline of historical studies and the possession of the historic spirit. Even in the domain of Literature and Fine Art, the mind that keeps up with the progress of the nation or the race; the mind that is able to go along with the great process of national or human development in this department; is the original and originant mind. Although in Poetry and Fine Art, freshness and originality seem to depend more upon the impulse of individual genius and less upon the general movement of the national or the universal mind, yet here, too, it is a fact, that the founders of particular schools; we mean schools of eminent and historic merit; have been men of extensive study, and liberal, universal sympathies. The great masters of the several schools of Italian Art, were diligent students of the Antique, and had minds open to truth and nature in all the schools that preceded them. They, moreover, cherished a historic feeling and spirit, by a most intimate and general intercourse with each other. The earnest rivalry that prevailed, sprung up from a close study of each other's productions. The view which Cellini presents us of the relations of the Italian artists to each other, and of the general spirit that prevailed among them, shows that there was very little that was bigoted and individual in those minds so remarkable for originality and productiveness within their own sphere.

A very fine and instructive illustration of the truth we are endeavoring to establish, is found in the department of literature in the poet Wordsworth. This man was a *student*. He cultivated the poetic faculty within him as sedulously as Newton cultivated the scientific genius within him. He retired up into the mountains, when he had once determined to make poetry the aim of his literary life, and by the thoughtful perusal of the English poets, as much as by his brooding contemplation of external nature, enlarged and strengthened his poetic power. By familiarizing himself with the spirit and principle, the *inward history*, of English poetry, he became largely imbued with the national spirit. And he was thorough in this course of study. He not only devoted himself to the works of the first English poets, the Chaucers, Spensers, Shakspeares and Miltons; but he patiently studied the productions of the second class, so much neglected by Englishmen, the Draytons, the Daniels, and the Donnes. The works of these latter are not distinguished for passion in sentiment or beauty in form, but they are remarkable for that thoroughly English property, thoughtful sterling sense. Wordsworth was undoubtedly attracted to these poets, not merely because he believed, with that most philosophic of English critics who was his friend and contemporary, that good sense is the body of poetry, but because he saw that an acquaintance with them was necessary to a thorough knowledge of English poetry considered as a historic process of development, as one phase of the English mind. For, although a poem like the Polyolbion of Drayton can by no means be put into the first class with the Faery Queen of Spenser, it yet contains more of the English temper, and exhibits more of the flesh and muscle of the native mind. These writers Wordsworth had patiently studied, as is indicated by that vein of strong sense which runs like a muscular cord through the more light and airy texture of his musings. It was because of this historical training as a poet, that Wordsworth's poetry breathes a far loftier and ampler spirit than it would have done had it been like that of Byron, for example, the product of an intense, but ignorant and narrow, individualism. And it was also because of this training, that Wordsworth, while preserving as original an individuality, certainly, as any writer of his time, acquired a much more national and universal poetic spirit than any of his contemporaries, and was the most productive poet of his age.

The result, then, of the discussion of the subject under this head is, that the individual mind acquires power of discernment and power of statement only by entering into a process already going on; into the great main movement of the common human mind. In no way can the educated man become genially recipient, and at the same time richly productive, but by a profound study of the development which truth has already attained in the history of man and the world.

III. The third characteristic of the historical mind is its union of moderation and enthusiasm.

One of the most distinct and impressive teachings of history is, that not every opinion which springs up and has currency in a particular age, is true for all time. History records the rise and great popularity, for a while, of many a theory which succeeding ages have consigned to oblivion, and which has exerted no permanent influence upon human progress. There always are, among the opinions and theories prevalent in any particular period, some, and perhaps many, that have not truth enough in them to preserve them. And yet these may be the very ones that seize upon the individual and local mind with most violence and most immediate effect. Because they are partial and narrow, they for this reason grasp the popular mind more fiercely and violently. Were they broader and more universal in their character, their immediate influence might be less visible, because it would extend over a far wider surface, and go down to a much lower depth. A blow upon a single point makes a deep dint, but displaces very few particles of matter, while a steady heavy pressure over the whole surface, changes the position of every atom, with but little superficial change.

The proper posture, therefore, of the individual mind, and, especially, of the educated mind, towards the current opinions of the age in which he lives, is, that of moderation. The educated man should keep his mind equable, and, in some degree, aloof from passing views and theories. He ought not to allow theories that have just come into existence to seize upon his understanding with all that assault and onset with which they take captive the uneducated, and, especially, the unhistoric mind. Of what use are the teachings of history if they do not serve to render the mind prudently distrustful in regard to new-born opinions, at the same time that they throw it wide open and fill it with a strong confidence towards all that has historically *proved* itself to be true? Is it for the cultivated man, the man of broad and general views, to throw himself without reserve and with all his weight, into what, for aught he yet knows, may be only a cross-current and eddy, instead of the main stream of truth?

Now it is only by the possession of a historic spirit that the individual can keep himself sufficiently above the course of things about him, to enable him to judge correctly concerning them. Knowing what the human mind has already accomplished in a particular direction, in art or science, in philosophy or religion, he very soon sees whether the particular movement of the time in any one of these directions, will or will not coincide with the preceding movement and be concurrent with it. He occupies a height, a vantage ground, by virtue of his extensive historical knowledge, and he stands upon it, not with the tremor and fervor of a partisan, but with the calmness and insight of a judge. Suppose the activity of an age, or of an individual, manifests itself in the production of a new theory in religion, of some new statement of Christian doctrine, the mind that is well versed in the history of the Christian church, and of Christian doctrine, will very quickly see whether the new joins on upon the old; whether it is an advance in the line of progress or a deviation from it. And his attitude will be accordingly. He will not be led astray with the multitude or even with the age. Through all the fervor and zeal of the period, he will preserve a moderate and temperate tone of mind; committing himself to current opinions no faster than he sees they will amalgamate with the truth which the human mind has already and confessedly discovered in past ages; with historic truth.

This moderation in adopting and maintaining current opinions is an infallible characteristic of a true scholar, of a ripe culture. And it is the fruit of that criticism and scepticism which is generated by historical study. For it is one of the effects of such studies to render the mind critical and sceptical; not, indeed, in respect to truth that has stood the test of time, but to truth that has just made its appearance. It would be untrue to say that the study of history genders absolute doubt and unbelief in the mind; that it tends generally and by its very nature to unsettle faith in the good and the true. This would be the case if there were no truth in the science; if it were substantially the record of dissension and disagreement; if, above the din and uproar of discordant voices, one clear and clarion-like voice did not make itself heard as the voice of universal history. We are all familiar with the story told of Raleigh, who is said to have destroyed the unpublished half of his work, because of several persons who professed to describe an occurrence in the Tower Court, which he had also witnessed from his prison window, each gave a different version of it, and his own differed from theirs. But history is not thus uncertain and unreliable. It teaches but one lesson. It reveals but one truth. Down through the ages and generations it traces one straight line, and in this one line of direction lies truth, and out of it lies error. Its record of the successes and triumphs of truth certainly teaches a correct lesson, and its record of the successes and triumphs of error is but the dark background from which truth stands out in still more bold and impressive reality. Whatever may be the case with particular accounts by particular individuals, the main current of this science runs in one direction, and its great lesson is in favor of truth and righteousness.

Not, then, towards well-tried and well-established truth, but towards apparent and newly-discovered truth, does history engender criticism and scepticism. The past is secure. That which has verified itself by the lapse of time, and the course of experiment, and the sifting of investigation, is commended as absolute and universal truth to the individual mind, and history bids it to believe and doubt not. But that which is current merely; that which in the novelty and youth of its existence is carrying all men away; must stand trial, must be brought to test, as all its predecessors have been. Towards the opinions and theories of the present, so far as they vary from those of the past, the historical mind is inquisitive, and critical, and sceptical, not for the purpose, be it remembered, of proving them to be false, but with the generous hope of evincing them to be true. For the scepticism of history is very different from scepticism in religion. The latter is always in some way biassed and interested. It springs out of a desire, conscious or unconscious, to overthrow that which the general mind has found to be true, and is resting in as truth. Scepticism in religion has always been in the minority; at war with the received opinions of the race, and consequently with all that is historic. There never was an individual sceptic, from Pyrrho to Strauss, who was not unhistorical; who did not take his stand outside of the great travelled road of human opinion; who did not try to disturb the human race in the possession of opinions that had come down from the beginning, besides having all the instincts of reason to corroborate them. But the scepticism of history has no desire to overthrow any opinion that has verified itself in the course of ages, and been organically assimilated, in the course of human development. All such opinion and all such truth constitutes the very substance of the science itself; its very vitality and charm for the human mind; and, therefore, can never be the object of doubt or attack for genuine historic scepticism. On the contrary, these sifting and critical methods have no other end or aim but to make a real addition to the existing stock of well-ascertained truth, and to prevent any erroneous opinion or theory from going into this sum-total, and thus receiving the sterling stamp and endorsement. This criticism and scepticism is simply for self-protection. These sceptical and sifting processes are gone through with, to preserve an all-sided science pure from the individual, the local, and the temporary, and to keep it universal and absolute in its contents and spirit.

Now it might seem at first glance, that this moderation of mind towards current opinions would preclude all earnestness and enthusiasm in the educated man; that the historic spirit must necessarily be cold and phlegmatic. It might seem that it would be impossible for such a mind to take an active and vigorous interest in the age in which it lived, and that it would be out of its element amid the stir and motion going on all around it. This is substantially the objection which the half-educated disciple of the present brings against history and historical views and opinions.

But this is a view that is false from defect; from not containing the *whole* truth. It arises from not taking the full idea of the science into the mind. This idea, like all strictly so-called ideas, contains two opposites, which, to the superficial glance, look like irreconcilable contraries, but to a deeper and more adequate intuition, are not only perfectly reconcilable, but are opposites in whose conciliation consists the vitality and fertility of the idea, and of the science founded upon it. History, as we have seen, is both continuous and complete; and continuity and completeness are opposite conceptions.— It is, in the first place, the record of a development that must unintermittently go on, and cannot cease, until the final consummation. And it is, in the second place, complete in its spirit, because at every point in the continuous process there are indications of the consummation; tendencies to an ultimate end. No part of history is irrelative. Even when it is but the account of a particular period, a small section of the great historic process, it exhibits this complete and universal spirit by clinging to what precedes and pointing to what succeeds; by its large discourse of reason looking before and after. But the objector does not reconcile these opposites in his own mind; he does not take this comprehensive and full view of the subject. Whether he acknowledges it or not, his view really is, that the many several ages of which history takes cognizance, have no inward connection with each other, nor any common tendency, and consequently that the whole entire past, in relation to the present, is a nonentity. It is gone, with all that it was and did, into "the dark backward and abysm" of time, and the present age, like every other, starts independent and alone upon its particular mission. His view of history is atomic. — On his theory, there is no such thing as either connected evolution or explanatory termination, in the course of the world. There is no human race, no common humanity, to be manifested in the millions of individuals, and the multitudes of ages and epochs. On this theory, there is and can be nothing in the past, in which the present has any *vital* interest; nothing in the past which has any *authority* for the present; nothing in the past which constitutes the root of the present, and nothing in the present which constitutes the germ of the future. History, on this theory, has no principle; no organization. It is a mere catalogue of events; a mere list of occurrences.

It is because the imperfectly educated disciple of the present, really takes this view, that he asserts that historic views and opinions are deadening in their influence upon the mind, and that the historic spirit is a lifeless spirit. If he believed in a living concatenation of events and a vital propagation of influences, he would not say that that which is truly historical, is virtually dead and buried. If he believed that no one age, any more than any one individual, contains the whole of human development within itself, but is only one fold of the great unfolding, he would suspect, at least, that there might be elements in the past so assimilated and wrought into the history of universal man that they are matters of living interest for every present age. If he believed that truth is reached only by the successive and consentaneous endeavors of many individual minds, each making use of all the labors of its predecessors, and each taking up the standing problem where its predecessors had dropped it; if the too zealous disciple of the present believed that truth is thus reached only by the efforts of the race; of the universal mind in distinction from the individual; he would find life all along the line of human history; he would see that in taking into his mind a historic view or opinion he was lodging there the highest intensity of mental life; the very purest and densest reason of the race.

Instead, therefore, of being cold, phlegmatical and lifeless, the historical mind is really the only truly living and enthusiastic mind. It is the only mind that is in communication. It is the only mind that is not isolated. — And in the mental world, intercommunication is not more necessary to a vital process, and isolation or breaking off is not more destructive of a vital process, than in the world of nature. That zeal, begotten by the narrow views of an individual, or a locality, or an age, which the unhistorical mind exhibits, is an altogether different thing from the enthusiasm of a spirit enlarged, educated, and liberalized, by an acquaintance with all ages and opinions. Enthusiasm springs out of the contemplation of a whole; zeal from the examination of a part. And there is no surer test and sign of intellectual vitality than enthusiasm; that deep and sustained interest which is grounded in the broad views and profound intuitions of history.

But while the well-read student of history preserves a wise and cautious moderation, in the outset, towards current opinions, yet, because of this genial and enthusiastic interest in the truth which the human mind has actually and without dispute arrived at, he in the end comes to take all the interest in the views and theories of the present, which they really deserve. The historical mind does no ultimate injustice. So far and so fast as it finds that the new movement of the present age is a natural continuation of the unfinished development of the past, does he acknowledge it as a step in advance, and receives the new element into his mind and into his culture with all the enthusiasm and all the feeling with which he adopts the great historic systems of antiquity. In this way the historical mind is actually more truly alive and interested even in relation to the present, than the man of the present. It appreciates the real excellence of the time more intelligently and profoundly, and it certainly has a far more inspiriting view of the connection of this excellence with the excellence that has preceded it, and which is the root of it. How much more inspiring and enlivening is that vision which sees the progress of the present linked to that of all the past, and contributing to make up that long line of development extending through the whole career of the human species, than that vision which sees but one thing at a time, and does not even know that it has any living references, or any organic connections whatever!

As an exemplification of the preceding remarks, contemplate for a moment the historian Niebuhr. His was a genuinely historical mind. He conceived and constructed in the true spirit of history. He always viewed events in the light of the organization by which they were shaped and of which they were elementary parts. He saw by a native sagacity, in which respect he never had a superior, the idea lying at the bottom of a historical process; such, for example, as the separate foundation of the city of Rome; the rise and formation of the

Roman population; the growth and consolidation of the plebeians; and built up his account of it, out of it and upon it. His written history thus corresponds with a fresh and vital correspondence with the actual history; with the living process itself. In this way he reproduced human life in his pages, and the student is carried along through the series with all the interest and charm of an actor in it. So sagacious was his intuition that, although two thousand years further off from them in time, he ha unquestionably so reconstructed the very facts of the early history of Rome, as to bring them nearer the actual matter of fact, than they appear in the legendary pages of Livy. It was the habit of his mind, both by nature and by an acquisition as minute as it was vast, to look at human life as an indivisible process, and to connect together all the ages, empires, civilizations, and literatures, of the secular world by the bond of a common development; thus organizing the immense amount of material contained in human history into a complete and symmetrical whole.

But slow and sequacious as the movements of such an organizing and thoroughly historic mind were, and must be from the nature of the case, we do not hesitate to affirm that the historian Niebuhr was one of the most vividly alive and profoundly enthusiastic minds in all literary history. He was not spared to complete his great work as it lay in him to have done, and as he would have done, immense as it was, had he lived to the appointed age of man. He left it a fragment. He left it a Torso which no man can complete. But from that fragment has gushed, as from many living centres, all the life and power not only of Roman history, but of history generally, since his day. It gave an impulse to this whole department which it still continues to feel, besides reproducing itself in particular schools and particular individuals. It is the work which more than any other one production, shaped the opinions of the most vigorous and enthusiastic of English historians, the late Dr. Arnold. And that serious spirit which we find in the science itself since the days of Niebuhr, when compared with the moral indifference characterizing it before his day and to a great extent during his day, is to be traced to his reverent recognition of a personal Deity in history, and his deep belief in the freedom and accountability of man.

But the man himself, as well as his works, was full of life, and he showed it nowhere more plainly than in his direct address to the minds of his pupils. "When he spoke," says one of them, "it always appeared as if the rapidity with which the thoughts occurred to him, obstructed his power of communicating them in regular order or succession. Nearly all his sentences, therefore, were anacoluths; for, before having finished one, he began another, perpetually mixing up one thought with another, without producing any one in its complete form. This peculiarity was more particularly striking when he was laboring under any mental excitement, which occurred the oftener, as, with his great sensitiveness, he felt that warmth of interest in treating of the history of past ages, which we are accustomed to witness only in discussions on the political affairs of our own time and country." The writer, after speaking of the difficulty of following him, owing to his rapid, and it should be added, entirely extemporaneous delivery (for he spoke without a scrap of paper before him), remarks, that "notwithstanding this deficiency of Niebuhr as a lecturer, there was an indescribable charm in the manner in which he treated his subject; the warmth of his feelings, the sympathy which he felt with the persons and things he was speaking of, his strong conviction of the truth of what he was saying, his earnestness, and, above all, the vividness with which he conceived and described the characters of the most prominent men, who were to him living realities, with souls, feelings and passions like ourselves, carried his hearers away, and produced effects which are usually the results only of the most powerful oratory.*"

How different from all this is the impression which we receive from the mind of one who, notwithstanding his great defects, must yet thus far be regarded as the first of English historians; from the mind of Gibbon. After a candid and full allowance of the ability of that mind and the great value of the History of the Decline and Fall of Rome, it must yet be said that it was not a vivid and vital mind, nor is its product. The autobiography of Gibbon, indeed, exhibits considerable native liveliness, but the perusal of his history does not even suggest the existence of such qualities as earnestness and enthusiasm. One is disposed to conclude from the picture which he gives of himself, that the historian had been endowed by his Maker with a more than average share of mental freshness and vitality, and most certainly if there had been in exercise enough of this quality; enough of the *vis vivida vitæ;* to have vivified his immense well-selected and well-arranged material, he would have approximated nearer than he has to the ideal of historical composition. But there was not, and, therefore, it is, that, throughout the whole of this great work, there reigns, so far as the human and moral interest of history is concerned, so far as all its higher religious problems are concerned, an utter sluggishness, apathy, and lifelessness; an apathy and

* Dr. Leonhard Schmitz. Preface to Vol. IV. of Niebuhr's Rome.

lifelessness as deep, unvarying, and monotonous, as if the forces of the period he described, the principles of decline and decay, had passed over into his own understanding and made it the theatre of their operations. We doubt whether there is another work in any literature whatever, possessing so many substantial excellences, and yet characterized by such a total destitution of glowing inspiration and earnest enthusiasm, as the History of the Decline and Fall of the Roman Empire.

The explanation of this fact will corroborate the truth of the position, that the *genuinely* historic mind is the only truly living and enthusiastic mind. Though nominally a historian, Gibbon was really utterly unhistorical in his spirit. His religious scepticism, besides paralyzing whatever natural vigor and earnestness of conception may have originally belonged to him, made it impossible for him to regard the processes of human life as so many parts of one grand plan of the world formed by one supreme presiding mind. History for him, consequently, had no organization and no moral significance. It was, therefore, strictly speaking, no *history* at all for him; no course of development with a divine plan at the bottom of it and a divine purpose at the termination of it. It was neither continuous in its nature, nor complete in its spirit and tendency. Everything that occurred in the world at large, or among a particular people, was for his mind irreferent, discontinuous, and sporadic. Not only did he fail to connect the History of the Decline and Fall of the Roman Empire with the general history of the race, or even with the general history of Rome, by exhibiting it in its relation to its antecedents and consequents, but he failed even to detect the historic principle lying at the bottom of the particular period itself. The great *moral and political causes* of the decline and fall of the Roman empire, do not stand out in bold and striking relief from the immense erudition and imposing rhetoric of that work. The reflecting reader, at the close of its perusal, feels the need of something more than a scenic representation of the period; something more than the pomp of a panorama; in order to a knowledge of the deep *ground* of all this decline and decay. He needs, in short, what Gibbon does not furnish, more of the philosophy of that organic decline, drawn from a profounder view of the nature of man and of human life, united with a deeper insight into the radical defect in the political constitution of the Roman empire; into that germ of corruption which came into existence immediately after the subjugation of the Italian tribes was completed, and in which the entire millennium of decline and decay lay coiled up.

We have thus far discussed the nature of the historic spirit on general grounds. We have mentioned only those general characteristics which are matters of interest to every cultivated mind; having reference chiefly to secular history and general education. We have now to speak of the importance of this spirit to the theologian, and must, therefore, discuss its more special nature, with a prevailing reference to Ecclesiastical History and Theological Education.

Before proceeding to the treatment of this part of the subject, it seems necessary to direct attention, for a moment, to the distinguishing difference between Secular and Church history.

Our Lord, in the most distinct manner, and repeatedly, affirms that His kingdom is not of this world. Throughout the Scriptures the church and the world are opposed to each other as direct contraries, mutually exclusive and expulsive of each other, so that "all that is in the world is not of the Father, but is of the world." There are, therefore two kingdoms, two courses of development, two histories, in the universal history of man on the globe. There is the account of the natural and spontaneous development of human nature as left to itself, guided only by the dictates of finite reason and impelled by the determination of the free, but fallen, human will, and the impulses of human passion. And there is the history of that supernatural and gracious development of human nature which has been begun and carried forward by means of a revelation from the Divine Mind made effectual by the direct efficiency of the Divine Spirit. The fact of sin, and the fact of redemption, constitute the substance of that great historic process which is involved in the origin, growth and final triumph of the Christian church. Had there been no fall of man, there would have been but one stream of history. The spontaneou development of the human race would have been normal and perfect, and there would have been no such distinction between the church and world as is recognized in Scripture. The race would not have been broken apart; one portion being left to a merely human and entirely false development, and the other portion being renovated and started upon a spiritual and heavenward career by the electing love of God. But sin in this, as in all its aspects, is dissension and dismemberment. The original unity of the race, *so far as a common religious character and a common blessed destiny are concerned*, is destroyed, and the two halves of one being, to borrow an illustration from the Platonic myth, are now and forever separated. The original single stream of human history was parted in the garden of Eden, and became into two heads, which have flowed on, each in its own channel, and will continue to do so, forevermore. For, although the church is to encroach upon the world, in the future, to an extent far surpassing anything that appears in the present and the past, we know, from the very best authority, that sin is to be an eternal fact in the universe of God, and as such must have its own awful and isolated development; its own awful and isolated history.

In passing, therefore, from secular to church history, we pass from the domain of merely human and sinful, to that of truly divine and holy, agencies. The subject-matter becomes extraordinary. The basis of fact in the career of the church is supernatural in both senses of the word. From the expulsion from Eden down to the close of miracles in the apostolic age, a positively miraculous intervention of Divine power lies under the series of events; momentarily withdrawn and momentarily reappearing, throughout the long line of Patriarchal, Jewish and Apostolic history; the very intermittency of the action indicating, like an Icelandic Geyser, the reality and constant proximity of the power. And if we pass from external events to that inward change that was constantly brought about in human character by which the church was called out from the mass of men and made to live and grow in the midst of an ignorant or a cultivated heathenism; if we pass from the miraculous to the simply spiritual manifestation of the Divine agency as it is seen in the inward life of the church, we find that we are in a far higher sphere than that of secular history. There is now a positive intercommunication between the human and the Divine mind, and the development which results constitutes a history far profounder, far purer and holier, far more encouraging and glorious, than that of the natural man and the secular world.

It is upon the fact of this direct and supernatural communication of the Supreme mind to the human mind, and this direct agency of the Divine Spirit upon the human soul, that we would take our stand as the point of departure in the remainder of this discussion. In treating of secular history, we have regarded the unaided reason of man as the source and origin of the development. We do not find in the history of the world, as the Scriptural antithesis of the church, any evidence of any special and direct intercommunication between man and God. We find only the ordinary workings of the human mind and such products as are confessedly within its competence to originate. We can, indeed, see the hand of an overruling Providence throughout this realm, employed chiefly in restraining the wrath of man, but through the whole long course of development we see no signs or products of a supernatural and peculiar interference of God in the affairs of men. Empires rise and fall; arts and sciences bloom and decay; the poet dreams his dream of the ideal, and the philosopher develops and tasks the utmost possibility of the finite reason; and still, so far as its highest interests are concerned, the condition and history of the race remain substantially the same. It is not until a communication is established between the mind of man and the mind of God; it is not until the Creator comes down by miracle and by revelation, by incarnation and by the Holy Ghost, that a new order of ages and a new species of history begins.

The Scriptures, therefore, as the revelation of the Eternal Mind, take the place of human reason within the sphere of church history. The individual man sustains the same relation to the Bible, in the sacred historic process, that he does to natural reason in the secular. The theologian expects to find in the history of the church that same comprehensive and approximately exhaustive development and realization of Scripture truth, which the philosopher hopes to find of the finite reason in the secular history of the race. It follows, consequently, that all that has been said of the influence of historical studies upon the literary man, applies with full force, when the distinguishing difference between secular and sacred history has been taken into account, to the education and culture of the theologian. The same spirit will work with the same results in both departments of knowledge, and the theologian, like the literary man, will become, in his own intellectual domain, both reverent and vigilant; both recipient and original; both deliberate and enthusiastic; as his mind feels the influences that come off from the history of the Christian religion and the Christian church.

Without, therefore, going again over the ground which we have travelled in the first part of the discourse, let us leave the general influences and characteristics of the historic spirit, and proceed to consider some of the most important of its specific influences within the department of theology and upon theological education. And, that we may not be embarrassed by the attempt to make use of all the materials that crowd in upon the mind on all sides, and from all parts, of this encyclopaedic subject, let us leave altogether untouched the external career of the church, and keep chiefly in view that most interesting and important branch of the department which is denominated Doctrinal Church History.

I. In the first place, a historic spirit within the department of theology promotes Scripturality.

We have already mentioned that the distinctive character of church history arises from the special presence and agency of the Divine Mind in the world. Subtract that presence, and that agency, and nothing is left but the spontaneous development of the natural man; nothing is left but secular history. Divine revelation, using the term in its widest signification, to denote the entire communication of God to man in the economy of grace, is the principle and germ of church history. That shaping of human events, and that formation and moulding of human character, which has resulted from the covenant of redemption, is the substance of sacred history. The church is the concrete and realized plan of redemption; and what is the plan of redemption but the sum-total of revelations which have been made to man by the Jehovah of the Old Testament and the Incarnate Word of the New, the infallible record of which is unchangeably fixed in the Scriptures? It follows, therefore, that the true and full history of the church of God on earth will be the Scriptures in the concrete. The plant is only the unfolded germ.

There is, consequently, no surer way to fill systematic theology with a Scriptural substance than to subject it to the influence of historical studies. As the theologian passes the several ages of the church in review, and becomes acquainted with the results to which the general mind of the church has come in interpreting the Scriptures, he runs little hazard of error in regard to their real teaching and contents. As in the domain of secular history we found that there was little danger of missing the true teachings of human reason, if we collect them from the continuous and self-defecating development of ages and epochs, so in the domain of sacred history we shall find that the real mind of the Spirit, the real teaching of Scripture, comes out plainer and clearer in the general growth and development of the Christian mind. Indeed we may regard church history, so far as it is mental and inward in its nature; so far as it is the record of a mental inquiry into the nature of Christianity and the contents of the Bible; as being as near to the infallibility of the written revelation, as anything that is still imperfect and fallible can be. The church is not infallible and never can be; but it is certainly not a very bold or dangerous affirmation to say that the church, the entire body of Christ, is wiser than any one of its members, and that the whole series of ages and generations of believers have penetrated more deeply into the substance of the Christian religion and have come nearer to an approximate exhaustion of Scripture truth, than any single age or single believer has.

So far, therefore, as a theological system contains historical elements, it is likely to contain Scriptural elements. So far as its statements of doctrine coincide with those of the creeds and symbols in which the wise, the learned, and the holy, of all ages have embodied the results of their continuous and self-correcting study of the Scriptures, so far it may be expected to coincide with the substance of inspiration itself.

Again, there is no surer way to imbue the theologian himself with a Scriptural spirit than to subject his mind to the full influence of a course of study in the history of the Christian religion and church. This is one of the best means which the individual mind can employ to reach the true end of a theological education; which is to get within the circle of inspired minds and see the truth exactly as they saw it. We believe, as the church has always believed, that the inspired writers were qualified and authorized to speak upon the subject of religion as no other human minds have been. They were the subjects of an illumination clearer and brighter than that of the purest Christian experience; and of a revelation that put them in possession of truths that are absolutely beyond the ken of the wisest human mind.— Within that inspired circle, therefore, there was a body of knowledge intrinsically inaccessible to the human mind; beyond the reach of its subtlest investigation, or its purest self-development. If those supernaturally taught minds had been prevented from fixing their knowledge in a written form; or if the written revelation had perished like the lost books of Livy; the human mind of the nineteenth century would have known no more upon moral and religious subjects, for substance, than the human mind of a Plato or Aristotle knew twenty-two centuries ago. For he must have an extravagant estimate of the inherent capacities of the finite mind, who supposes that the rolling round of two millenniums, or of ten, would have witnessed in any one individual case, a more central, or a more defecated, development of the pure rationality of mere man than was witnessed in Aristotle. And he must have a very ardent belief in the omnipotence of the finite, who supposes, that, without that communication of truth and of spirit; of light and of life; which God in Christ has made to the race, ages upon ages of merely spontaneous and secular history would have produced a more beautiful development of the human imagination than appears in the Grecian Art and Literature, or a more profound development of the human reason than appears in the Grecian Philosophy and the Grecian Ethics.

The Scriptures have, accordingly, been the source of religious knowledge and progress for the Christian, as antithetic to the secular, mind, and will continue to be, until they are superseded by some other and fuller revelation in another mode of being than that of earth. It has, consequently, been the aim and endeavor of the church in all ages, to be Scriptural; to work itself into the very heart of the written revelation; to stand upon the very same point of view with the few inspired minds, and see objects precisely as they saw them. But this, though possible and a duty, is no easy task, as the whole history of Christian doctrines shows. Truth in the Scriptures is full and entire. The Scriptural idea is never defective, but contains all the elements. Hence its very perfection and completeness is an obstacle to its full apprehension. It is difficult for the human mind to take in the *whole* great thought. It is often exceedingly difficult for the human mind oppressed, first, by the vastness and mystery of the revealed truth, and, secondly, by its own singular tendency to one-sided and imperfect perception, to gather the full idea from the artless and unsystematized contents of Scripture, and then state it in the imperfect language of man. The doctrine of the Trinity, for example, is fully revealed in the Bible. *All* the elements of that great mystery; the whole truth respecting the real triune nature of God, may be found in that book. But the elements are uncombined and unexpanded, and hence one source of the heresies respecting this doctrine. Arius and Sabellius both appealed to Scripture. Neither of them took the position of the infidel. Each acknowledged the authority of the written word, and endeavored to support his position from it.—But in these instances the individual mind merely picked up Scriptural elements as they lie scattered upon the page and in the letter of Scripture, and, without combining them with others that lie just as plainly upon the very same pages, moulded them into a defective, and therefore erroneous, statement. Heresy is individual and not historic in its nature.

Now it is the characteristic of the general mind of the church; of the historic Christian mind; that it reproduces in its intuition, and in its statement, the *complex* and *complete* Scriptural idea. So far as it has any intuition it all, it sees *all* the sides; so far as it makes any statement at all, it brings into it *all* the fundamentals. By this is not meant that even the mind of the church has perfected the expansion of Scripture elements and made the fullest possible statement of the doctrine of the Trinity. There may, possibly, be a further exhaustion of the contents of revelation in this direction. There may, possibly, be a statement of this doctrine that will be yet fuller; still closer up to the Scriptural matter; than that one which the church has generally accepted since the date of the Councils of Nice and Constantinople. But there will never be a form of statement that will flatly contradict this form, or that will add any new fundamentals to it. All that is new and different must be in the way of expansion and not of addition; in the way of development and not of denial. A closer study of the teachings of Scripture, and a deeper reflection upon them, may carry the theological mind further along on the line, but will give it no diagonal or retrograde movement.

Now is it not perfectly plain that the close and thorough study of this continuous and self-correcting endeavor of the Christian church to enucleate the real meaning of Scripture; an endeavor which has been put forth by the wisest, the most reverent, and the holiest, minds in its history, tasking their own powers to the utmost, and invoking and receiving Divine illumination, during the whole of the process; an endeavor which has to a great extent formed and fixed the religious experience of ages and generations, by its results embodied in the creeds and symbols of the church: a series of mental constructions, which, even if we contemplate only their human characteristics, their scientific coherence and systematic compactness, are more than worthy to be placed side by side with the best dialectics of the secular mind, is it not perfectly plain, we say, that the close and thorough study of such a strenuous endeavor, as this has been, to reach the inmost heart and fibre of Scripture, will tend irresistibly to render the theologian Scriptural in head and in heart? May we not expect that such a student will be *intensely* Scriptural? Will not this distinct and thorough knowledge of revelation be so wrought into his mental texture that he will see and judge of everything through this medium? Will he not have so thought in that same range and region in which his inspired teachers thought, that doubt and perplexity in regard to Divine revelation would be nearly as impossible for him, as for Isaiah while under the Divine afflatus, or for Paul when in the third heavens? To borrow an illustration from the kindred science of Law: if it is the effect of the continued and thoughtful study of Law Reports and Political Constitutions and Commentaries upon Political Constitutions; a body of literature which, as it originates out of the organic idea of law, breathes the purest spirit of the legal reason; if it is the effect of such study to render the individual mind legal and judicial in its tone and temper, must it not be the effect of the study of that body of symbolic literature which has come slowly but consecutively into existence through the endeavor of the theological mind to reach a perfect understanding of Scripture, to render the individual mind Scriptural in its tone and temper?

II. And this leads us to say, in the second place, that a historic spirit in the theologian, induces a correct estimate of Creeds and Systematic Theology.

One of the most interesting features in the present condition of the theological world is a revived interest in the department of church history. This interest has been slowly increasing for the last half century, and promises to become a leading interest for some time to come. In Germany, in America, and in England, scholars and thinking men are turning their attention away, somewhat, from the purely secular history of mankind, to that more solemn and momentous career which a part of the human family have been running for nearly six thousand years. They have become aware that the history of the church of God is a peculiar movement that has been silently going on in the heart of the race from the beginning of time, and which, while it has not by any means left the secular historic processes untouched and unaffected, has yet kept on in its own solitary and sublime line of direction. They are now disposed to look and see how and where

> * * the sacred river ran
> Through caverns measureless to man
> Down to the sunlit sea.

But it would be an error to suppose that this interest has been awakened merely or mainly by the external history of the Christian Church. "The battles, sieges, fortunes it hath passed;" its conflicts with persecuting Paganism, Mohammedanism, and Romanism; its influence upon art, upon literature and science, upon society and government; these are not the charm which is now drawing as by a spell the best thinking of Christendom towards church history. It is not the secular and worldly elements in this history into which the mind of the time most desires to look. The great march of profane history brings to view a pomp and prodigality of such elements that has already dulled and satiated the tired sensibilities. Thinking minds now desire to look into the distinctively supernatural elements in this historic process; to see if it really has, as it claims to have, a direct connection with the Creator of the race and the Author of the human mind. It is for this reason that the revived interest in this department of knowledge has shown itself most powerfully and influentially in investigating the origin and nature of the *doctrines* of the church, as they are found speculatively in creeds and symbols, and practically in the Christian consciousness. The mind of Germany, for example, after ranging over the whole field of cultivated heathenism, and sounding the lowest depths of the finite reason, in a vain search for that absolute truth in which alone the human soul can rest, has betaken itself to the domain of Christian revelation and Christian history. Its interest in Greek and Roman culture, in Mediaeval Art, and in its own speculative systems, has given way to a deeper interest in the Christian religion; in some instances with a clear perception, in others with a dim intimation, that, if the truth which the human mind needs, is not to be found here, the last resource has failed; and that then

> The pillared firmament is rottenness
> And earth's base built on stubble.

This revived interest in church history, therefore, is in reality a search after truth, rather than after a mere dramatic scene or spectacle. The mind of the time is anxious to understand that *revealed doctrinal system*, which it now sees, has, from the beginning, been the "rock" on which the church of God has been founded, and the "quarry" out of which it has been built. Knowing this, it believes it will then have the key to the process. Knowing this, it believes it will know the whole secret; the secret of that charmed life which has borne the church of God through all the mutations and extinctions of secular history, and that unearthly life which in all ages has secured to the believer a serene or an ecstatic passage into the unknown and dreadful future.

Now this interest in a doctrinal system, which thus lies at the bottom of this general interest in church history, will be shared by the individual student. He, too, cannot stop with the scene, the spectacle, the drama. He, too, cannot stop with those characteristics which ecclesiastical history has in common with secular, but will pass on to those which are distinctive and peculiar. For him, too, the history of a single mind, like that of Augustine or Anselm; or of a single doctrine, like that of the Atonement or of the Trinity; will have a charm and fruitfulness not to be found in the entire rise of the worldly Papacy, or in centuries of merely external and earthly movement like the Crusades. The whole influence of his studies in this direction will be spiritual and spiritualizing.

But, without enlarging upon the general nature of the estimate which the historic spirit puts upon the internal as compared with the external history of the church, let us notice two particulars which fall under this head.

1. Notice, first, the interest awakened by historical studies in the creeds and symbols of the Christian church *as containing the Philosophy of Christianity.*

We have spoken of the symbolic literature of the Christian church as a growth out of Scripture soil; as a fruitage full of the flavor and juices of its germ. A Christian creed is not the product of the individual, or the general, human mind evolving out of itself those truths of natural reason and natural religion which are connate and inborn. It is not the self-development of the human mind, but the development of Scripture matter. The

Christian mind, as we have seen, is occupied, from age to age, with an endeavor to fathom the depths of Divine revelation; to make the fullest possible expression and expansion of all the truths that have been communicated from God to man. This endeavor necessarily assumes a scientific form. The practical explanation, illustration, and application, is going on continually in the popular representations of the pulpit and the sermon, but this cannot satisfy all the wants of the church. Simultaneously with this there is a constant effort to obtain a still more scientific apprehension of Scripture and make a still more full and self-consistent statement of its contents. The Christian mind, as well as the secular, is scientific; has a scientific feeling, and scientific wants. A creed is as necessary to a theologian, as a philosophical system is to the secular student.

It follows, therefore, that the philosophy, by which is meant the rationality, of the Christian religion, is to be found in these creeds and symbols. For reasonableness and self-consistence are qualities not to be carried into Christianity from without, as if they were not to be found in it, but to be brought out from within, because they belong to its intrinsic nature. The philosophy, that is, the rational necessity, of the Christian religion, is not an importation but an evolution. This religion is to be taken just as it is given in the Scriptures; just as it reappears in the close and systematic statement of the creeds; and its intrinsic truth and reasonableness evinced by what it furnishes itself. For whoever shows the *inward* necessity and reasonableness of a Doctrine of Christianity does by the very act and fact show the harmony of philosophy and religion. Whoever takes a doctrine of Christianity and without anxiously troubling himself with the tenets of this or that particular philosophical system, derives out of the very elements of the doctrine and the very terms of the statement itself, a reasonableness that irresistibly commends itself to the spontaneous reason and instinctive judgment of universal man, by this very process demonstrates the *inward, central*, unity of faith and reason. Instead, therefore, of setting the two sciences over against each other and endeavoring, by modifications upon one or both sides, to bring about the adjustment, the theologian should take the Christian system precisely as it is given in Scripture, in all its comprehension, depth, and strictness, and without being diverted by any side references to particular philosophical schools, simply exhibit the *intrinsic* truthfulness, rationality, and necessity, of the system. In this way he establishes the position, that philosophy and revelation are harmonious, in a manner that admits of no contradiction. The greater necessarily includes the less. When the theologian has demonstrated the inward necessity of Christianity, out of its own self-sufficient and independent rationality, his demonstration is perfect. For reason cannot be contrary to reason. A rational necessity anywhere, is a philosophical necessity everywhere.

The correctness of this method of finding and establishing the rationality of Christianity, is beginning to be acknowledged in that country where the conflict between reason and revelation has been hottest. It begins to be seen that the harmony between philosophy and Christianity is not to be brought about, by first assuming that the infallibility is on the side of the human reason; and that, too, as it appears in a *single* and *particular* philosophical system; and then insisting that all the adjustment, conformity, and coalescence, shall be on the side of the Divine revelation. It begins to be seen that philosophy is in reality an abstract and universal term which, by its very etymology, denotes, not that it has already attained and now possesses the truth, but that it is seeking for it.* It begins to be seen that both Aristotle and Bacon were right in calling it an *organon;* an *instrument* for getting at the truth, and neither the truth itself nor even its containing source.† It begins to be seen that philosophy is only another term for rationality, and that to exhibit the philosophy of a department, like religion, or history, or philosophy, or natural science, is simply to exhibit the real and reasonable truth that is *in* it. It begins to be seen, consequently, that each branch of knowledge, each subject of investigation, must be treated *genetically* in order to be treated philosophically; must be allowed to furnish its own matter, make its own statements, out of which, and not out of what may be carried over into it from some other quarter, its acceptance or its rejection by the human mind should be determined.

We are aware that the barrenness of those later systems of speculative philosophy, with which the German mind has been so intensely busied for the last fifty years, has been one great means of bringing it back to this moderate and true estimate of the nature and functions of philosophy; but this revived interest in the history of Christianity

* The *love* of wisdom, implies a present seeking for it.

† Kant, says William Humboldt, did not so much teach philosophy, as how to philosophize. Correspondence with Schiller: *Vorerinnerung.*

It is the greatest merit of Schleiermacher that he saw and asserted the independent and self-subsistent position of Christian theology in relation to philosophical systems. If he had sought the *sources* of this theology more in the objective revelation and less in the subjective Christian consciousness, he would have accomplished more than he has towards evincing the harmony of the two sciences, while his own system would have had more agreement than it now has with the general theology of the Christian church.

and profounder study of its symbols, has also contributed, greatly, to produce this disposition to let revealed religion stand or fall upon its own merits. For this study has disclosed the fact that it has philosophical and scientific merits of its own; that, in the unsystematized statements and simple but prolific teachings of the Bible, there lies the substance of a *system* deeper and wider and loftier than the whole department of philosophy, and that this substance has actually been expanded and combined by the historic mind of the church into a series of doctrines respecting the nature of God and man and the universe with their mutual relations, with which the corresponding statements upon the same subjects, of the Greek Theism or the German Pantheism cannot compare for a moment. Probably nothing has done more to exhibit the Christian system in its true nature and proportions, and thereby to render it grand and venerable to the modern scientific mind, than this history of its origin and formation. As the scientific man studies the articles of a creed, which one of the most naturally scientific minds of the race, aided by the wisdom of predecessors and contemporaries, derived from the written revelation; as the rigorous and dialectic man follows Athanasius down into those depths of the Divine nature, which yawn like a gulf of darkness before the unaided human mind; if he finds nothing to love and adore, he finds something to respect; if he finds no food for his affections, he finds some matter for his thoughts. Here, too, is science. Here, too, is the profound intuition expressed in the clear but inadequate conception; the most thorough unions, guarded against the slightest confusions; analysis and synthesis; opposite conceptions reconciled in their higher and original unities; in short, all the forms of science, filled up in this instance as in no other, with the truth of eternal necessary fact and eternal necessary being.

And this same kind of influence, only in much greater degree, is exerted by historical studies upon the mind of the theologian. As he becomes better acquainted with the history of Christian doctrines, he becomes more disposed to find his philosophy of human nature and of the Divine nature in them, rather than in human systems. As he studies the development of that great doctrine, the doctrine of sin, he becomes convinced, if he was not before, that the powers, and capacities, and possible destiny, of the human soul, have received their most profound examination within the sphere of Christian theology. As he studies the history of that other great doctrine, the doctrine of the atonement, he sees plainly that the ideas of law and justice and government, of guilt and punishment and expiation; ideas that are the life and lifeblood of the Aristotelian ethics, the best and purest ethical system which the human reason was able to construct; that these great parent ideas show truest, fullest, largest, and clearest, by far, within the consciousness of the Christian mind.

What surer method, therefore, of making his mind *grow* into the philosophy of Christianity can the theologian employ, than the historic method? In what better way can he arm himself for the contest with ignorant or with cultivated scepticism, than by getting possession, through the reproductive study of dogmatic history, of the exact contents of Scripture as expanded and systematized by the consentaneous and connected studies of the Fathers, the Reformers, and the Divines, the Councils, the Synods, and the Assemblies, of the Church universal?

2. Secondly, notice the interest awakened by histori-

cal studies in the creeds and symbols of the Christian church *as marks of development and progress in theology*.

If we have truly enunciated the idea of history, in the first part of this discourse, it follows that all *genuine* development is a *historical* development, and all *true* progress is a *historical* progress. For the *true* history of anything is the account of its development according to its true idea and necessary law. The history of a natural object, like a crystal, for example, is the account of its rigorously geometric collection and upbuilding about a nucleus. Crystallization is a *necessary* process, for it is a petrified geometry. The history of a tree is the account of its spontaneous and *inevitable* evolution out of a germ. The process itself, in both of these instances, is predetermined and fixed. The account of the process, therefore, if it is exactly conformed to the actual matter of fact, has a fixed and predetermined character also. For, if nature herself goes forward in a straight and undeviating line, the history of nature must follow on after, and tread in her very and exactest footsteps. Hence, true legitimate history, of any kind, is neither arbitrary nor capricious. It corresponds to real fact, and real fact is the process of real nature. The matter and method of nature, therefore, dictate the matter and method of the history of nature.

And the same holds true, when we pass from history in the sphere of nature, to history in the realm of mind and spirit. The matter and method of a spiritual idea dictate the matter and method of the unfolding, and, consequently, of the history, of that idea. In the case now under discussion, the real nature and inward structure of Christianity determine what does, and what does not, belong to its true historical development. The *true* his tory of Christianity, therefore, is the history of true Christianity.* The church historian is, indeed, obliged to take into account the deviations from the true Scriptural ideal, because, unlike the naturalist, he is within the sphere of freedom, and of false development, and because redemption itself is a mixed process of dying to sin and living to righteousness. But he notices the deviations not for the purpose, it should be carefully observed, of letting them make up part of the *true* and *normal* history of Scriptural Christianity. The church historian is obliged to watch the rise and growth of heresies, not surely because they constitute an integrant part of the legitimate development and true history of Scripture truth. The account of a heresy has only a negative historical value. All the positive and genuine history of Christian doctrine is to be made up out of that correct apprehension and unfolding which Scripture has received from the Catholic as antithetic to the Heretical mind. Temporary departures from the real nature of Scripture truth, and deductions from it that are illegitimate, may possibly have contributed to a return to a deeper and clearer knowledge of revelation on the part of some few minds, and have unquestionably elicited a more full and comprehensive statement and defence of Christianity on the part of others, and in this way the heresies that appear all along the line of church history, throw light upon the

* The reader will notice the value of the qualifying adjective here. The term history is used in two senses; a general and a special. In the former sense, it denotes *all* that occurred, right or wrong, normal or abnormal. In the latter sense, in which alone it is employed above, it denotes only that which *ought* to occur. It is the proper function of the philosophic historian of the Christian religion and church, to reduce the general to the special history, by throwing out of the former all that is miscellaneous and heterogeneous, and retaining only that which accords with the supernatural law and principle that constitutes the basis of sacred, as distinguished from secular, history.

true course of doctrinal development and help to bring out the true history. But these heretical processes themselves, cannot be regarded as integrant and necessary parts of the great historic process, any more than the diseases of the human body can be regarded, equally with the healthy processes of growth, as the normal development of the organism. Nosology is not a chapter in physiology.

It follows, consequently, that the *true* and *proper* history of Christianity will exhibit a *true* and *proper* theological progress. It will show that the Scripture germ implanted by God, has been slowly but correctly unfolding in the doctrine and science of the church. We cannot grant that historical theology is anti-scriptural and radically wrong; that the Bible has had no true and legitimate apprehension in the ages and generations of believers. There has been, notwithstanding all the attacks of infidelity from without, and controversies from within, a substantial agreement, and a steady advance, in understanding the written revelation. This is very plainly to be seen in the history of doctrines, and from this we may draw the most forcible proofs and illustrations. Let any one compare the first with the latest Christian creed, and he will see the development which the Scripture mustard-seed has undergone. Let any one place the Apostles' creed beside that of the Westminster Assembly, and see what a vast expansion of revealed truth has taken place. The former was all that the mind of the church in that age of infancy was able to eliminate and systematize out of the Scriptures; and this simple statement was sufficient to satisfy the imperfectly developed scientific wants of the early church. The latter creed was what the mind of the church was able to construct out of the elements of the very same written revelation, after fifteen hundred years of study and reflection upon them. The "words," the doctrinal elements, of Scripture, are "spirit and life," and hence, like all spirit and all life, are capable of expansion. Upon them the historic Christian mind, age after age, has expended its best reflection, and now the result is an enlarged and systematized statement, such as the early church could not have made, and did not need.

Compare, again, the statement of the doctrine of the Trinity in the Apostles' creed with that in the Nicene creed. The erroneous and defective statements of Arius, compelled the orthodox mind to a more profound reflection upon the matter of Scripture, and the result was a creed in which the implication and potentiality of revelation was so far explicated and evolved as to present a distinct and unequivocal denial of the doctrine of a created Son of God. But, besides this negative value, this systematic construction of the Scripture doctrine of the Trinity has a great positive worth. It opens before the human mind the great abyss of the Divine nature; and, though it cannot impart to the finite intelligence that absolutely full and perfect knowledge of the Godhead which only God himself can have, it yet furnishes a form of apprehension which accords with the real nature of God, and will, therefore, preserve the mind that accepts it from both the Dualistic and the Pantheistic ideas of the Supreme Being. Abstruse and dialectic as that creed has appeared to some minds and some ages in the Christian church; little connection as it has seemed to them to have with so practical a matter as vital religion; it would not be difficult to show that those councils at Nice and Constantinople, did a work in the years 325 and 381, of which the church universal will feel the salutary effects to the end of time, both in practial and scientific respects. For, if all right religious feeling towards Jesus Christ is grounded in the unassailable conviction that he is truly and verily God; "begotten, not made, being of one substance with the Father;" then this creed laid down the systematic basis of all the true worship and acceptable adoration which the church universal have paid to the Redeemer of the world.* And if a correct metaphysical conception of the Divine Being is necessary in order to all right philosophizing upon God and the universe, then this Christian doctrine of the Trinity is the only statement that is adequate to the wants of science, and the only one that can keep the philosophic mind from the Pantheistic and Dualistic deviation to which, when left to itself, it is so liable.

The importance of historical studies and the historic spirit in an age of the world that more than any other suffers from false notions regarding the nature of pro-

* By this is not meant that there can be no true worship until a creed has been systematically formed and laid down, but that all true worship is grounded in a practical belief which, when examined, is found to harmonize exactly with the speculative results reached by the Christian Scientific mind. So far as the great body of believers is concerned, their case is like that of Hilary of Poictiers, who has left one of the best of the patristic treatises upon the Trinity, but who, in his retired bishopric in Gaul, did not hear of the Nicene creed until many years after its origin. He "found in it that very same doctrine of the unity of essence in the Father and the Son, which he had, before this, ascertained to be the true doctrine, from the study of the New Testament, and had received into his Christian experience, without being aware that the faith which he bore in his heart, had been laid down in the form of a creed." — Torrey's Neander, ii. 396.

Consonant with this, Hagenbach, after speaking of the highly scientific character of the *Symbolum Quicumque*, its endeavor, namely, to express the ineffable by its series of affirmations and guarding negations, adds, that "such formulae nevertheless have their edifying no less than their scientific side, inasmuch as they testify to the struggle of the Christian mind after a satisfactory expression of that which has its full truth only in the depths of the believing heart and character." — Dogmengeschichte, third edition, p. 249, note.

gress and development, cannot be exaggerated. But he who is able to see in the creeds and symbols of the Christian church so many steps of real progress; he who knows that outside of that line of symbolic literature there is nothing but deviation from the real matter of Scripture, will not be likely to be carried away with the notion of a sudden and great improvement upon all that has hitherto been accomplished in the department of theology. He will know that, as all the past development has been historic; restatement shooting out of prestatement; the fuller creed bursting out of the narrower; the expanded treatise swelling forth growth-like from the more slender; so all the present and future development in theology must be historic also. He will see, especially, that elements that have already been examined and rejected by the Christian mind, as unscriptural and foreign, can never again be rightfully introduced into creeds and symbols; that history cannot undo history; that the progress of the present and the future must be homogeneous and kindred with the progress of the past.

III. In the third place, a historic spirit in the theologian protects him from false notions respecting the nature of the visible church, and from a false church feeling.

We can devote but a moment to this branch of the discussion, unusually important just at this time.

We have seen that the most important part of the history of the church is its inward history. We have found that the external history of Christianity derives all its interest for a thoughtful mind from its connection with that dispensation of truth and of spirit which lies beneath it as its animating soul. The whole influence, consequently, of genuine and comprehensive historical study is to magnify the substance and subordinate the form to exalt truth, doctrine, and life, over rites, ceremonies, and polities.

It is undoubtedly true, that the study of ecclesiastical history, in some minds, and in some branches of the church, has strengthened a strong formalizing tendency, and promoted ecclesiasticism. The Papacy has from time immemorial appealed to tradition; and those portions of the Protestant church which have been least successful in freeing themselves from the materialism of the Papacy, have said much about the past history of the church. Hence, in some quarters in the Protestant church, there are, and always have been, apprehensions lest history should interfere with the great right of private judgment, and put a stop to all legitimate progress. But it only needs a comprehensive idea of the nature of history to allay these apprehensions. It only needs to be remembered that the history of Christianity is something more than the history of the Nicene period or of the Scholastic age. It only needs to be recollected that the history of Christianity denotes a course of development from the beginning of the world down to the present moment; that it includes the whole of that Divine economy which began with the first promise, and which manifested itself first in the Patriarchal, next in the Jewish, and finally in the Christian, church.* The

* Probably the most serious defect in the construction of the history of Christianity by the school of Schleiermacher, springs from regarding the incarnation as the beginning of church history. Even if this is not always formally said, as it sometimes is, the notion itself moulds and forms the whole account. The golden position of Augustine, *Novum Testamentum in Vetere latet, Vetus in Novo patet*, is forgotten, and the Jewish religion, as it came from God, is confounded with that corruption of it which we find in the days of our Saviour, but against which the evangelical prophet Isaiah inveighs as earnestly as the evangelical apostle Paul. "He is not a Jew

influence of the study of this *whole* great process, especially if the eye is kept fastened upon the spiritual substance of it, is anything but formalizing and sectarian. — If, therefore, a papistic and anti-catholic temper has ever shown itself in connection with the study of ecclesiastical history, it was because the inward history was neglected, and even the external history was studied in sections only. He who selects a particular period merely and neglects all that has preceded and all that has followed, will be liable to a sectarian view of the nature and history of the church of God. He who reproduces within his mind the views and feelings of a single age merely, will be individual and bigoted in his temper. — He who confines his studies, for example, as so many

which is one outwardly, neither is that circumcision which is outward in the flesh." Judaism is not Phariseeism. There is, therefore, no *inward* and *essential* difference between true Judaism and true Christianity. The former looked forward and the latter looks backward to the same central Person and the same central Cross. The manifested Jehovah of the Old Testament was the incarnate Word of the New. "The religion," says Edwards, "that the church of God has professed from the first founding of the church after the fall to this time, has always been the same. Though the dispensations have been altered, yet the religion which the church has professed, has always, as to its essentials, been the same. The church of God, from the beginning, has been one society. The Christian church which has been since Christ's ascension, is manifestly the same society continued, with the church that was before Christ came. The Christian church is grafted on their root; they are built upon the same foundation. — The revelation upon which both have depended, is essentially the same; for, as the Christian church is built on the Holy Scriptures, so was the Jewish church, though now the Scriptures be enlarged by the addition of the New Testament; but still it is essentially the same revelation with that which was given in the Old Testament, only the subjects of Divine revelation are now more clearly recorded in the New Testament than they were in the Old. But the sum and substance of both the Old Testament and the New, is Christ and His redemption. The church of God has always been on the foundation of Divine revelation, and always on those revelations that were essentially the same, and which were summarily comprehended in the Holy Scriptures." — Edwards's Work of Redemption, i. 47[illegible]

have done, and are doing, to that period from Constantine to Hildebrand, which witnessed the rise and formation of the Papacy; and, especially, he, who in this period studies merely the archaeology and the polity, without the doctrines, the morality, and the life; he, who confines himself to those tracts of Augustine which emphasize the idea of the church in opposition to ancient radicals and disorganizers, but studiously avoids those other and greater and more elaborate treatises of this earnest spiritualist, which thunder the idea of the truth, in opposition to all heretics and all formalists; he, in short, who goes to the study of ecclesiastical history with a predetermined purpose, and carries into it an antecedent interpreting idea, derived from his denomination, and not from Scripture, will undoubtedly become more and more Romish and less and less historic.

Such a disposition as this, is directly crossed and mortified by a comprehensive and philosophic conception of history. Especially will the history of doctrines destroy the belief in the infallibility, or *paramount* authority, of any particular portion of the church universal. The eye is now turned away from those external and imposing features of the history which have such a natural effect to carnalize the mind, to those simpler truths and interior living principles, which have a natural effect to spiritualize it. An interest in the theology of the church is very different from an interest in the polity of the church. It is a fact that as the one rises, the other declines; and there would be no surer method of destroying the formalism that exists in some portions of the church, than to compel their clergy to the continuous and close study of the entire history of Christian doctrines.

IV. In the fourth place, a historic spirit in theologians

promotes a profound and genial agreement on essential points, and a genial disagreement on non-essentials.

It is plain that the study of church history tends to establish and to magnify the distinction between real orthodoxy and real heterodoxy. History is discriminating and cannot be made to mingle the immiscible. In regard, therefore, to the great main currents of truth and of error, the historic mind is clear in its insight and decided in its opinions. It knows that the Christian religion has been both truly and falsely apprehended by the human mind, and that, consequently, two lines of belief can be traced down the ages and generations; that in only one of these two, is Scriptural Christianity to be found.

But its wide and catholic survey, also enables the historic mind to see as the unhistoric mind cannot, that the line of orthodoxy is not a mathematical line. It has some breadth. It is a path, upon which the church can travel, and not merely a direction in which it can look. It is a high and royal road, where Christian men may go abreast; may pass each other, and carry on the practical business of a Christian life; and not a mere hair-line down which nought can go but the one-eyed sighting of either speculative or provincial bigotry.

Hence historical studies banish both provincialism and bigotry from a theological system, and imbue it with that practical and catholic spirit which renders it interesting and influential through the whole church and world. A system of theology may be true and yet not contain the whole truth. It may have seized upon some fundamental positions, or cardinal doctrines, with a too violent energy, and have given them an exorbitant expansion, to the neglect of other equally fundamental truths. In this case, historical knowledge is one of the best correctives

A wider knowledge of the course of theological speculation; a more profound acquaintance with the origin and formation of the leading systems of the church universal; tends to produce that equilibrium of the parts and that comprehensiveness of the whole, which are so apt to be lacking in a provincial creed or system.

A similar liberalizing influence is exerted by the study of church history upon the theologian himself. He sees that men on the same side of the line which divides real orthodoxy from real heterodoxy, have differed from each other, and sometimes upon very important, though never upon vital, points. The history of Christian doctrine compels him to acknowledge that there is a theological space, within which it is safe for the theological scientific mind to expatiate and career; that this is a liberty conceded to the theologian by the unsystematized form in which the written revelation has been given to man, and a liberty, too, which, when it is not abused, greatly promotes that clearer and fuller understanding of the Scriptures, which we have seen the historic Christian mind is continually striving after.

But this scientific liberality among theologians leads directly to a more profound and genial agreement among them upon all practical and essential points. The liberality of the historic mind is very far removed from that mere indifferentism which sometimes usurps this name. There *is* a truth for which the disagreeing, and perhaps (owing to imperfectly sanctified hearts) the bitterly disagreeing, theologians would both be tied to one stake and be burnt with one fire. There is a vital and necessary doctrine for which, if it were assailed by a third party, a bitter unevangelic enemy, both of the contending orthodox divines would fight under one and the same shield. That truth which history shows has been the life of the church and without which it must die; that historic truth, which is the heritage and the joy of the whole family in heaven and on earth, is dear to both hearts alike.

But what tends to make differing theologians agree, profoundly and thoroughly, upon essential points, also tends to make them differ generously and genially upon non-essentials. Those who know that, after all, they are one, in fundamental character, and in fundamental belief; that, after all their disputing, they have but one Lord, one faith and one baptism; find it more difficult to maintain a bitter tone and to employ an exasperated accent toward each other. The common Christian consciousness wells up from the lower depths of the soul, and, as in those deep inland lakes which are fed from subterranean fountains, the sweet waters neutralize and change those bitter or brackish surface currents that have in them the taint of the shores; perhaps the washings of civilization.

While, therefore, a wide acquaintance with the varieties of statement which appear in scientific orthodoxy, does not in the least render the mind indifferent to that essential truth which every man must believe or be lost eternally, it at the same time induces a generous and genial temper among differing theologians. The controversies of the Christian church have unquestionably been a benefit to systematic theology, and that mind must have a very meagre idea of the comprehensiveness and pregnancy of Divine revelation, who supposes that the Christian mind could have derived out of it that great system of doctrinal knowledge which is to outlive all the constructions of the philosophic mind, without any sharp controversy, or keen examination among theologians. That structure did not and could not rise like Thebes, at the mellifluous sound of Amphion's lute; it did not re-

itself up like the Jewish temple without sound of hammer, or axe, or any tool of iron. Slowly, and with difficulty, was it upreared, by hard toil, amid opposition from foes without and foes within, and through much earnest mental conflict. And so will it continue to be reared and beautified in the ages that are to come. We cannot alter this course of things so long as the truth is infinite, and the mind is finite and sees through a glass darkly.

What is needed, therefore, is a sweet and generous temper in all parties as the work goes on. The theologian needs that great ability: *the ability to differ genially.* It has been the misery and the disgrace of the church, that too many theologians who have held the truth, and have held it, too, in its best forms, have held it, like the heathen, in unrighteousness; have held it in narrowness and bigotry. They have differed in a hard, dry, ungenial way. They have forgotten that the rich man can afford to be liberal; that the strong man need not be constantly anxious; that a scientific and rigorous orthodoxy should ever look out of a beaming, and not a sullen, eye.

Let us be thankful that some ages in the history of the church furnish examples that cheer and instruct. Look back at that most interesting period, the period of the Reformation, and contemplate the profound agreement upon essentials and the genial disagreement upon non-essentials, that prevailed among the leaders then. Martin Luther and John Calvin were two theologians who differed as greatly in mental structure, and in their spontaneous mode of contemplating and constructing doctrines, as is possible for two minds upon the same side of the great controversy between orthodoxy and heresy. No man will say that the differences between Lutheranism and Calvinism are minor or unimportant. Probably any one would say that, if those two men were able to feel the common Christian fellowship; to enjoy the communion of saints; and to realize with tenderness their common relationship to the Head of the church; there is no reason why all men who are properly within the pale of orthodoxy should not do the same.

Turn now to the letters of both of these men; written in the midst of that controversy which was going on between the two portions of the Reformed, and which resulted, not, however, through the desire or the influence of these two great men, but through the bitterness of their adherents, in their division into two distinct churches; and witness the common genial feeling that prevailed. Hear Luther in his letter to Bucer sending his cordial greeting to Calvin, whose books he has read with singular pleasure: *cum singulari voluptate.* Hear Calvin declaring his willing and glad readiness to subscribe to the Augsburg Confession, interpreting it upon the sacramental question as the Lutherans themselves authorized him to do.* Above all, turn to that burst, from Calvin, of affectionate feeling towards Melanchthon, which gives itself vent in the midst of one of his stern controversial tracts, like the music of flutes silencing for a moment the clang of war-cymbals and the blare of the trumpet: "O Philip Melanchthon, to thee I address myself, to thee who art now living in the presence of God with

* Henry's Life of Calvin, II. pp. 96, 99. It is interesting and instructive to witness the liberal feeling of the scientific and rigorously orthodox Athanasius towards the Semiarians themselves, whose statement of the doctrine of the Trinity he regarded to be inadequate. See the quotation from *Athanasius de Synodis*, § 41, in Giesceler, Chap. II. § 83, and the reference to *Hilarius de Synodis*, § 76. Says Augustine: "they who do not pertinaciously defend their opinion, false and perverse though it be, especially when it does not spring from the audacity of their own presumption, while they seek the truth with cautious solicitude, and are prepared to correct themselves when they have found it, are by no means to be ranked among heretics."—Epistle 43, Newman's Library Version.

esus Christ, and there awaitest us, till death shall unite s in the enjoyment of Divine peace. A hundred times ast thou said to me, when weary with so much labor nd oppressed with so many burdens, thou laidst thy ead upon my breast, 'God grant, God grant, that I nay now die!'"*

The theology of Richard Baxter differs from the theol- gy of John Owen by some important modifications, and ach of these two types of Calvinism will probably per- etuate itself in the church to the end of time; but the onfidence which both of these great men cherished to- vards each other, should go along down with these sys- ems through the ages and generations of time.

But what surer method can be employed to produce nd perpetuate this catholic and liberal feeling among ne various types and schools of orthodox theology, than) impart to all of them the broad views of history? nd what surer method than this can be taken to dimin- h the number and bring about more unity of opinion n the department of systematic theology? For it is one reat effect of history to coalesce and harmonize. It intro- uces mutual modifications, by showing opponents that neir predecessors were nearer together than they them- elves are, by tracing the now widely separated opinions ack to that point of departure where they were once ery near together; and, above all, by causing all parties) remember, what all are so liable to forget in the heat f controversy, that all forms of orthodoxy took their first rigin in the Scriptures, and that, therefore, all theologi- al controversy should be carried on with a constant eference to this one infallible standard, which can teach ut one infallible system.

* Henry's Life of Calvin, I. 239.

I have thus considered the nature of the historic spirit and its influence both upon the secular and theological mind, in order to indicate my own deep sense of the importance of the department in which I have been called to give instruction by the guardians of this Institution. The first instinctive feelings would have shrunk from the weight of the great burden imposed, and the extent of the very great field opened; though in an institution where the pleasant years of professional study were all spent; though in an ancient institution, made illustrious and influential, through the land and the world, by the labors of the venerated dead and the honored living. But it does not become the individual to yield to his individuality. The stream of Divine Providence, so signally conspicuous in the life of the church, and of its members, is the stream upon which the diffident as well as the confident must alike cast themselves. And he who enters upon a new course of labor for the church of God, with just views of the greatness and glory of the kingdom and of the comparative unimportance of any individual member, will be most likely to perform a work that will best harmonize with the development and progress of the great whole.

THE RELATION OF LANGUAGE, AND STYLE, TO THOUGHT.*

"It is a truth," (says Hartung in beginning his subtle and profound work on the Greek Particles,) "as simple as it is fruitful, that language is no arbitrary, artificial, and gradual invention of the reflective understanding, but a necessary and organic product of human nature, appearing contemporaneously with the activity of thought. Speech is the correlate of thought; both require and condition each other like body and soul, and are developed at the same time and in the same degree, both in the case of the individual and the nation. Words are the coinage of conceptions freeing themselves from the dark chaos of intimations and feelings, and gaining shape and clearness. In so far as a man uses and is master of language, has he also attained clearness of thought; the developed and spoken language of a people is its expressed intelligence."† Consonant with this, William Humboldt remarks that "speech must be regarded as naturally inherent in man, for it is altogether inexplicable as a work of his inventive understanding. We are none the better for allowing thousands of years for its invention.

* Reprinted from the Bibliotheca Sacra; Numbers XX. and XXXI.

† Partikeln Lehre, Bd. I. §§ 1, 2.

There could be no invention of language unless its type already existed in the human mind. Man is man only by means of speech; but in order to invent speech he must be already man."

In these extracts it is asserted that language is an *organic* product of which thought is the organizing and vitalizing principle. Writers upon language have generally acknowledged a connection of some sort between thought and language, but they have not been unanimous with respect to the nature of the connection. The common assertions that language is the "dress" of thought — is the "vehicle" of thought — point to an outward and mechanical connection between the two: while the fine remark of Wordsworth that "language is not so much the dress of thought as its incarnation," and the frequent comparison of the relation which they bear to each other, with that which exists between the body and the soul, indicate that a *vital* connection is believed to exist between language and thought.

The correctness of this latter doctrine becomes apparent when it is considered that everything growing out of human nature, in the process of its development and meeting its felt wants, is of necessity *living* in its essence, and cannot be regarded as a dead mechanical contrivance. That language has such a natural and spontaneous origin is evident from the fact, that history gives no account of any language which was the direct invention of any one man, or set of men, to supply the wants of a nation utterly destitute of the ability to *express* its thought. Individuals have bestowed an alphabet, a written code of laws, useful mechanical inventions, upon their countrymen, but no individual ever bestowed a language. This has its origin in human nature, or rather in that constitutional necessity, under which hu man nature in common with all creation is placed by Him who sees the end from the beginning, which compels the invisible to become visible, the formless to take form, the intelligible to corporealize itself. That thought is invisible and spiritual in essence, is granted by all systems of philosophy except the coarsest and most unphilosophic materialism. It is therefore subject to the universal law, and *must* become sensuous — must be *communicated.*

In the case of the primitive language, spoken by the first human pair, we must conceive of it as a *gift* from the Creator, perfectly correspondent, like all their other endowments, to the wants of a *living soul.* As in this first instance the bodily form reached its height of being and of beauty, not through the ordinary processes of generation, birth, and growth, but as an instantaneous creation; so too the form of thought, language, passed through no stages of development (as some teach) from the inarticulate cry of the brute, to the articulate and intelligent tones of cultivated man, but came into full and finished existence simultaneously with the fiat that called the full-formed soul and body into being. It would not have been a perfect creation, had the first man stood mute in mature manhood, and that too in his unfallen state and amidst the beauty and glory of Eden. As the posterity of the first man come into existence by a process, and as both soul and body in their case undergo development before reaching the points of bloom and maturity, language also in their case is a slow and gradual formation. It begins with the dawn of reflective consciousness, and unfolds itself as this becomes deeper and clearer. In the infancy of a nation it is exquisitely fitted for the lyrical expression of those thoughts and feelings which rise simple and sincere in the national mind and heart, before philosophical reflection has rendered them complex, or advancing civilization has dried up their freshness. As the period of fancy and feeling passes by and that of reason and reflection comes in, language becomes more rigid and precise in its structure, conforms itself to the expression of profound thought, and history and philosophy take the place of the ballad and the chronicle.

Now the point to be observed here is, that this whole process is spontaneous and natural; is a growth and not a manufacture. Thought embodies itself, even as the merely animal life becomes sensuous and sensible through its own tendency and activity. When investigating language, therefore, we are really within the sphere of life and living organization, and to attempt its comprehension by means of mechanical principles would be as absurd as to attempt to apprehend the phenomena of the animal kingdom by the principles that regulate the investigation of inorganic nature. It is only by the application of dynamical principles, of the doctrine of life, that we can get a true view of language or be enabled to use it with power.

It is assumed then that thought is the life of language; and this too in no figurative sense of the word, but in its strict scientific signification as denoting the principle that organizes and vivifies the form in which it makes its appearance. It is assumed that thought is as really the living principle of language as the soul is the life of the body, and the assumption verifies itself by the clearness which it introduces into the investigation of the subject, and by the light which it flares into its darker and more mysterious parts. That *fusion*, for instance, of the thoughts with the words, which renders the discourse of the poet glowing and tremulous with feeling and life.

can be explained upon no other supposition than that the immaterial entity born of beauty in the poet's mind actually materializes itself, and thus enlivens the otherwise lifeless syllables. Nothing but a *vital* connection with the thoughts that breathe, can account for the words that burn.

We are not therefore to look upon language as having intrinsic existence, separate from the thought which it conveys, but as being *external* thought, *expressed* thought. Words were not first invented, and then assigned to conceptions as their arbitrary, and intrinsically, meaningless signs; mere indices, having no more inward connection with the things indicated, than the algebraic marks, + and —, have with the notions of increase and diminution. In the order of nature, language follows rather than precedes thought, and is subject to all its modifications from its first rise in the consciousness of the individual and the nation, up to that of the philosopher and the philosophic age in a nation's history. Language in essence is thought, is thought in an outward form, and consequently cannot exist, or be the object of reflection dissevered from the vital principle which substantiates it. The words of the most thoughtless man do nevertheless contain some meaning, and words have effect upon us only in proportion as they are filled with thought.

And this fulness must not be conceived of as flowing into empty moulds already prepared. It is a statement of one of the most profound investigators of physical life, that the living power merely *added* to the dead organ is not life;* i. e. that no intensity whatever of physical life

* Carus' Physiologie, Bd. 1 Vorrede. He denies the correctness of the following formula upon which, he affirms, the mechanical school of physiologists proceeds: todtes Organ + Kraft = Leben.

streamed upon and through a *dead* hand lying upon a dissecting table can produce life in the form of the living member. The living member cannot come into existence except as growing out of a living body, and the living body cannot come into existence unless life, the immaterial and invisible, harden into the materiality and burst into the visibility of a minute seminal point which teems and swells with the whole future organism; a point or dot of life from which as a centre, the radiation, the organization, and the circulation may commence. In like manner it is impossible, if it were conceivable, to produce human language by the superinduction of thought upon, or by the assignation of meaning to, a mass of unmeaning sounds already in existence. When a conception comes into the consciousness of one mind, and seeks expression that it may enter the consciousness of another mind, it must be conceived of as uttering itself in a word which is not taken at hap-hazard, and which might have been any other arbitrary sound, but which is *prompted* and *formed* by the creative thought struggling out of the world of mind, and making use of the vocal organs in order to enter the world of sense.

We cannot, it is true, verify all this by reference to all the words we are in the habit of using every day, because we are too far off from the period of their origin, and because they are oftentimes combinations of simple sounds that were originally formed by vocal organs differing from our own by marked peculiarities, yet the simplicity and naturalness of the Greek of Homer, or the English of Chaucer, which is no other than the affinity of the language with the thought, the sympathy of the sound with the sense, cause us to *feel* what in the present state of philology most certainly cannot be proved in the case of every single word, that primarily, in the root and heart, language is self-embodied thought. Yet though it is impossible at present in the case of every single word to verify the assumption upon which we have gone, it is not difficult to do this in the case of that portion of the language in which there is emphasis and intensity of meaning. The verb, by which action and suffering (which in the animal world is but a calmer and more intense activity) are expressed, is a word often and evidently suited to the thought. Those nouns which are names not of things but of acts and energies, are likewise exceedingly significant of the things signified. The motions of the mouth, the position of the organs, and the tension of the muscles of speech, in the utterance of such words as shock, smite, writhe, slake, quench, are produced by the force and energy and character of the conceptions which these words communicate, just as the prolonged relaxation of the organs and muscles in the pronunciation of soothe, breathe, dream, calm, and the like, results naturally from the nature of the thought of which they are the vocal embodiment.

And this leads us to notice that this view of the origin and nature of language acquires additional support from considering that the vocal sound is the product of physical organs which are started into action and directed in their motion by the soul itself.* Even the tones of the animal are suited to the inward feeling by the particular play of muscles and organs of utterance. The feeling of pleasure *could* not, so long as nature is herself, twist these muscles and organs into the emission of the sharp scream of physical agony, any more than it could light up the eye with the glare and flash of rage.

Now if this is true in the low sphere of animal exist-

* See on this point Wallis's English Grammar, and Hearne's Langtofts Chronicle, Vol. I. Preface.

ence, it is still more true in the sphere of intellectual and moral existence. If life is true to itself in the lower, it is true to itself in the higher realm of its manifestation. When full of earnest thought and feeling the mind *uses* the body at will, and the latter naturally and spontaneously subserves the former. As thought becomes more and more earnest, and feeling more and more glowing, the body bends and yields with increasing pliancy, down to its minutest fibres and most delicate tissues, to the working of the engaged mind; the organs of speech become one with the soul, and are swayed and wielded by it. The word is, as it were, *put into the mouth*, by the vehement and excited spirit.

> When the mind is quickened, out of doubt,
> The organs, though defunct and dead before,
> Break up their drowsy grave and newly move
> With casted slough and fresh legerity.*

As well might it be said that there is no vital and natural connection between the feeling and the blush in which it mantles, or the tear in which it finds vent, as that the word—the "*winged word*"—has only an arbitrary and dead relation to the thought.

Again, it is generally conceded that there is an inherent fitness of gesture, attitude and look, to the thought or feeling conveyed by them; but do attitude, gesture, and look, sustain a more intimate relation to thought and feeling than language does; language, at once the most universal as well as most particular in its application, the most exhaustive and perfect, of all the media of communication between mind and mind, between heart and heart? The truth is, that *all* the media through which thought becomes sensuous and communi-

* Henry IV. Act IV. Sc. 1.

able are in greater or less degree, yet in *some* degree, *homogeneous and con-natural with thought itself.* In other words they all, in a greater or less degree, possess manifest propriety.

It is to be borne in mind here, that the question is not whether thought could not have embodied itself in other forms than it has, whether other languages could not have arisen, but whether the existing forms possess adaptedness to the thought they convey. Life is not compelled to manifest itself in one only form, or in one particular set of forms, in any of the kingdoms, but it *is* compelled to make the form in which it does appear, vital like itself. The forms, for aught that we know, may be infinite in number, in which the invisible principle may become sensible, but the *corpse* is no one of them.

Thought as the substance of discourse is logical, necessary, and immutable, in its nature, while language as the form is variable. The language of a people is continually undergoing a change, so that those who speak it in its later periods, (it very often happens,) would be unintelligible to those who spoke it in its earlier ages. Chaucer cannot be read by Englishmen of the present day without a glossary.* Again, the languages of different nations differ from each other. There is great variety in the changes of the verb to express the passive form. The subject is sometimes included in the verb, sometimes is prefixed, and sometimes is suffixed to it. The Malay language assumes the plural instead of the

* Yet even in this case, as Wordsworth truly remarks, "the *affecting* parts are almost always expressed in language pure, and universally intelligible even to this day."—*Preface to Lyrical Ballads.* The more *intense* and *vital* the thought, the nearer the form approaches the essence, the more universal does it become.

singular as the basis of number, all nouns primarily denoting the plural. Some use the dual and some do not; some give gender and number to adjectives, and others do not; some have the article and some have not. And yet all these different languages are equally embodiments of thought, and of the same thought substantially. For the human mind is everywhere, and at all times, subject to the invariable laws of its own constitution, and that logical, immutable, truth which stands over against it as its correlative object, is developed in much the same way among all nations in whom the intellect obtains a development. The vital principle—logical, immutable, truth in the form of human thought—is here seen embodying itself in manifold forms, with freedom and originality and with an expressive suitableness in every instance.

That a foreign language does not seem expressive to the stranger is no argument against the fundamental hypothesis. It is expressive to the native-born, and become so to the stranger in proportion as he acquires (not a mere mechanical and book knowledge, but) a vital and vernacular knowledge of it. And this expressiveness is not the result of custom. Apart from the instinctive association of a certain word with a certain conception, there is an instinctive sense of its intrinsic fitness to communicate the thought intended—of its expressiveness. For why should some words be *more* expressive than others, if they all equally depend upon the law of association for their significance? And why is a certain portion of every language more positive, emphatic, and intense, than the remaining portions? There is in every language a class of words which are its life and life-blood, a class to which the mind, in its fervor and glow, *instinctively* betakes itself in order to free itself of its thoughts in the most effective and satisfactory ma er. But this is irreconcilable with the hypothesis that l words are but lifeless signs, acquiring their significaon and *apparent* suitableness from use and custom, and ll consequently being upon the same dead level with spect to expressiveness.

Still another proof that the connection between lanuage and thought is organic, is found in the fact that e relation between the two is evidently that of actior nd reaction.

We have seen that language is the produce of thought ut this is not to be understood as though language were mere *effect*, of which thought is the mere *cause*. The ere effect cannot *react* upon the pure cause. It is rown off and away from its cause (as the cannon ball from the cannon), so that it stands insulated and inlependent with respect to its origin.

This is not the case with language. Originated by hought, and undergoing modifications as thought is deeloped, it, in turn, exerts a reflex influence upon its oriinating cause. In proportion as language is an exact nd sincere expression, does thought itself become exact nd sincere. The more appropriate and expressive the anguage, the more correct will be the thought, and the more expressive and powerful will be the direction which thought takes.

But if language were a mechanical invention, no such eaction as this could take place upon the inventor. While connected with thought only by an arbitrary compact on the part of those who made use of it, it would be *separated* from thought by origin and by nature. Not being a living and organic product, it could sustain to hought only the external and lifeless relation of cause nd effect, and consequently would remain one and the same amid all the life, motion, and modification, which the immaterial principle might undergo.

Of course if such were the relation between the two, it would be impossible to account for all that unconscious but real *change* ever going on in a spoken language, which we call *growth* and *progress*. Language upon such an hypothesis would remain stationary in substance, and at best could be altered only by aggregation from without. New words might be invented and added to the number already in existence, but no change could occur in the spirit of the language, if it may be allowed to speak of spirit in such a connection.

Furthermore, if there is no vital relation between language and thought, it would be absurd to speak of the beneficial influence upon mental development (which is but the development of thought) of the study of philology. If in strict literality the relation of language to thought is that of the invention to the mind of the inventor, then the study of this outward, and in itself lifeless instrument, would be of no worth in developing an essence so intensely vital, so full of motion, and with such an irrepressible tendency to development, as the human mind.

It is however a truth and a fact that the study of a well organized language is one of the very best means of mental education. It brings the mind of the student into communication with the whole mind of a nation, and infuses into his culture its good and bad elements —the whole genius and spirit of the people of whose mind it is the evolution. In no way can the mind of the individual be made to feel the power and influence of the mind of the race, and thereby receive the greatest possible enlargement and liberalizing, so well as by the hilosophic study of language A rational method of ducation makes use of this study as an indispensable iscipline, and selects for this purpose two languages istinguished for the intimate relation which they susain to the particular forms of thought they respectively xpress. For the Greek language is so fused and one vith Grecian thought, that it is living to this day, and as been the source of life to literature ever since its evival in the fifteenth century; and the rigid but majesic Latin is the exact embodiment of the organizing and mperial ideas of Rome.

These languages exhibit the changes of thought in the Greek and Roman mind. They take their form and lerive their spirit from the peculiarities of these nations. Hence the strong and original influence which they exrt upon the modern mind. If these languages really ontained no tincture of the intellect that made them nd made use of them, if they communicated none of he spirit of antiquity, they would indeed be "dead" languages for all purposes of mental enlivening and develpment.

But it is not so. The Greek and Roman mind with ill that passed through it, whether it were thought or eeling, whether it were individual or national, instead of remaining in the sphere of consciousness merely, and hus being kept from the ken of all after ages, projected tself, as it were, into these fine languages, into these noble forms, and not only became a *κτῆμα ἐς ἀεί* for mankind, but also a possession with whose characteristics the possessor is in sympathy, and from which he derives ntellectual nourishment and strength.

A further proof that language has a living connection with thought, is found in the fact that feeling and passion uggest language.

Feeling and passion are the most vital of all the activities of the human soul, flowing as they do from the heart, and that which is prompted by them may safely be affirmed to have life. That words the most expressive and powerful fly from the lips of the impassioned thinker is notorious. The man who is naturally of few words, becomes both fluent and appropriate in the use of language, when his mind glows with his subject and feeling is awakened.

But the use of language is the same in kind and character with its origin. The processes through which language passes from the beginning to the end of its existence are all of the same nature. As in the wide sphere of the universe, preservation is a constant creation, and the things that are, are sustained and perpetuated on principles in accordance with the character impressed upon them by the creative fiat, so in all the narrower spheres of the finite, the use and development are coincident and harmonious with the origin and nature. We may therefore argue back from the use and development to the origin and nature; and when we find that in all periods of its history human language is suggested, and that too in its most expressive form, by feeling and passion, we may infer that these had to do in its origin, and have left something of themselves in its nature. For how could there be a point and surface of communication between words and feeling, so that the latter should start out the former in all the freshness of a new creation, if there were no *interior* connection between them. For language as it falls from the lips of passion is tremulous with life—with the life of the soul and imparts the life of the soul to all who hear it.

If, then, in the actual every-day use of language, we find it to be suggested by passion, and to be undergoin changes both in form and signification, without the intervention of a formal compact on the part of men, it is just to infer that no such compact called it into existence. If, upon watching the progress and growth of a language, we find it in continual flux and reflux, and detect everywhere in it, change and motion, without any consciously directed effort to this end on the part of those who speak it, it is safe to infer that the same unconscious spontaneousness characterized it in its beginning. Moreover, if in every-day life we unconsciously, yet really, use language not as a lifeless sign of our thought, but believe that in employing it we are really expressing our mind, and furthermore, if we never in any way agreed to use the tongue which we drank in with our mother's milk, but were born into it and grew up into its use, even as we were born into and grew up under the intellectual and moral constitution imposed upon human nature by its Creator, we may safely conclude that language, too, is a provision on the part of the author of our being, and consequently is organic and alive.

Indeed, necessity of speech, like necessity of religion and government and social existence, is laid upon man by his constitution, and as in these latter instances whatever secondary arrangements may be made by circumstances, the primary basis and central form is fixed in human nature, so in the case of language, whatever may be the secondary modifications growing out of national differences and peculiarities of vocal organs, the deep ground and source of language is the human constitution itself.

Frederick Schlegel, after quoting Schiller's lines:

> Thy knowledge, thou sharest with superior spirits;
> Art, oh man! thou hast alone,

calls language "the general, all-embracing *art* of man." This is truth. For language is embodiment — the embodiment not indeed of one particular idea in a material form, but of thought at large, in an immaterial yet sensible form. And the fact that the material used is sound — the most ethereal of media — imparts to this "all embracing art" a spirituality of character that raises it above many of the fine arts, strictly so called. It is an embodiment of the spiritual, yet not in the coarse elements of matter. When the spiritual passes from the intelligible to the sensible world by means of art, there is a coming down from the pure ether and element of *incorporeal* beauty into the lower sphere of the defined and sensuous. The pure abstract idea necessarily loses something of its purity and abstractedness by becoming embodied. By coming into appearance for the sense it ceases to be in its ineffable, original, highest state for the reason — for the pure intelligence. Art, therefore, is degradation — a stooping to the limitations and imperfections of the material world of sense, and the feeling awakened by the form, however full it may be of the idea, is not equal in purity, depth, and elevation, to the direct beholding of the idea itself in spirit and in truth.*

We may, therefore, add to the assertion of Schlegel, and say, that language is also the highest art of man. — With the exceptions of poetry and oratory, all the fine arts are hampered in the full, free, expression of the idea by the uncomplying material. Poetry and oratory, in

* It is interesting in this connection to notice that the Puritan, though generally charged with a barbarian ignorance of the worth of art, nevertheless in practice took the only strictly philosophic view of it. That stripping flaying hatred of form, *per se*, which he manifested, grew out of a (practically) intensely philosophic mind which clearly saw the true relation of the form to the idea — of the sensible to the spiritual.

ommon with language, by employing the most ethereal f media, approach as near as is possible for embodiments o the nature of that which they embody, but the latter s infinitely superior to the two former, by virtue of its nfinitely greater range, and power of exhaustive expres-ion. Poetry and eloquence are confined to the particu-ar and individual, while language seeks to embody hought in all its relations and transitions, and feeling in ll its manifoldness and depth. The sphere in which it noves, and of which it seeks to give an outward manifes-ation is the whole human consciousness, from its rise in he individual, on through all its modifications in the ace. It seeks to give expression to an inward experi-ence, that is "co-infinite with human life itself."

Viewed in this aspect, human language ceases to be he insignificant and uninteresting phenomenon it is so ften represented to be, and appears in all its real mean-ng and mystery. It is an *organization*, as wonderful as ny in the realm of creation, built up by a necessary ten-lency of human nature seeking to provide for its wants, nd constructed too, upon the principles of that universal nature, which Sir Thomas Brown truly affirms to be "the art of God." * Contemplate, for a moment, the Greek language as the product of this tendency, and necessity, to express his thought imposed upon man by creation. This wonderful structure could not have been put together by the cunning contrivance, and adopted by the formal consent, of the nation, and it certainly was not preserved and improved in this manner. Its pliancy and copiousness and precision and vitality and harmony,

* Die philosophische Bildung der Sprachen, die vorzuglich noch an den ursprünglichen sichtbar wird, ist ein wahrhaftes durch den Mechanismus des menschlichen Geistes gewirktes Wunder. — Schelling's vom Ich. u. s. w. § 3.

whereby it is capable of expressing all forms of thought, from the simplicity of Herodotus to the depth of Plato, are qualities which the unaided and mechanizing understanding of man could not have produced. They grew spontaneously, and gradually, out of the fundamental characteristics of the Grecian mind, and are the natural and pure expression of Grecian thought. Contemplate, again, our own mother tongue as the product of this same foundation for speech laid in human nature by its constitution. Its native strength and energy and vividness, and its acquired copiousness and harmony, as exhibited in the simple artlessness of Chaucer, and "the stately and regal argument" of Milton, are what might be expected to characterize the Latinized Saxon.

A creative power, deeper and more truly artistic than the inventive understanding, produced these languages. It was that plastic power, by which man creates form for the formless, and which, whether it show itself universally in the production of a living language, or particularly in the works of the poet or painter, is the crowning power of humanity. In view of the wonderful harmonies and symmetrical gradations of these languages, may we not apply the language of Wordsworth:

> Point not these mysteries to an art
> Lodged above the starry pole,
> Pure *modulations* flowing from the heart
> Of Divine love, where wisdom, beauty, truth,
> With order dwell, in endless youth.*

We should not, however, have a complete view of the relation of language to thought, if we failed to notice that in its best estate it is an imperfect expression.— Philosophy ever labors under the difficulty of finding

* Power of Sound.

terms by which to communicate its subtle and profound discoveries, and there are feelings that are absolutely unutterable. Especially is this true of religious thought and feeling. There is a limit within this profound domain beyond which human speech cannot go, and the hushed and breathless spirit must remain absorbed in the awful intuition. Here, as throughout the whole world of life, the principle obtains but an imperfect embodiment. There is ever something more perfect and more glorious beyond what appears. The intelligible world cannot be entirely exhausted, and therefore it is the never-failing source of substantial principle and creative life. In the case before us, truth is entirely exhausted by no language whatever. There are depths not yet penetrated by consciousness, and who will say that even the consciousness of such a thinker as Plato can have had a complete expression, even through such a wonderful medium as the Greek tongue? The human mind is connected with the Divine mind, and thereby with the whole abyss of truth; and hence the impossibility of completely sounding even the human mind, or of giving complete utterance to it; and hence the possibility and the basis of an unending development for the mind and an unending growth for language.

We are aware that the charge of obscurity may be brought against the theory here presented, by an advocate of the other theory of the origin and nature of language. We have no disposition to deny the truth of the charge, only adding that the obscurity, so far as it pertains to the theory (in distinction from the presentation of the theory, for which the individual is responsible,) is such as grows out of the very nature and depth and absolute truth of the theory itself. We have gone upon the supposition that human language, as a form, is neither hollow nor lifeless — that it has a living principle, and that this principle is thought. Now life is and must be mysterious; and at no point more so than when it begins to organize itself into a body. Furthermore, the spontaneous, and to a great extent, *unconscious* processes of life, are and must be mysterious. The method of genius — one of the highest forms of life — in the production of a Hamlet, or Paradise Lost, or the Transfiguration, has not yet been *explained*, and the method of human nature, by which it constructs for itself its wonderful medium of communication — by which it externalizes the whole inner world of thought and feeling — cannot be rendered plain like the working of a well poised and smoothly running machine throwing off its manufactures.

Simply asking then of him who would render all things clear by rendering all things shallow, *by whom*, *when*, *where*, and *how*, the Greek language, for example, was invented, and by what historical compact it came to be the language of the nation, we would turn away to that nobler, more exciting, and more rational theory, which regards language to be "a necessary and organic product of human nature, appearing contemporaneously and parallel with the activity of thought." This theory of the origin of language throws light over all departments of the great subject of philology, finds its gradual and unceasing verification as philological science advances under a spur and impulse derived from this very theory, and ends in that philosophical insight into language, which, after all, is but the clear and full intuition of its mystery — of its life.

Having thus specified the general relation of language to thought, we naturally turn to the uses and applications of the theory itself. Its truth, value, and fruitfulness, are nowhere more apparent than in the department of Rhetoric and Criticism. For this department takes special cognizance of the more living and animated forms of speech — of the glow of the poet, and the fire of the orator. It also investigates all those peculiarities of construction, and form, in human composition that spring out of individual characteristics. It is, therefore, natural to suppose that a theory of language which recognizes a power in human thought to organize and vivify and modify the forms in which it appears, will afford the best light in which to examine those forms; just as it is natural to suppose that the commonly received theory of physical life, will furnish a better light in which to examine vegetable and animal productions, than a theory like that of Descartes, e. g. which maintains that the forms and functions in the animal kingdom are the result of a mechanical principle. Life itself is the best light in which to contemplate living things.

We propose therefore in the remainder of this essay to follow the same general method already pursued, and examine the nature of style, by pointing out its relation to thought.

Style is the particular manner in which thought flows out, in the case of the individual mind, and upon a particular subject. When, therefore, it has, as it always should have, a free and spontaneous origin, it partakes of the peculiarity both of the individual and of the topic upon which he thinks. A genuine style, therefore, is the free and pure expression of the individuality of the thinker and the speciality of the subject of thought. — Uniformity of style is consequently found in the productions of the same general cast of mind, applied to the same general class of subjects, so that there is no distinguishable period in the history of a nation's literature, but what exhibits a style of its own. The spirit of the age appears in the general style of its literary composition, and the spirit of the individual — the tone of his mind — nowhere comes out more clearly than in his manner of handling a subject. The grave, lofty, and calm, style of the Elizabethan age is an exact representation of the spirit of its thinking men. The intellectual temperament of the age of Queen Anne flows out in the clear, but diffuse and nerveless, style of the essayists.

From this it is easy to see that style, like language, has a spontaneous and natural origin, and a living connection with thought. It is not a manner of composing, arbitrarily or even designedly chosen, but rises of its own accord, and in its own way, in the general process of mental development. The more unconscious its origin, and the more strongly it partakes of the individuality of the mind, the more genuine is style. Only let it be carefully observed in this connection, that a *pure* and *sincere* expression of the individual peculiarity is intended. Affectation of originality and studied effort after peculiarity produce *mannerism*, in distinction from that manner of pure nature, which alone merits the name of style.

If this be true, it is evident that the union of all styles, or of a portion of them, would not constitute a perfect style. On the contrary, the excellence of style consists in its having a bold and determined character of its own — in its bearing the genuine image and superscription of an individual mind at work upon a particular subject. In a union of many different styles, there would be nothing simple, bold, and individual. The union would be a mixture, rather than a union, in which each ingredient would be neutralized by all, and all by each, leaving a residuum characterless, spiritless, and lifeless.

Style, in proportion as it is genuine and excellent, is

incere and artless. It is the free and unconscious emaiation of the individual nature. It alters as the individual alters. In early life it is ardent and adorned; in nature life it is calm and grave. In youth it is flushed vith fancy and feeling; in manhood it is sobered by reaon and reflection. But in both periods it is the genune expression of the man. The gay manner of L'Allegro and Comus is as truly natural and spontaneous, as he grave and stately style of Paradise Regained and Samson Agonistes. The individuality of a man like Milon passes through great varieties of culture and of mood, ind there is seen a corresponding variety in the ways in which it communicates itself; yet through this variety here runs the unity of nature; each sort of style is the incere and pure manner of the same individual taken in a particular stage of his development.

No one style, therefore, can be said to be the best of ll absolutely, but only relatively. That is the best style elatively to the individual, in which his particular cast of thought best utters itself, and in which the peculiarity of the individual has the fullest and freest play. That nay be called a good style generally, in which every word *tells* — in which the language is full of thought, ind alive with thought, and so fresh and vigorous as to seem to have been just created — while at the same time he characteristics of the mind that is pouring out in this particular manner, are all in every part, as the constructng and vivifying principle.

The truth of this view of style is both confirmed and llustrated by considering the unity in variety exhibited by the human mind itself. The mind of man is one and he same in its constitution and necessary laws, so that he human race may be said to be possessed of one universal intelligence. In the language of one of the most elegant and philosophic of English critics,* "It is no unpleasing speculation to see how the *same reason*, has at all times prevailed: how there is *one truth*, like one sun, that has enlightened human intelligence through every age, and saved it from the darkness of sophistry and error." Upon this sameness of intelligence rest all absolute statements, and all universal appeals. Over against this universal human mind, as its corresponding object and counterpart, stands truth, universal in its nature and one and the same in its essence.

But besides this unity of the universal, there is the variety of the individual, mind. Truth, consequently, coming into consciousness in the form of thought in an individual mind, undergoes modifications. It is now contemplated not as universal and abstract, but as concrete and in its practical relations. It is, moreover, seen, not as an unity, but in its parts, and one side at a time. Philosophical truth in Plato differs from philosophical truth in Aristotle, by a very marked modification. Poetical truth is one thing in Homer and another in Virgil. Religious truth assumes a strikingly different form in Paul and Luther, from that which it wears in John and Melanchthon. And yet poetry, philosophy, and religion, have each their universal principles — their one abstract nature. Each, however, *appears* in the form imposed upon it by the individual mind; each wears that tinge of the mind through which it has passed, which is denominated style.

No man has yet appeared whose individuality was so comprehensive and universal, and who was such a master of form, that he exhausted the whole material of poetry, or philosophy, or religion, and exhibited it in a style

* Harris. Preface to Hermes.

nd form absolutely universal and final. Enough is ever ·ft of truth, even after the most comprehensive presenta- on, for another individuality to show it in still a new nd original form. For there is no limit to the manner f contemplating infinite and universal truth. Provided nly there be a peculiarity — a particular type of the hu- ıan mind — there will be a peculiarity of intuition, and onsequently of exhibition.

The most comprehensive and universal individual ıind was that of Shakspeare, and hence his productions ave less of style, of peculiar manner, than all other lite- ary productions. Who can describe the style of Shak- peare? Who is aware of his style? The style of Mil- on is apparent in every line, for he was one of the most *ui-generic* of men. But the form which truth takes in Shakspeare, is as comprehensive and universal as the rama, as all mankind. This is owing to that Protean ower by which, for the purposes of dramatic art, he con- erts himself into other men, takes their consciousness, nd thereby temporarily loses his own limited individual- ty. But that Shakspeare was an individual, that a pecu- ar type of humanity formed the basis of his personal eing, and that he had a style of thought of his own, it vould be absurd to doubt. And had he attempted other pecies of composition than the drama, (which by its ery nature requires that the individuality of the author e sunk and lost entirely in the various characters,) had e taken, like Milton, a particular theme as the "great rgument" for his poetic power, doubtless the *man*, the *ndividual*, would have come into sight.*

* In corroboration of this, it may be remarked that we have far more ense of the *individuality* of Shakspeare, while perusing his poems and onnets, than while studying his dramas.

Style of expression thus springing out of the style of thought, is therefore immediately connected with the structure and character of the individual mind. It consequently has an unconscious origin. On the basis laid in the individual's characteristics, and by and through the individual's mental growth, his manner of expression is formed. There is a certain style which fits the individual — which, and no other, is *his* style. It is that manner of presenting thought, into which he naturally falls, when his mind is deeply absorbed in a subject, and when he gives no heed to the form into which his thought is running.

It is not to be inferred from this, that style has no connection with culture. It has a most immediate and vital connection with the individual's education. Not only all that he is by nature, but all that he becomes by culture, tends to form his style of thought and expression; but, be it observed, *unconsciously* to him. For an incessant aim, a conscious, anxious effort to form a given style, is the destruction of style. Under such an inspection and oversight, Nature cannot work, even if the mind under such circumstances, could absorb itself in the theme of reflection. There must be no consciousness during the time and process of composing, but of the subject. The subject being all in all, for the thinker, the form into which his thought runs, with all the modification and coloring which it really, though *unconsciously* to him, receives from his individualism, and from the whole past of his education, is his *style* — his genuine and true manner.

The point to be observed here is, that style is the *consequent*, so far as it is related to culture. For, the culture itself takes its direction and character from the original tendency of the individual, (for every one in the end obains a mental development coincident with his mental bias,) and style is but the unconscious manifestation of this culture. Style — genuine style — can never be the conscious antecedent of culture. It cannot be first selected, and then the whole individuality of the mind, and the whole course of education, be forced to contribute to its realization. One cannot antecedently choose the style of Burke, e. g. as that which he would have for his own, and then deliberately realize his choice. It is true that a mind similar to that of Burke in its structure, and in sympathy with him through a similarly fruitful and opulent culture, would spontaneously form its style upon, and with, his. But the process, in this case, would not be a deliberate and conscious imitation, but an unconscious and genial reproduction. It would be the consequent of nature and of culture, and not the antecedent. The individual would not distinctly know that his was the style of Burke, until it became apparent to others that it actually was.

Here, too, as in every sphere in which the *living* soul of man works, do we find the genuine and beautiful product originating freely, spontaneously, and unconsciously. Freely, for it might have been a false and deformed product, yet spontaneously and unconsciously, for it cannot be the subject of reflection and matter of distinct knowledge until *after* it has come into existence. By the thronging stress and tendency of the human soul, which is so created as to contain within itself the principle and direction of its own movement, is the product originated, which then, and not till then, is the possible and legitimate subject of consciousness, analysis, and criticism. The style of a thinking mind is no exception to this universal law. It is formed, when formed according to nature — when formed as it was destined to be, by that creative idea which prescribes the whole never-ending development of the creature — it is formed out of what is laid in the individual constitution, and through what is brought in by the individual culture, unconsciously to the subject of the process, and yet freely, so far as his nature and constitution are concerned.

If the view that has been taken of style, be correct, it is evident, that in the formation of style, no attempt should be made to change the fundamental character imposed upon it by the individual constitution. The type is fixed by nature, and no one should strive, by forcing nature, to obtain a manner essentially alien and foreign to him. The sort of style which belongs to the individual by his intellectual constitution is to be taken as given. The direction which all culture in this relation takes, should proceed from this as a point of departure, and all discipline and effort should end in an acquisition that is homogeneous with this *substantial ground* of style. Or still more accurately, the individuality itself is to be deepened and made more capacious and distinct, by culture, and is then to be poured forth in that *hearty unconscious* purity of manner which is its proper and genuine style.

And this leads us to consider the true method of forming and cultivating style.

If the general view that has been presented of the nature both of language and style be correct, it is plain that the mind itself, rather than the style itself, should receive the formation and the cultivation. Both language and style are but *forms* in which the human mind embodies its thought, and therefore the *mind*, considered as the originating power — as that which is to find an utterance and expression — should be the chief object of culture, even in relation to style. A cultivated mind con ains within itself resources sufficient for all its purposes. The direct cultivation of the mind, is the indirect cultivation of all that stands connected with it.

And this is eminently true of the formal, in distinction from the material departments of knowledge — of those "organic (or instrumental) arts," as Milton calls them, "which enable men to discourse and write perspicuously, elegantly, and according to the fitted style of lofty, mean or lowly." For inasmuch as these formal departments of knowledge are not self-sufficient, but derive their substance from the material departments, it is plain that they can be cultivated with power and success only through the cultivation of these latter. Rhetoric, in order to be anything more than an idle play with words and figures of speech — in order to a substantial existence, and an energetic power — must spring out of logic; and logic again, in order to be something more than a dry and useless permutation of the members of syllogisms, must be grounded in the necessary laws of thought, and so become but the inevitable and the living movement of reason. Thus are we led in from the external to the internal as the solid ground of action and origination, and are made to see that the culture must begin here, in every instance, and work out. All these arts and sciences are the architecture of the rational and thinking mind of man, and all changes in them, either in the way of growth or decline, proceed from a change that has first taken place in their originating ground. They are in reality the index of the human mind, and show with most delicate sensibility all that is passing, in this ever-moving principle. What are the languages literatures, laws, governments, and (with one exception) religions of the globe but the history of the human mind — the outstanding monument of what it has *thought!*

It may be said with perfect truth, therefore, that the formation and cultivation of the mind, is the true method of forming and cultivating style. And there are two qualities in mental culture which exert such a direct and powerful influence upon style as to merit in this connection a particular and close examination. They are depth and clearness.

(1) By depth of culture is meant that development of the mind *from its centre*, which enables it to exert its very best power, and to accomplish the utmost of which it is capable. The individual mind differs in respect to innate capacity. Some men are created with a richer and more powerful intellectual constitution than others. But all are capable of a *profound* culture; of a development that shall bring out the entire contents and capacity be they more or less. By going to the centre of the mind — by setting into play those profounder faculties which though differing in degree, are yet the same in kind, in every man — a culture is attained that exerts a most powerful and excellent influence upon style. Such mental education gives *body* to style. It furnishes the material which is to *fill* the language and *solidify* the discourse. The form in which a profoundly cultivated mind expresses itself is never hollow; the language which it employs not being alone — mere words — is never dead. It may, perhaps, be silent at times, for such a mind is not necessarily fluent, but when it *does* speak, the product has a marked character. The thought and its expression form an identity; are coined at one stroke.

For a deeply educated mind spontaneously seeks to know truth in its reality, and to express it in its simplicity. Unconsciously, because it is its nature to do so, it penetrates to the heart of a subject, and discourses upon it with a simplicity and directness which precludes any separation between the thought and the words in which it is conveyed. The mind which has but a superficial knowledge of the subject-matter of its discourse cannot render the language it employs *consubstantial* with its thought. We feel that the words have been *hunted up* by a vacant mind, instead of *prompted* by a full one.—Thought and language stand apart, because thought has not reached that degree of profundity, and that point of clear intuition, and that height of energy, in consciousness, at which it utters itself in language that is truly one with itself, and alive with itself. Whenever a profoundly cultivated mind directs itself to an object of contemplation it becomes identical with it, while in the act of contemplation. The distinction between the contemplating subject, and the contemplated object, vanishes for the time being; the mind, as we say popularly, and yet with strict philosophic truth, is *lost* in the theme, and the theme during this temporary process, becomes but a particular state of the mind. The object of contemplation, which at first was *before* the mind is now *in* the mind; that to which the mind came up as to a thing objective and extant, has now been transmuted into the very consciousness of the mind itself, and is therefore the mind itself, *taken and held in this temporary process.** It follows, consequently, that the *style* in which this

* The doctrine of the identity of subject and object in the act of consciousness is a true and safe one, it seems to us, only when stated with the limitation above; only when the identity is regarded as merely *relative*—as existing only *in, and during the act of consciousness.* If, however, the identity is regarded as *absolute* and *essential*—if it be asserted that, apart from consciousness and back of consciousness, the subject and object, the mind and the truth, are absolutely but one essence—then we see no difference between the doctrine and that of the "substantia una et unica" of Spinoza. The identity in this case, notwithstanding the disclaimer of Schelling, is *sameness* of substance, and there is but one substance in the universe. The

fusion of truth with intellect flows out, must be as near the perfection of form as it can be. The style of such a mind is similar to the style of the Infinite mind, as it is seen in nature. It is characterized by the simplicity and freedom of nature itself. Nor let this be regarded either as irreverent or extravagant. We are confessedly within the sphere of the finite and the created, and therefore are at an infinite remove from Him "who is wonderful in working," and yet there is something strongly resembling the workings of creative power, in the operations of a mind deeply absorbed in truth and full of the idea. As the Divine idea becomes a phenomenon — manifests itself in external nature — by its own movement and guidance, it necessarily assumes the very perfection of manner. — The great attributes of nature, the sublimity and beauty of creation, arise from the oneness of the form with the idea — the transfusion of mind into matter. In like manner, though in an infinitely lower sphere and degree, the human idea, profound, full, and clear in consciousness, throws itself out into language, in a style, free, simple, beautiful, and, it may be, sublime like nature itself. And all this arises because thought does its own perfect work — because truth arrived at in the consciousness of the profound thinker is simply suffered to exercise its own vitality, and to organize itself into existence. It is not so much because the individual makes an effort to embody the results of his meditation, as because these results have their own way, and take their own form, that the style of their appearance is so grand. It has been asserted above, that style, in its most abstract definition, is the universal appearing in the particular. In

truth is, that subject and object are not, absolutely, one essence, but two; but *become* one temporarily, in the act of consciousness, by virtue of a *homogeneity* rather than an absolute identity, of essence.

other words, it is the particular and peculiar manner in which the individual mind conceives and expresses truth, which is universal. Now it is only by and through *depth* of mental cultivation, that truth, in its absolute reality and in its vital energy, is reached at all. A superficial education never reaches the heart of a subject — never brings the mind into contact and fusion with the real substance of the topic of discourse. Of course, a mind thus superficially educated in reality has nothing to express. It has not reached that depth of apprehension, that central point where the solid and real truth lies, at which, and only at which, it is qualified to discourse. — It may, it is true, speak *about* the given topic, but before it can speak it *out*, in a grand, impressive style, and in discourse which, while it is weighty and solid, also dilates and thrills and glows with the living verity, it must, by deep thought, have effected that *mental union* with it of which we have spoken.

A mind, on the contrary, that has received a central development, and whose power of contemplation is strong, instead of working at the surface, and about the accidents, strikes down into the heart and essence, and obtains an actual view of truth; and under the impulse imparted by it, and by the light radiated from it at all points, simply represents it. In all this there is no effort at expression — no endeavor at style — on the part of the individual. He is but the medium of communication, now that, by his own voluntary thought, the union between his mind and truth has been brought about. — All that he needs to do is, to absorb himself still more profoundly in the great theme, and to let it use him as its organ. It will flow through his individualism, and take form and hue from it, as inevitably as the formless and colorless light, acquires both form and color by coming into the beautiful arch of the sky.

(2) By clearness, as an element in culture, is meant such an education of the mind, as arms it with a penetrating and clear vision, so that it beholds objects in distinct outline. When united with depth of culture, this element is of great worth, and diffuses through the productions of the mind some of the most desirable qualities. Depth, without clearness of intuition, is obscurity. Though there may be substantial thinking, and real truth may be reached by the mind, yet like the ὕλη out of which the material universe was formed, according to the ancient philosophy, it needs to be irradiated by light, before it becomes a defined, distinct, and beautiful form. Indeed, without clearness of intuition, truth must remain in the depths of the mind, and cannot be really expressed. The mind, without close and clear thinking, is but a dark chaos of ideas, intimations, and feelings. It is true, that in these is the substance of truth, for the human mind is, by its constitution, full of truth; yet these its contents need to be *elaborated.* These undefined ideas need to become clear conceptions; these dark and pregnant intimations need to be converted into substantial verities; and these swelling but vague feelings must acquire definition and shape; not merely that the consciousness of one mind may be conveyed over into that of another, but also in order to the mind's full understanding of itself.

And such culture manifests itself in the purity and perspicuity of the style in which it conveys its thoughts. Having a distinctly clear apprehension of truth, the mind utters its conceptions with all that simplicity and pertinence of language which characterizes the narrative of an honest eye-witness. Nothing intervenes between thought and expression. The clear, direct, view, *instantaneously* becomes the clear, direct, statement. And when the clear conception is thus united with the profound intuition, thought assumes its most perfect form. The form in which it appears, is full and round with solid truth, and yet distinct and transparent. The immaterial principle is embodied in just the right amount of matter; the former does not overflow, nor does the latter overlay. The discourse exhibits the same opposite and counterbalancing excellencies which we see in the forms of nature—the simplicity and the richness, the negligence and the niceness, the solid opacity and the aërial transparence.*

* Shakspeare affords innumerable exemplifications of the characteristic here spoken of. In the following passages notice the *purity* and *cleanliness* of the style in which he exhibits his thought. As in a perfect embodiment in nature, there is nothing ragged, or to be sloughed off:

> * * * Chaste as the icicle
> That's curded by the frost from purest snow,
> And hangs on Dian's temple.
>
> *Coriolanus*, V. 3.

> * * * * * This hand
> As soft as dove's down, and as white as it;
> Or Ethiopian's tooth, or the fann'd snow,
> That's bolted by the northern blasts twice o'er.
>
> *Winter's Tale*, IV. 3.

> Or if that surly spirit, melancholy,
> Had baked thy blood, and made it heavy, thick;
> Which else runs tickling up and down the veins.
>
> *King John*, III. 3.

> And I, of ladies most deject and wretched,
> That sucked the honey of his music vows,
> Now see that noble and most sovereign reason,
> Like sweet bells jangled, out of tune, and harsh.
>
> *Hamlet*, III. 1.

It is rare to find such a union of the two main elements of culture, and consequently rare to find them in style. A profoundly contemplative mind is often mystic and vague in its discourse, because it has not come to a clear, as well as profound, consciousness—because distinctness, has not gone along with depth, of apprehension. The discourse of such a mind is thoughtful and suggestive it may be, but is lacking in that scientific, logical, power which penetrates and illumines. It has warmth and glow, it may be, but it is the warmth of the stove (to use the comparison of another)—warmth without light.

On the other hand it often happens that the culture of the mind is clear but shallow. In this case nothing but the merest and most obvious commonplace is uttered, in a manner intelligible and plain enough to be sure, but without force or weight, or even genuine fire, of style. Shallow waters show a very clear bottom, and but little intensity of light is needed in order to display the pebbles and clean sand. That must be a "purest ray serene"—a pencil of strongest light—which discloses the black, rich, wreck-strown depths. For the clearness of depth is very different from the clearness of shallowness. The former is a positive quality. It is the positive and powerful irradiation of that which is solid and dark, by that which is ethereal and light. The latter is a negative quality. It is the mere absence of darkness, because there is no substance to be dark—no *body* in which (if we may be allowed the expression) darkness can inhere. Nothing is more luminous than solid fire; nothing is more flashy than an ignited void.

These two fundamental characteristics of mental culture, lie at the foundation of style. Even if the secondary qualities of style could exist, without the weightiness and clearness of manner which spring from the union of profound with distinct apprehension, they would exist in vain. The ornament is worthless, if there is nothing to sustain it. The bas-relief is valueless, without the slab to support it. But these secondary qualities of style—the beauty, and the elegance, and the harmony—derive all their charm and power from springing out of the primary qualities, and in this way, ultimately, out of the deep and clear culture of the mind itself—from being the white flower of the black root.

Style, when having this mental and natural origin, is to be put into the first class of fine forms. It is the form of thought; and, as a piece of art, is as worthy of study and admiration, as those glorious material forms which embody the ideas of Phidias, Michael Angelo, and Raphael. It is the form in which the human mind manifests its freest, purest, and most mysterious activity—its thinking. There is nothing mechanical in its origin, or stale in its nature. It is plastic and fresh as the immortal energy, of which it is the air and bearing.

THE DOCTRINE OF ORIGINAL SIN.*

Die christliche Lehre von der Sünde, dargestellt von Julius Müller.

We have placed the title of this work of Müller at the head of our article, not for the purpose of entering into an analysis and criticism of it at this time, but rather, as a strong and convenient shelter under which to labor upon the much vexed and much vexing doctrine of Original Sin. We are the more inclined to connect our reflections upon this subject with this work, in even this slight and external manner, first, because they coincide substantially with what we suppose to be the general theory presented in this thorough and thoroughly elaborated treatise, though differing from it, as may be seen, on the point of the nature of the connection of the individual with Adam, and by such other modifications as would naturally result from considering the subject from other points of view, and with reference to questions current among a theological public, differing very considerably from that in the midst of which this work originated; and, secondly, because it gives us countenance in the

* Reprinted from the Christian Review, Number LXVII.

attempt to investigate the doctrine from a metaphysical, and not merely psychological, position. For it is the misfortune of the theology in vogue for the last hundred years, as it seems to us, that sin has been contemplated in its phenomenal aspects, rather than in its hidden sources. The majority of treatises that have been written upon this subject since the middle of the eighteenth century, have been occupied principally with *conscious*, and (technically so called) *actual* transgression; while sin, in the form of a nature, deeper than consciousness, and the very fountain of all consciousness itself, on this subject, has too generally been neglected. While, therefore, the psychology of sin has been diligently investigated, and with as much success as could have been expected under the circumstances, the metaphysical side of the doctrine has made little or no progress. If we turn to the treatises of an elder day—to the doctrinal statements on this subject of Augustine or Calvin, or Turretine, or Owen, or the elder Edwards—we find the reverse to be the fact. Here the essence of sin is regarded as a nature, or state of the soul, which manifests itself in a conscious and actual transgression that derives all its malignity and guilt from this, its deeper source. With this source itself—this metaphysical ground of the psychological or conscious transgression—the profound intellect and acute speculation of these men were chiefly occupied, knowing that if all the contradiction and all the mystery on this difficult doctrine, could be cleared up at this point, the question would be settled once for all. Instead, however, of advancing in the general line of advance, marked and deeply scored into all the best theology of the past, the theological mind for the last century has stopped short, as it seems to us, and has contented itself with investigating the mere superficies of the subject—ignoring, and in some instances denying, the existence of its solid substance. The effect of this species of theologizing is every way deleterious. In the first place, the problem itself can never be solved by this method, any more than the mystery of life can be made clearer by a mere examination of the leaves and blossoms of a tree The creed statement of the doctrine of original sin has made no advance since the statement made in 1643, by the Westminster Assembly. There has been much acute and intense speculation upon the doctrine since that time,—for mysterious as it is, and repulsive as it is, to fallen human nature, it will ever charm like the serpent's eye,—but we know of no distinct and strict wording of the doctrine made since then, that contains a fuller and clearer and less contradictory statement than that of the Catechism. It is plain, that there will be no "progress in Theology" by this route. In the second place, this neglect of the sinful nature, and this fastening of the eye upon the sinful exercises only, is greatly injurious to the interests of practical religion. The attention of man is directed to the mere surface of his character. His eye is not made to penetrate into what he *is*, because he is constantly occupied with what he *does*. The standard of character itself is lowered; while, as all church history shows, the grade of character actually reached is far lower than that attained on another theory and view of sin.

Finally, less unanimity among theologians is the natural result of this neglect of the metaphysical side of the doctrine of sin. We know that it is one of the most popular of fallacies, that nothing is less settled than metaphysics,—that the brain of a thorough-bred metaphysician is as confused as his heart, according to Burke, is hard. Still, in the face of the fallacy, we re-affirm that nothing but a return to the old ground occupied by the combatants of an earlier day, will enable theologians to range themselves into two, and only two, divisions, instead of the present variety of "schools," whose name is legion. The questions that arise, and the answers that are compelled, by a metaphysical method, as distinguished from a merely empirical one, *locate* the theologian, on one side or the other of the line; because, by this method, terms are used in their strict signification, and the conceptions denoted by them are distinct.

Suppose, for example, that the term "sinful," when applied to the nature of fallen man, instead of being employed in the sense of "innocent," as it sometimes is at the present day, had but the one uniform and constant signification of "guilty,"— would not all who hold and teach the doctrine of a sinful nature see eye to eye on that point? Suppose again, that the word "imputation" were employed to denote the charge of guilt upon the absolutely guilty, and never an arbitrary charge of any sort,— would not all who hold to the imputation of a sinful nature be at one on this point? And yet the loose use of these and kindred terms, and the multiplication of schools in theology thereby, can be prevented only by that method of investigation which passes by all manifestations and phenomena, and having reached the nature itself, asks — is it innocent, or is it culpable? — is this nature as justly and properly imputable, and so, as worthy of punishment, in the case of the individual, as of Adam, or is it not? Here the subject lies in a nutshell; and while the "yea, yea," locates the theologian on one side of the line first sharply drawn in the days of Augustine, and the "nay, nay," locates him on the other side, what is still better, this strict handling of terms leads to a deeper and more satisfactory enucleation and establishment of the truth itself.

For, if a man affirm that the fallen nature is sin itself, and not the mere occasion of sin; is guilt itself, and not the mere occasion of guilt; and also, that all this is as true of the posterity of Adam as of the individual Adam himself, he is not only bound to explain this on rational grounds, but he is driven to the attempt to explain it by the inevitable movement of his own mind. And this was the case with the men whom we have mentioned. They never shrank from affirming that the ultimate form of sin is a nature, that this nature is guilt, and that the wrath of God justly rests upon every individual of the human race because of it. And when pressed with the difficulties that beset this, and every other one of the "deep things of God," by as acute and able opponents as the world has ever seen, instead of relaxing the statement, or betaking themselves to a loose and equivocal use of words, they stuck to terms, and endeavored to think through, and establish, on philosophical grounds, a form of doctrine which they first and heartily adopted, on experimental and Scriptural grounds. We do not say that they completely solved the problem, but we verily believe that they were in the way of its solution, and that theological speculation must join on where they left off, and move forward in their line of advance. No one age, however wise and learned, can furnish a finished Theology for all the ages to come; but if we would have substantial advance, each and every age must be in communication with the wisdom and truth of the preceding, and form a piece of continuity with it.

Returning to this point of unanimity, consider for a moment the variety of opinions among us in regard to this subject of a sinful nature. What divisions and controversies exist among those who all alike profess to be Calvinists! How little unanimity exists upon this doctrine among those who all alike repel the charge of Arminianism! One portion or school teach, that there is a corrupt nature in man, but deny that it is really and strictly sinful. Another portion or school teach, that there is a nature in man to which the epithet "sinful" is properly applied, who yet, when pressed with the inquiry — is it *crime*, and deserving of the wrath of God? — shrink from the right answer, and return an uncertain sound, of which the substance is, that its contrariety to law, and not its voluntariness, is the essence of sin. Again, there are those who are prepared to fall back upon the ground of the elder Calvinists, up to a certain point, but who resolve the whole matter when pressed by their opponents, into the arbitrary will and sovereignty of God, and deprecate all attempts to construct the doctrine on grounds of reason and philosophy. And finally, there are some who are inclined not only to the doctrinal statement of Augustine and Owen and the elder Edwards, but also to their method of establishing and defending it, by means of the doctrine of the real oneness of Adam and his posterity, in the fall of the human soul. And yet Calvinism is one in its nature and theory. Using this term to denote not merely that particular scheme of Christian doctrine drawn up by Calvin, but that doctrinal system which had its origin in the controversy of Augustine with Pelagius, and which received a further development through the reformed theologians on the continent, and the puritan divines of England; we may say that Calvinism teaches but one thing in regard to the existence of a sinful nature in fallen man, and but one thing in regard to the meaning of the term sinful. During those ages of controversy

—the 16th and 17th centuries—those who held the doctrine of a sinful nature, and of a sinful nature that is guilt, stood upon one side, and stood all together; and those who rejected this doctrine stood upon the other side, and also stood all together.* The Christian church

* This is evident from the symbols of the three great divisions of the modern Protestant church, viz: the Lutheran, the Reformed (Calvinistic), and the Puritan.

Item docent, quod post lapsum Adae omnes homines, secundum naturam propagati, nascantur cum peccato, hoc est, sine metu Dei, sine fiducia erga Deum, et cum concupiscentia, *quodque hic morbus, seu vitium originis vere sit peccatum, damnans et afferens aeternam mortem.*

Damnant Pelagianos et alios, qui vitium originis negant esse peccatum. Confessio Augustana, Articulus II.

Est peccatum originis corruptio totius naturae, et vitium hereditarium, * * * * * estque tam foedum *atque execrabile coram Deo, ut ad universi generis humani condemnationem sufficiat.* Confessio Belgica, Articulus XV.

Peccatum originis, est vitium et depravatio naturae cuiuslibet hominis ex Adamo naturaliter propagati, qua fit ut ab originali justitia quam longissime distet, ad malum sua natura propendeat, et caro semper adversus spiritum concupiscat, *unde in unoquoque nascentium iram Dei atque damnationem meretur.* Articuli XXXIX, Articulus IX.

Qua transgressione, quae vulgo dicitur originale peccatum, prorsus deformata est illa Dei in homine imago, ipseque et ejus posteri natura facti sunt inimici Dei, mancipia Satanae, et servi peccati, *adeo ut mors aeterna habuerit et habitura est potentiam et dominium in omnes*, qui non fuerunt, non sunt coelitus regeniti. Confessio Scoticana, III.

Peccatum omne *cum originale* tum actuale, quum justae Dei legis transgressio sit eique contraria, peccatori suapte natura *reatum infert, quo ad iram Dei, ac maledictionem legis subeundam obligatur, adeoque redditur obnoxius morti simul et miseriis omnibus spiritualibus, temporalibus, ac aeternis.* Westminster Confessio fidei, Cap. VI. § 6.

Every sin, both *original* and actual, being a transgression of the righteous law of God, and contrary thereunto, doth in its own nature bring guilt upon the sinner, whereby he is bound over to the wrath of God, and curse of the law, and so made subject to death, with all miseries spiritual, temporal, and eternal. Boston Confession of Faith, Chapter VI.

Q. What are the effects of this first sin of man? A. 1. Guilt; whereby they are bound to undergo due punishment for their fault. 2. Punishment; which is the just wrath of God, with the effects of it upon them for the filth of sin. Davenport's New Haven Catechism.

vas divided into two divisions, and no more. And this, because the controversy was a thorough one, owing to the profound view of sin taken by the disputants on the Augustinian side; the metaphysical, rather than merely psychological aspect of the doctrine being uppermost.

It is therefore in this connection that we rejoice at the appearance, in this age, of a work like that of Müller, which recognizes a deeper source and form of sin than particular and conscious choices, and invites the theologian to contemplate the origin and essential character of that *nature* and *state* of the human soul, from which all conscious transgression proceeds. Whether it adopt all the views of the author or not, we are confident the reflecting mind that has made itself acquainted with the history of the doctrine of original sin, will find no difficulty in deciding on which side of the great controversy this treatise is; and furthermore, that it is on the whole a substantial advance towards a complete philosophical statement of the theological statement contained germinally in the works of Augustine, and formally in all the best symbols of the church.

In commencing the investigation of the doctrine of original sin, we naturally start from one distinct and unambiguous statement of Scripture; and we know of no one at once so plain and full as the affirmation of St Paul, that man is by nature a child of wrath. The doctrine of a guilty nature in man is taught either by implication, or by an explicit detail, in other passages in Paul's Epistles, in the Psalms of David, in the Epistles of John, in the Prophecies of Isaiah and Jeremiah, and in the teachings of Christ; but perhaps no single text of Scripture enounces the doctrine so briefly and comprehensively as this. It makes specific mention of the two principal characteristics of human sinfulness: (1.) its depth, and, by implication, its universality; and (2.) its guilt. After all that may be said upon this boundless subject, in its various relations to man, to the universe, and to God, the whole substance of the doctrine may be crowded into a very narrow compass. When we have said, that man is *by nature a child of wrath*—when we have said, that sin is a nature, and that this nature is guilt—we have said in substance all that can be said. The most exhaustive investigation of the subject will not reveal any feature or element that is not contained by implication in this brief statement.

The true method of investigating the doctrine is thus prescribed by the terms in which it is stated in Scripture, and we shall endeavor to follow it rigidly. We shall endeavor to exhibit the Scriptural doctrine of original sin, not by merely reciting a series of texts, and there leaving the matter, but by seizing upon the most significant and pregnant text of all, and rigorously developing it. If we are not mistaken, the simple contents of this one proposition of St. Paul, will unfold themselves by close reflection into a detailed view, and a doctrinal statement, that will be found to harmonize also with reason and the Christian experience.

I. This passage of inspiration teaches, that sin is a *nature*. "We were φύσεί—*by nature*—children of wrath." The Greek word φυσις, like the Latin, *natura*, always denotes something original and innate, in contradistinction to something acquired by practice or habit. Whenever we wish to represent an attribute or quality, as residing in a subject in the most deep and total manner possible, we say that it is in it by nature, or as a nature; and when in our investigations we are brought ıck to a nature, as a fundamental basis, we think we ıve reached the bottom.*

When we search for the essence of human sinfulness, ·e find it in the form of a nature in the man. Suppose we

* The word "nature" for some minds conveys only the meaning of "cre-ed substance," so that to assert that sin is a nature, is tantamount, for ıem, to the assertion that it is the substance or essence of man. This is ɔt its use in this essay. Sin is not substance but agency: it is not the es-ınce of the will but its action; not the constitution of this faculty but its ıotion. The term "nature," consequently, when applied to moral agency, equivalent to "natural disposition."

None were more careful to guard against the Manichaean doctrine, that n is substance, than those who have held the doctrine that man has a sin-ıl nature and that this nature is guilt. Augustine carefully distinguishes etween the work of the Creator and that of the creature. The work of ıe former he often designates by the term *natura*. Employed in *this* sense e denies that sin is nature, or belongs to the course and constitution of na-ıre. Omne autem vitium *naturae nocet*, ac per hoc *contra naturam* est. (De ïiv. Dei XII. 1). The entire argument in Chapter 6 of Book XII. of the De Civitate Dei, endeavors to prove that moral evil is the pure self-motion f the will of the creature.

Consonant with this, Calvin (Institutes B. II. C. I. § 11) remarks "We say, herefore, that man is corrupted by a natural depravity, but which did not riginate from nature. We deny that it proceeded from nature, to signify hat it is rather an adventitious quality or accident, than a *substantial prop-rty* originally innate. Yet we call it natural, that no one may suppose it o be contracted by each individual from corrupt habit." Again (Inst. B. I. C. XIV. § 3) "neither the depravity and wickedness of men and devils, nor he sins which proceed from that source, are from *mere nature*, but from a orruption of nature." Again (Inst. B. I. C. XV. § 1), "we must beware est, in precisely pointing out the *natural* evils of man, we seem to refer them to the Author of nature." Again (Inst. B. I. C. XV. § 1), "it would redound to the dishonor of God, if nature could be proved to have had any innate depravity at its formation."

The *Formula Concordiae* is careful to assert, in opposition to the doctrine of an extreme party in the Lutheran church, "peccatum originale non esse ipsam hominis *naturam*, aut *essentiam*, hoc est, ipsius hominis *corpus* et *animam*, (quae hodie in nobis, etiam post lapsum sunt, manentque Dei opus et creatura) sed malum illud originis esse aliquid *in* ipsa hominis natura, corpore, anima, omnibusque viribus humanis." Hase's Libri Sym bolici, p. 639.

arrest the sinner in the outward act, and fix our attention upon sin in this form, we are immediately compelled, by the operation of our own mind, to let go of this outward act, and to seek for the reality of his sin within him. The outward act, we see in an instant, is but an effect of a cause; and we instinctively turn our eye inward, and fasten it upon the cause. The outward act of transgression drives us, by the very laws of thought, to the power that produced it — to the particular volition that originated it. No mind that thinks at all upon sin can possibly stop with the outward act. Its own rational reflection hurries it away, almost instantaneously, from the blow of the murderer — from the momentary gleam of the knife — to the *volition* within that strung the muscle, and nerved the blow.

But the mind cannot stop here in its search for the essential reality of sin. When we have reached the sphere — the *inward* sphere — of volitions, we have by no means reached the ultimate ground and form of sin. We may suppose, that because we have gone beyond the outward act — because we are now *within* the man — we have found sin in its last form. But we are mistaken. Closer thinking, and what is still better, a deeper experience, will disclose to us a depth in our souls, lower than that in which volitions occur, and a form of sin in that depth, and to the bottom of it, very different from the sin of single volitions.

The thinking mind which cannot stop with mere effects, but seeks for first causes, and especially the heart that knows its own plague, cannot stop with that quite superficial action of the will which manifests itself in a volition. This action is too isolated — too intermittent — and, in reality, too feeble, to account for so steady and uniform a state of character as human sinfulness.

For these particular volitions, ending in particular outward actions, the mind instinctively seeks a common ground. For these innumerable volitions, occurring each by itself and separately, the mind instinctively seeks *one single indivisible nature* from which they spring. When the mind has got back to this point, it stops content, because it has reached a central point. When it has traced all these outward acts and inward volitions to one common principle and source, it stops content, because it has introduced unity into the subject of its investigation. When the human mind has attained a view that is both central and simple, it is satisfied.

It is not more certain, that we are compelled by the laws of our minds to refer properties to a substance, than that by the operation of the same laws, we are compelled to refer sinful volitions to a sinful disposition. When we see exercises of the soul, we as instinctively refer them to a natural character in that soul, as we refer the the properties of a body to the substance of that body. In both cases the human mind is seeking for unity and simplicity in its perceptions. It cannot be content with merely looking at these various properties of matter, this impenetrability, this extension in space, this form, this color, and stopping here. It wants unity of perception, and simplicity of perception, and therefore it goes farther, and *refers* all these properties to one simple substance, of which they are the manifestation. In like manner, the human mind cannot be content with merely looking at all these exercises—these unnumbered volitions of the soul. It craves unity and simplicity of perception here too, and *refers* these innumerable, sinful volitions, to a sinful *nature* in man, one and indivisible, of which they are the manifestations.

Again: the argument from the Christian experience is

20

as strong as that from the nature of the human mind, in favor of the position that the ultimate form — the essential reality — of sin, is a nature. Although in the first period of conviction of sin, the attention of the man may be directed mainly to actions and volitions; and although this may be the case to a considerable extent, even in the first stages of the Christian experience, it is yet safe to say, that the Christian man is troubled through the Christian life on earth, mainly, and permanently, by his sinful *nature.* The reality of sin, for every man whose experience is worth being taken as testimony, is not in particular volitions of his will, but in its abiding state — not in what he chooses to do now and then, but in that unceasing, uninterrupted determination of self to evil. This is the torment of his life — that below his volitions to sin — below his resolutions to reform — even below his deepest self-examination, and his most distinct self-knowledge — below all the conscious exercises and operations of his soul, there is a sinful *heart*, a dark ground of moral evil.

We are aware of the mysteriousness which is thrown over the subject of sin, by the assumption of a form of sin which is deeper than consciousness. But we must take things as we find them, whether they are mysterious or not; whether we can explain them or not. The contents which we are to analyze are given to our hand, and whether we succeed or not in the analysis, they have the same fixed and real nature of their own. And, we may add, the true way to arrive at the unfolding of a mystery, is to recognize in the outset, the existence of all that belongs to it. The true way to arrive at the successful solution of a dark problem, is to retain all the terms of its statement. To throw out one or more of the terms which properly belong to the problem, and in which its real nature is contained, because it seems to be a troublesome term to manage, is to utterly prevent the solution; and the attempt to unfold the deep mystery of original sin, while rejecting in the outset an element that is essential — the sin that is deeper than consciousness, or the sinful nature, as distinguished from sinful volitions — simply because it darkens a subject that is confessedly mysterious, must inevitably be a failure.

Without troubling ourselves, therefore, at this point in the investigation, about the mysteriousness of a sin of which we are not conscious, because it is the basis and explanation of consciousness, and therefore of necessity below its range and plane, let us here and now settle the fact, whether there *is* any such sin.

(1.) And, in the first place, is it not a fact, that in regard to the matter of sin, we do refer all the conscious processes of our souls to something back of these processes? The materials that make up our consciousness as sinners — the innumerable items of which it is composed — the thousands of wrong volitions, and the hundreds of thousands of wrong emotions, and the millions of wrong thoughts — do we not, as a matter of fact, refer them all to some *one* thing, out of which they spring? Can we, and as matter of fact do we, continue to chase these innumerable and constantly vanishing particulars, dropping one as soon as we have reached the next succeeding, because the mind can grasp but one thing at a time, and thus lose the mind in an endless series, instead of collecting it in one act of contemplation and reflection; or do we, with David, cease this attempt to number our iniquities, and having acknowledged that they are more than the hairs of our head, (Ps. xl. 12,) with him confess a *one* sin of heart and of nature at the bottom of them all? No man who has had any experience on this subject at all, will deny that such is the fact.—Whatever his theory may be, every man does, in his private reflections and secret confession to God, find a form of sin within him which he regards as the fountain and cause of all his particular and conscious transgressions. He finds an original sin from which these particular wrong thoughts, emotions, and volitions, proceed.

(2.) And now, in the second place, is it not a fact, that we are never conscious of this source itself of transgressions, but only of what flows from it? We are undeniably conscious of these thoughts, these emotions, these volitions—of these items which go to make up the sum of our experience—of these various materials of consciousness. But, are we, as matter of fact, ever conscious of that *principle* of evil—that sinful *nature*, to which, as we have seen, we instinctively refer all our conscious transgressions? We have only to reflect a moment to see that we are never conscious of this sinful *nature* itself, but only of what proceeds from it. The evil *principle* to which we refer all these manifestations of evil, remains ever below the plane of consciousness. These manifestations may, themselves, become more and more profound, and may carry us down into deeper and deeper regions, but we find the sinful nature ever below us; as we go down into the depths of our apostate souls, and know still more and still more of the plague of our hearts, we are all along, and at every lower point, obliged to assume the existence of a yet deeper sin than our consciousness has grasped. We never reach the bottom; we never come, in consciousness, to the lowest and ultimate form of sin; or, which is the same thing, we never see the time when we have become conscious of all our sinfulness, and there are no further discoveries for us to make. The prayer of David is the proper prayer for us to the day of our death: "Search me, O Lord, and try me, and see what evil ways are within me; cleanse Thou me from *secret* faults." A prayer, it may be remarked, that is utterly unintelligible on the hypothesis that there is no sin deeper than consciousness.

This sinful nature, as distinguished from the conscious transgressions that proceed from it, is not a part of our experience, but something which we *infer* from our experience, as the origin and explanation of it. It is the metaphysical ground of the physical — *i. e.*, psychological — phenomena. We find within consciousness, an innumerable amount of particulars — an endless series of wrong thoughts, emotions, and volitions — each occurring by itself; and this is all we do or can find in consciousness. And if we were confined merely to what we are *conscious* of — if we were shut up to the series of our *experiences* merely — we should never come to the knowledge of a sinful nature. We should be compelled to stop with the phenomenal merely. But when in reflection, and for the purposes of science, we arrest all these processes of consciousness — when we bring this ever-flowing stream of conscious transgressions to a stand-still — that we may look at them, and find the origin and first cause of them, then we are obliged to *assume* a principle below them all, to *infer* a nature back of them all.— Thus, this sinful nature is an *inference*, an *assumption*, or, to use a word borrowed from geometry, a *postulate*, which the mind is obliged to grant, in order to find a key that will unlock, and explain, its own experience.

"But granting," the objector may say, "granting that, as matter of fact, we do infer and assume, from what we find in our consciousness, the existence of a nature deeper than consciousness, to which we refer the data of experience, and by which we explain them, what evidence is there, that there is in reality any such thing? By your own confession, it is entirely beyond the sphere of human consciousness; and though it may be a convenient a priori postulate, under which to group and generalize the various particulars in our experience, what evidence is there, that there is an actual correspondent to it in the human soul?" We answer: The evidence in this case is precisely the same with that which exists in the case of any and every purely *metaphysical* truth. The evidence cannot of course be derived from consciousness, because we are seeking the ground and explanation of consciousness itself; and therefore must be sought for in that *normal and necessary movement of our rational intellect*, by which we are compelled to the a priori assumption.—We find ourselves *necessitated*, in every instance that we attempt to find an adequate origin for our particular transgressions, to assume the existence of a sinful nature, and this *rational necessity* in the case, is the evidence that we need. When we find that the mind is driven by the *very laws of thought* to an a priori assumption, and that it is *invariably* driven to it whenever it reflects at all upon its experience, we have all the evidence that can be had for a metaphysical truth — all the evidence that can rationally be required, that the assumption corresponds to the truth and reality in the case. Reason cannot impose upon itself, and invariably teach a truth of knowing, that is no truth of being — a truth of logic and science, that is no truth of fact; and therefore it is, that men will always believe that there is a substance in which accidents inhere, and a nature from which manifestations proceed, though there is no evidence from consciousness for either. The fact, that the human mind, in the exercise of its sober reflection upon the data of consciousness, is *invariably* and *unavoidably* compelled to a given assumption, is evidence that the assumption has rational grounds, and corresponds to truth and reality.—If it is not, then a lie has been built into the very structure of the human mind, and it is not to be trusted in regard to any a priori truth. If, when following the laws of thought, and trusting to the constitution imposed upon it by the Creator, there is no certainty that the assumptions which it is compelled to make, as the sufficient ground and adequate explanation of its experimental consciousness, correspond to the truth of things, the human mind might as well stop thinking altogether.

And what shall we do in this connection with the sense of guilt? This sinful nature, as matter of fact, is the source of remorse, and the cause of the most poignant self-reproach in those whose senses have been exercised to discern good and evil. Can we suppose that there is a lie here too, and that pangs come into the human soul, and exist there, with no valid reason for them, no real ground for them to rest upon? Can we suppose that all the remorse and self-reproach that has resulted in the souls of men, from a knowledge of their *nature* and *character*, and not merely of their particular acts, was un-called for, because there is in reality no such nature? Can we suppose that He who looks on things precisely as they are, *knows* that there is no just cause for this mental distress in His creatures?

In addition to these arguments derived from the nature of the human mind, and the sense of guilt, (which latter point opens a wide and most interesting field of investigation,) we may add, that the history of Christian doctrine shows that the church has in all ages believed in a sinful nature, as distinguished from conscious transgressions. The soundest, and, as we believe, the profoundest symbols, all teach the existence of a form of human sinfulness running deeper than even the most thorough and searching Christian experience — or, which is the same thing, that the Divine Eye beholds a corruption in man, more radical and more profound than has ever been seen by the eye of man himself.

II. Assuming, then, that the fact of a sinful nature has been established, we pass to the second statement of St. Paul, that man is by nature *a child of wrath.* We pass from his statement, that sin, in its ultimate form, is a nature, to his statement, that this nature is *guilt.* And we need not say, that in so doing, we are passing over into the darkest and most dangerous district in the whole domain of theological speculation. The recondite nature of the subject, the difficulty of clearly expressing one's conceptions, even when they lie distinct in one's own mind, the liability to push a point too far, the failure to guard one's statements with sufficient care, and many other causes that might be specified, conspire to render this side of the doctrine of original sin one of the most difficult of all topics of discussion. And before we venture out into this region, we wish to say beforehand, that we should regret and dread above all things, to advance any views on this important doctrine that would conflict with the Christian's experience of the plague of his heart—any views that would be in the least degree prejudicial to that profound view of sin which the soul does actually have when under the teaching and influence of the Holy Spirit. We most heartily and religiously acknowledge, that here the Practical must have preference to the Speculative; and we would immediately give up any speculative view or theory of sin that we might have formed, the moment that we saw that it would go, or tend in the least, to disparage a thoroughgoing statement of the doctrine in a creed, or to pro-note an imperfect and shallow experience of it in the heart.

The apostle teaches, that sinful man is a child of wrath. Now, none but a *guilty* being can be the object of the righteous and holy displeasure of God. The doctrine of the Divine Anger is tenable only on the supposition that the objects upon whom it expends itself are *really ill deserving* — are *really criminal.* It becomes necessary therefore to show, that that sinful nature of man, on account of which he becomes a child of wrath, and obnoxious to the Divine anger, is a *guilty nature.* In doing this, we shall be led to discuss sin in its relation to the human Will, and to Adam, the first man.

(1.) In regard to the first point, the position taken is, that this sinful nature is in the Will, and is the product of the Will. We say that it is in the Will, in contradistinction to the physical nature of man. One statement of the doctrine of original sin makes it to consist in the depravation of man's sensuous nature merely. In this case, the Will is conceived to be extraneous to this corrupted nature, and merely the executor of it. Original sin, in this case, is not in the voluntary part of man, but in the involuntary part of him; and guilt cleaves to him when the voluntary part executes the promptings of the involuntary part; and guilt does not cleave to him until this does take place. The adherents of this view insist, (and properly too, if this statement is correct,) that the term " sinful," in the sense of guilty or criminal, cannot be applied to this depraved physical nature — to this (so-called) original sin.

In opposition to this view, we affirm that original sin does not consist in the depravation of man's sensuous or physical nature, but in *the depravation of his Will itself.* The corruption of the physical nature of man is one of the consequences of original sin, but not original sin itself. This is a depravation of a far deeper and more central faculty than that of sense — a corruption of the voluntary power itself. It is because the human *Will* — the *governing* power in the soul — first fell away from God, that the other faculties of man are in the condition they are, that the affections are carnal, that the understanding is darkened, that the physical nature is depraved; and these effects of apostasy should never be put in the place of their cause — of that corruption of the Will which is the origin of them all.

But the examination of a single instance of the gratification of a sensuous propensity, is enough to show that sin lies elsewhere than in the physical nature. A man, we will suppose, gratifies the sensuous craving for strong drink. The sin in the case does not lie in this craving of the sensuous nature, corrupted though it be. The sin in the case lies further back, in the Will; and, be it observed, not solely in that particular volition of the Will by which the act of drinking was performed, but ultimately in that *abiding state* of the Will — that *selfishness*, or *selfish nature* in the Will — which prompted and permitted the volition. Here, as in every instance, we are led back to a sinful nature, as the essence of sin; and this nature we find in the Will itself; we find it to be a particular state of the Will itself.

But, besides saying that this sinful nature is in the Will, we have said, furthermore, that it is the product of the Will. By this we mean, that the efficient producing author of this sinful nature is the Will itself; in other words, that this nature is a *self-willed*, a *self-determined* nature. Before proceeding further with this part of the subject, we wish to premise a few remarks upon these terms, "self-willed" and "self-determined."

It is unfortunate for the cause of truth, and especially or the scientific development of the doctrine of original in, that the term self-determination has been appropria-ed by the Arminian School in Theology; and still more unfortunate, that the conception denoted by it has been, and still is, such a defective and inadequate one. Both Arminians and their modern opponents have understood, and still do understand, by this term, an ability in the Will, at any moment, to choose or refuse some particu-lar thing. The Will accordingly, both for Arminians and their opponents, is merely the faculty of single choices — the faculty of particular volitions; and self-de-termination for both parties denotes the ability to put forth a single volition, or not, at pleasure. The Will for both parties is simply that faculty of particular choices, by which we raise a hand or let it drop — a species of voluntary power which the horse employs, in common with man, when he chooses clover and refuses burdock.

This is the notion attached to the term self-determina-tion in the treatise of Edwards — the ability, viz., to resolve this way or that, at any moment, and under all circumstances; and if this is the only self-deter-mination of which we can have any conception, then Edwards was correct in denying the doctrine. So far as his work combats this defective and inadequate no-tion of self-determination — so far as it seeks to over-throw the *Arminian* self-determination — it is one of great value. From such a superficial view of the Will, as being merely the faculty of single isolated volitions, and from such an inadequate notion of self-determination, as being merely the ability to choose or refuse a particular thing, in a particular case, nothing but the most shallow view both of sin and of regeneration could result. The great merit of Edwards in this polemic treatise, it seems to us, consists more in his powerful and successful resistance of a false theology, in connection with a thorough view of the *fallen* and *corrupt* Will, than in his own positive statements concerning the ideal and original nature of this faculty.*

In saying, therefore, that the sinful nature of man is the product of his Will, we do not mean to teach, that it has its origin in the Will considered as the faculty of choices, or particular volitions. We no more believe that original sin was produced by a volition, than that it can be destroyed by one. And if we can have no idea of the Will except as such a faculty of single choices, and no idea of voluntary action except such as we are conscious of in our volitions and resolutions, then we grant that the sinful nature must be referred to some other producing cause than the human Will, and that the epithets, "self-determined," and "self-originated," cannot be applied to it.

But it seems to us that we can have a fuller and more adequate idea of the voluntary power in man than this comes to. It seems to us that our idea of the human Will is by no means exhausted of its contents, when we have taken into view merely that ability which a man has, to regulate his conduct in a particular instance. It seems to us that we do believe in the existence of a controlling power in the soul, that is far more central and profound than the quite superficial faculty by which we regulate the movement of our limbs outwardly, or inwardly summon up our energies to the performance of particular acts. It seems to us, that by the Will, is meant a voluntary power that lies at the very centre of the soul, and whose movements consist, not so much in

* Edwards's work on "The Affections," contains much that is of great value for the construction of a philosophic theory of the Will.

choosing or refusing, in reference to particular circumstances, as *in determining the whole man with reference to some great and ultimate end of living*. The characteristic of the Will proper, as distinguished from the volitionary faculty, is *determination of the whole being to an ultimate end*, rather than selection of means for attaining that end in a particular case.* The difference between the voluntary and the volitionary power — between the Will proper and the faculty of choices — may be seen by considering a particular instance of the exercise of the latter. Suppose that a man chooses to indulge one of his appetites in a particular instance — the appetite for alcoholic stimulus, *e. g.*—and that he actually does gratify it. In this instance, he puts forth one single volition, and performs one particular act. By an act of the faculty of choices, of which he is distinctly conscious, and over which he has arbitrary power, he drinks, and gratifies his appetite. But why does he thus choose in this particular instance? In other words, is there not a deeper ground for this single volition? Is not this particular act of the choice determined by a far deeper and pre-existing *determination of his whole inward being* to self, as an ultimate end of living? And now, if the Will should be widened out and deepened, so as to contain this whole inward state of the man — this entire *tendency* of the soul to self and sin — is it not plain that it would be a very different power from that which put forth the particular volition? Would not the Will, as thus conceived, cover a far wider surface of the soul, and reach down to a far deeper depth in it, than that faculty

* This distinction between the Will proper, and the faculty of choices, is marked in Latin by the two words, *Voluntas* and *Arbitrium;* and in that one of the modern tongues whose vocabulary for Philosophy is the richest of all, by the two words, *Wille* and *Willkühr*.

of single choices which covers but a single point on the surface, and never goes below the surface? — Would not a faculty comprehensive enough to include the *whole* man, and sufficiently deep and central to be the origin and basis of a *nature*, *a character*, *a permanent moral state*, be a very different faculty from that volitionary power whose activity is merely on the surface, and whose products are single resolutions, and transient volitions?

Now, by the Will, we mean such a faculty. We mean by it a voluntary power that lies at the very foundation of the human soul, constituting its central, active principle, containing the whole moral state, and all the moral affections. We mean by it a voluntary power that carries the *whole* inward being along with it when it moves; a power, in short, which is the man himself — the *ego*, the *person*.

It will be seen from this view, that the voluntary power in man is the deepest and most central power within him. We sometimes hear the human soul spoken of as composed fundamentally of Intellect and of Feeling, and only superficially of Will; as if man were an Intellect at bottom, or a Heart at bottom, and then a Will were superinduced as the executive of these. But this cannot be so, for man is a person, and the bottom of personality is free Will. Man at bottom is a Will — a self-determining creature — and his other faculties of knowing and feeling are grafted into this stock and root; and hence he is responsible from centre to circumference.*

* This more capacious idea of the Will is the most common one in doctrinal history. " Voluntas est quippe in omnibus: *imo omnes nihil aliud quam voluntates sunt.* Nam quid est cupiditas, et lætitia, nisi voluntas in eorum consensionem quæ volumus? Et quid est metus atque tristitia, nisi voluntas in dissensionem ab his quæ nolumus." Aug. De civitate Dei, Lib. XIV., Cap. VI.

The Will, as thus defined, we affirm to be the responsible and guilty author of the sinful nature. *Indeed, this sinful nature is nothing more nor less than the state of the*

"The Will is in the soul like the *primum mobile* in the heavens, that doth carry all the inferior orbs away with its own motion. This is the *whole* of a man; a man is not what he knoweth, or what he remembereth, but what he *Willeth.* The Will is the Queen sitting upon its throne, exercising its dominion over the other parts of the soul. The Will is the proper seat of all our sin; and if there could be a *summum malum* as there is a *summum bonum*, this would be in the Will."—Burgess. Original Sin. Part III. chap. XIV. Sec. 1.

"In the Will, we are to conceive suitable and proportionate affections to those we call passions in the sensitive part. Thus, in the Will, (as it is a rational appetite,) there are love, joy, desire, fear, and hatred. * * * So that the Will loveth, the Will rejoiceth, and the Will desireth," etc.—Burgess. Part III. chap. IV. Sec. 2.

"The heart in Scripture is variously used; sometimes for the mind and understanding; *sometimes for the Will;* sometimes for the affections; sometimes for the conscience; sometimes for the whole soul. Generally it denotes the whole soul of man, and all the faculties of it, not absolutely, *but as they are one principle of moral operations, as they all concur in our doing good or evil.*"—Owen. Indwelling Sin. Chapter III.

"And then, likewise, there is a consequent averse or transverse posture in the affections of the soul, *whereof, indeed, the Will is the seat and subject;* desires, fears, hopes, delights, anger, sorrow, all transversed in a quite contrary course and being, to what they should be."—Howe's Oracles of God. Sec. 25. Also compare pp. 1204, 1128, 891. New York Ed.

.."As to spiritual duties or acts, or any good thing in the state or immanent acts of the Will itself, or of the affections (*which are only certain modes of the exercise of the Will*), etc.—Edwards on the Will. Part III. Sec. 4.

"The Will, and the affections of the soul, are not two faculties; *the affections are not essentially distinct from the Will, nor do they differ from the mere actings of the Will, and inclination of the soul,* but only in the liveliness and sensibleness of exercise."—Edwards on the Affections. Works, III. p. 3.

Edwards everywhere dichotomizes. For example, speaking of the difference between the knowledge of the natural man and that of the regenerate, he remarks: "In the former is exercised merely the speculative faculty, or the *understanding*, strictly so called, or as spoken of in distinction from the *Will, or disposition of the soul.* In the latter, the *Will, or inclination, or heart*, is mainly concerned."—Reality of Spiritual Light. Works, IV. 442.

The terms "heart" and "will" are everywhere used as equivalents by Calvin. See e. g. Institutes. Book II. Chap. III. Sec. 5–11.

Will; nothing more nor less than its constant and total determination to self, as the ultimate end of living. This voluntary power lying at the bottom of the soul, as its elementary base, and carrying all the faculties and powers of the man along with it, whenever it moves, and wherever it goes, has turned away from God as an ultimate end; and this self-direction — this permanent and entire determination of itself — this *state* of the Will — is the sinful nature of man.

Here then we have a depraved nature, and a depraved nature that is guilt, because it is a self-originated nature.* Here, then, is the child of wrath. Were this nature created and put into man, as an intellectual nature, or as a particular temperament, is put into him, by the Creator of all things, it would not be a responsible and guilty nature, nor would man be a child of wrath. But it does not thus originate. It has its origin in the free and responsible use of that voluntary power which God has created and placed in the human soul, as its most central, most mysterious, and most hazardous endowment. It is a self-determined nature — *i. e., a nature originated in a Will, and by a Will.*†

* To use a scholastic distinction — it is peccatum *originans*, and not merely originatum.

† The Will is the principle, the next seat and cause of obedience and disobedience. Moral actions are unto us, or in us, so far good or evil as they partake of the consent of the Will. He spoke truth of old who said "Omne peccatum est adeo voluntarium, ut non sit peccatum nisi sit voluntarium"—Owen, Indwelling Sin, Chapter XII.

"I mean hereby those first acts of the soul which are thus far involuntary as that they have not the actual [i. e., deliberately conscious] consent of the Will to them; *but are voluntary, as far as sin has its residence in the Will.* I know no greater burden in the life of a believer than these involuntary surprisals of the soul; involuntary, I say, as to the actual [i. e., deliberately conscious] consent of the Will, *but not so in respect of that corruption which is in the Will, and is the principle of them.*

Owen, Indwelling Sin, Chapter VI.

It will be apparent, from what has been said, that we regard the Arminian idea of the Will, and of self-determination, to be altogether inadequate to the purpose intended by it. The *motive* of this school, we are charitable enough to believe, was in many instances a good one. It desired to vindicate the ways of God to man — to make man responsible for his character — but it ended in the annihilation of all sin except that of volitions; of all sin except what is technically called *actual* sin, because its view of the Will was not profound enough. And as we wish to bring out into as clear a light as possible the difference between the Arminian self-determination, and what we suppose to be the true doctrine, let us for a moment exhibit the relation of both theories to "the doctrine of inability," as it is familiarly styled.

According to the Arminian school, the Will is merely the faculty of choices; and its action consists solely in volitions. Self-determination, consequently, is the ability to put forth a volition. Now, as a volition is confessedly under the arbitrary control of a man, it follows, that he has the ability to put forth (so-called) holy or sinful volitions at pleasure; and inasmuch as no deeper action of the Will than this volitionary action is recognized in the scheme, it follows, that he has the ability to be holy or sinful at pleasure. This is the "power to the contrary," which even sinful man has, although the more

Owen, in the above extract plainly distinguishes between voluntary and volitionary action: between the immanent self-determination of the *Voluntas*, and the deliberate and conscious ("actual") action of the *Arbitrium*. The old writers often denominate the disposition or nature in the Will, *activity*. Owen speaks of the Christian affections as the "*actings*" of the soul; e. g., "Christians are able to discern spiritual things, sweetly and genuinely to *act* faith, love, submission to God, and that in a high and eminent manner." (On Forgiveness Rule VI.). Edwards speaks of original sin as the "leading *act*, or inclination."

thoughtful portion of the school freely acknowledge that it is never exercised, as matter of fact, except under the co-operating influence of the Holy Spirit. This view of the Will, and of self-determination, then, teaches theoretically, at all events, the doctrine of man's ability to regenerate himself. There is no other action of the Will than that of single volitions, and over these man has arbitrary power.

But the true idea of the Will, and of self-determination, while bringing man in guilty for his sinful nature and conduct, forbids the attribution to him of a self-regenerating power. According to the Arminian theory, all the action of the Will consists of volitions, and one volition being as much within the power of the man as another, a succeeding volition can at any moment reverse and undo the preceding. But, according to what we suppose to be the true view of the Will, there is an action of this voluntary power far deeper, and consequently far less easily managed than that of single choices. We have spoken of a deep and central action of the Will, which consists in the determination and tendency of the *whole* soul and of the soul as a *whole*, and which results in the origination of an inclination, a disposition, a nature, in distinction from a volition, or a resolution. We have spoken of a movement in the voluntary power that carries the whole inward being along with it. Now it is plain that such a power as this — including so much, and running so deep — cannot, from the very nature of the case, be such a facile and easily managed power, as that by which we resolve to do some particular thing in every day life. While, therefore, we affirm that the Will, using the term in the comprehensive sense in which we have defined it, is a freely self-determined power, we deny, that having once taken its direction, it can reverse its motion by a volition or resolution. If the Will were *only* the faculty of choices or volitions, this might be the case; but that deep under current, that central self-determination, that great main tendency of the Will to self and sin as an ultimate end, cannot be reversed and overcome by any power less profound and central, to say the very least, than itself. Surface action cannot reverse and overcome central action. And we have only to take the Will as thus conceived, and steadily eye it in this free process of self-determination, to see that there is no power in this *central* tendency itself, from the very nature of the case, by which the direction of its movement can be altered. Take and hold the sinful Will of man, in this steady, this inmost, this total determination of itself to self as the ultimate end of its existence, and say how the power that is to reverse all this process can possibly come out of the Will, *thus shut up, and entirely swallowed, in the process.** How is the process to destroy itself, and turn into its own contrary? How is Satan to cast out Satan? Having once set itself, with *all* its energy, in a given direction, and towards a *final* end, the human Will becomes a current that is unmanageable — a power too strong for itself to turn back — not because of any com-

* The Will in the time of a *leading act or inclination* that is diverse from or opposite to the command of God, and when actually under the influence of it, *is not able to exert itself to the contrary*, to make an alteration in order to a compliance. The inclination *is unable to change itself:* and that for this plain reason that it is unable to *incline* to change itself. Present choice cannot at present choose to be otherwise: for that would be *at present* to choose something diverse from what is *at present* chosen. If the will, all things now considered, inclines or chooses to go that way, then it cannot choose, all things now considered, to go the other way, and so cannot choose to be made to go the other way. To suppose that the mind is now sincerely inclined to change itself to a different inclination, is to suppose the mind is now truly inclined otherwise than it is now inclined.

Edwards on the Will, Part III. Section 4.

pulsion or stress from without, be it observed, but simply because of its own momentum and comprehensiveness — simply because of the obstinate and all-engrossing energy with which it is perversely going in the contrary direction. For the *whole* Will is determined, if determined at all. The depravity is *total.* Consequently, when a tendency or determination, as distinguished from a volition, has been taken, there is no remainder of uncommitted power in reserve, (as it were behind the existing determination or tendency,) by which the present moral state of the Will can be reversed. For this determination or permanent state of the Will, as we have observed again and again, is something very different from a volition, which does not carry the *whole* soul along with it, and which therefore may be reversed by another volition back of it. When a determination has occurred, and a nature has been originated, the Will proper — the *whole* voluntary power — *is in for it;* and hence, in the case of sin, the bondage in the very seat of freedom — the absolute inability to be holy, springing out of, and identical with, the total determination to be evil — which is a self-determination.*

* This non-returning character of the will, is noticed by that subtlest and most spiritual of the Schoolmen, Anselm. Justo namque judicio Dei decretum erat, et quasi chirographo confirmatum, ut homo, qui sponte peccaverat, nec peccatum, nec poenam peccati, per se vitare posset; *est enim spiritus* (by which Anselm here means *voluntas*) *vadens, et non rediens;* et qui facit peccatum, *servus* est peccati.

Cur Deus Homo. Liber I. Cap. VII.

It may be briefly remarked here, that the whole controversy respecting original Sin has turned upon the conception of voluntary action held by the disputing parties. In the Latin anthropology, this was, simply and only, the power of *self*-determination. That which is *self*-moved is voluntary, by virtue of this bare fact of *self*-motion. Neither the presence nor the absence of a power to the contrary, can destroy the existing fact that the will is moving spontaneously and without external compulsion, and hence the

It will be seen, that according to this theory, the freedom of the Will does not consist in the ability to originate a holy or sinful nature at any instant, and according to the caprice of the individual. It does not consist in the ability to determine itself to good or evil, as an ultimate end of existence, with the same facility and agility with which single choices can be exercised. It does not consist in an ability to jerk over from one moral *state* of the will, into a contrary moral *state*, at any moment, by a violent or a resolute effort. The doctrine of the freedom of the Will does indeed require us to affirm that the Will is primarily and constantly *self*-moved — that its permanent tendency and character is not imposed upon it, as the tendency of the brute is imposed upon it, by the creative act; but the doctrine does not require us to affirm, that when the Will has once freely formed its character, and responsibly originated its nature, it can then, ad libitum, or by any power then possessed by it, form a contrary character, and originate an entirely contrary nature within itself. All that is to be claimed is, that at the initial point in the history of the human Will, a free and responsible start shall be taken, a self-determination shall begin and *continue*. It is not to be affirmed, for it contradicts the experience of every man who has had any valuable experience upon this subject, that there is power in the will to cross and re-cross from a sinful to a holy *state*, and back again, at any moment —

power to the contrary did not enter as a *sine qua non* into the Latin idea of moral agency. It might be lost, and actually had been, and the will still be a *self*-determined faculty. In the Greek anthropology, on the contrary, voluntariness was *in*determination. The will, whether fallen or unfallen, at all times and in all conditions, could either choose or refuse the same object. But that it might do so, it must be itself in a state of equilibrium or indifferency, and not actually *committed* or *determined* either one way or the other.

that the Will is in such an *indifferent* state in regard to the two great ultimate ends of action — God and self — that it stands affected in precisely the same way towards both, and by a volition can choose either at pleasure.

(2.) The foregoing statement, it is hoped, will be sufficient to exhibit, so far as the limits of an article will allow, what is conceived to be the true idea of the Will, and of self-determination, in distinction from the Arminian view of them. We turn now to the relation of original sin to Adam, the head and representative of the race of mankind. There is not space to examine the passages of Scripture which speak of the connection of the individual with Adam. We shall assume, that such a connection is plainly taught in Scripture, particularly in the 5th chapter of Romans; and at the same time barely call attention to the fact, that the soundest creeds of the Church, and that of the Westminster Assembly in particular, have all recognized the connection. Our object is to see if the views that have been presented will not throw some light upon one of the darkest points in speculative theology.

It will be recollected, that in the first part of this article, it was shown that the deepest and ultimate form of sin is below the sphere of consciousness — that we are not conscious of the sinful nature, but only of what proceeds from it. It will also be remembered, that this original sin, or sinful nature, has been traced to the Will as its originating cause, and thereby found to be a guilty nature. If, now, these two points have been made out, it follows as a corollary, that there is an action of the human Will deeper than the ordinary consciousness of man reaches. If man is not conscious of his sinful nature, and if, nevertheless, that nature is the product of his Will — is the very state of the Will itself — it follows, hat his Will can put forth an action of which he is not ;onscious. And if this be so, it furthermore follows, that listinct consciousness is not an indispensable condition o the origin and existence of sin and guilt in the human soul.

We are as well aware as any body, that a statement ike this seems to carry on the very face of it, not a mysery merely, but an absurdity. At first sight, it seems to e self-contradictory to affirm, that the responsible action f a free moral agent can go on in utter unconsciousness f the action — that the human Will can put forth its nost important action, (action the most criminal, and he most tremendous in its consequences,) in a sphere oo deep for the agent to know what he is doing. On he contrary, it seems to be plain as an axiom, that nowledge must in every instance precede action — that he Will cannot act without first distinctly knowing vhat it is going to do. And accordingly, this is the poition laid down in the beginning of all the current treaises on the Will.

Now, without entering into any process of ratiocinaion to support a mere theory, we wish to raise a simple uestion of fact. Is it, then, a fact, that man is conscious f all the action of his will? Is it a fact, that from the ommencement of his existence, on and down through very moment of his existence, he is unintermittently *selfonscious* of what he is all the while doing as a moral agent? Is it a fact, that the impenitent sinner — the *thoughtless* sinner, as we so often call him in our sermons — is *aware* every moment of what he is about? No man will pretend that such is the fact. Saying nothing in egard to that deeper action of the Will, which we have denominated its determination, no one will say that a man is distinctly conscious of all his volitions even. f each and every one of the millions of choices which he is exercising from the cradle to the grave. Even here, so near the surface of the soul, and with reference to its most palpable exercises, no one will be bold enough to affirm a distinct consciousness in every instance. Volition after volition, choice after choice, is exercised by the *unawakened, unanxious* sinner, with all the unconsciousness and mechanism, so to speak, with which the two thousand volitions by which he lifts his legs two thousand times in walking a single mile, are exercised.*

Take the first sinful man you meet, and say how much of his daily existence goes on within the sphere of self-consciousness. During how many moments of the day is this moral agent aware of what he is doing, as a moral agent? Of how many of the volitions which he puts forth in the attainment of his ends of living is he distinctly conscious? How many of his emotions are exercised in the clear light of self-consciousness, so that he has a distinct knowledge and sense of their moral character? Is it not safe to say, that whole days, it may be whole weeks, and it may be whole months, pass in the lives of many men, during which there is not a single instant of distinct consciousness, in regard to the nature of the agencies going on within their souls? And will it do to say, that all this while there is no action of the Will?

The truth is, we cannot lay aside pre-conceived opinions, and look at the simple facts of the case, without being compelled to the position, that there not only can be, but there actually is, action of the Will that is not

* That the action in this instance is voluntary, in the sense that the muscles and limbs are moved ultimately by acts of the choice, is proved by the fact, that the man can *stop* walking. If it were strictly mechanical and in voluntary, the walker must go on like a clock until his ambulatory appara tus ran down.

self-conscious action, and a vast amount of it. And this too, whether the Will be regarded as the volitionary or as the voluntary faculty. If we believe the Scripture doctrine, that man is evil *continually*, we must also believe, that the Will of man is in *continual* action — absorbed in an *uninterrupted* tendency and determination to self. The motion — the *κινήσις*, — is incessant. But we know from observation, and as a matter of fact, that man is not distinctly conscious of a thousandth part of this process, which is nevertheless steadily going on, whether he thinks of it or not, whether he is aware of it or not. If, now, while affirming, as we must, that there is no responsible action but action of the Will, we also affirm, as we must not, that there is no action of the Will but conscious action, we remove responsibility from the greater part of human life. Responsibility and criminality would, in this case, cleave only to that comparatively infinitesimal part of a man's life during which he sinned deliberately, and with the consciousness that he was sinning. Furthermore, it would follow, from this doctrine, that the more entire the man's absorption in evil — the more thoughtless and unconscious his life became in regard to sin — the less responsible he would be; the more depraved, the less guilty.

But in this instance again, as in a former, whatever may be our theory, we do practically acknowledge the truth of the doctrine of the responsible action of the human Will, even when there is, or has been, no distinct consciousness of it. The great aim of every awakening sermon that we preach, is to bring the sinner to the distinct perception of what he *is*, and *is doing*, as a free moral agent. And observe, the aim of the sermon is not simply to aid the memory of the sinner — to furnish him an inventory or catalogue of his past transgressions — but, in the strict meaning of the expressive phrase, *to bring him to* — *to bring him to himself.* The object of every awakening sermon, and the end had in view by the Holy Spirit when He sets it home, is to bring the sinner to a distinct self-consciousness in regard to sin — to make him realize the awful truth, that during his whole past life of thoughtlessness and unconsciousness of what he has been, and been about, his Will has been active, and that from the inmost centre to the outward circumference, this action has been criminal; and still more than this, to make him realize, that *now*, at this very instant, his Will is setting itself with a deep, and as yet to him, *unconscious* determination towards evil, as an ultimate end of action. The object of conviction, in short, is to impart to the sinner a conscious knowledge of that sin, the major part of which came into existence without his conscious knowledge, but by no means without his Will.

We need only take a passage that frequently occurs in the common Christian experience to see the truth of the view here presented. How often the Christian *finds* himself already in a train of thought, or of feeling, that is contrary to the divine law. Notice that he did not go into this train of thought or feeling deliberately, and with a distinct consciousness of what he was doing. The first he knows is, that he is already caught in the process. Thought and feeling in this instance have been *unconsciously* exercised in accordance with that central and abiding determination of the Will towards self, of which we have spoken; in other words, the Will has been *unconsciously* putting forth its action, in and through the powers of thought and feeling, as the self-reproach and sense of guilt consequent upon such exercises of the soul, are proof positive.* The moment the Christian man comes to distinct consciousness in regard to this action that has been going on, "without his thinking of it," (as we say in common parlance,) he acknowledges it as criminal action, responsible action, action of the Will. The fact that he was not thinking—that the Will was acting unconsciously—subtracts nothing from his sense of guilt in the case.

And if there is unconscious action of the Will in these instances, which occur in the every-day experience of the individual Christian, much more should we expect to find unconscious action in the case of that deepest and primal movement of the Will which is denominated the Fall. If, in the instance of the development or unfolding of sin, there is much of this unconscious voluntary action, much more should we expect to find it in that instance when the profound basis itself, for this development, was laid. If there is mystery in the stalk above ground, much more must we expect to find it in the dark long root under ground. The fall of the human Will unquestionably occurs back of consciousness, and in a region beyond the reach of it. Certainly no one of the posterity of Adam was ever conscious of that act whereby his Will fell from God; and even with regard to Adam himself, the remark of Augustine is true—that he had already fallen before he ate the forbidden fruit. This remark is strictly true, and characterized by those two traits in which Augustine never had a superior—depth and penetration. The act of conscious transgression in the case of Adam sprung from an evil

* It is evident that there may be thinking without *thinking* of thinking, as there may be acting without *thinking* of acting. In these instances there is both thought and action without self-consciousness of either.

nature that had already been unconsciously generated in his Will. He would not have eaten of the tree, if he had not in his soul already fallen from God.

We may, in this connection, add furthermore, that the other great change which occurs in the human Will — viz., its renovation by the Holy Spirit, and its determination to God as an ultimate end, consequent thereon — also occurs below the sphere of consciousness. All acknowledge that there is no consciousness of the regenerating act itself, but only of its consequences; and yet even the most careful theologian must acknowledge, that there is action of the Will of some sort in this instance; that the renovating action is in the Will and in accordance with its freedom, though by no means, as in the case of sin, to be referred solely to the Will.

Enough has been said to show, that, unless we would unclothe most of human existence of its responsibility, we must assume the possibility and reality of an action of the Will, which is unaccompanied by distinct consciousness on the part of the individual man. And this is eminently true of that deepest action of the Will, by which a nature is generated, and a character is originated. That action of the human Will, which is denominated its fall, which lies under the whole sinful history and development of the individual man — which is the ground and source of all his conscious transgression — is, without contradiction, unconscious action. The moral consciousness of man, taken at its very rise, is the consciousness of guilt — which fact shows that the responsible action, lying under it, as its just cause and valid ground, *has already occurred. If there is any guilt in falling from God, the human soul incurs that guilt in every instance, without distinct consciousness of the process by which it is brought about.* If the origination of a sinful nature—of an abiding wrong state of the Will—is a criminal procedure on the part of the soul, and justly exposes it to the Divine Anger, it is yet a procedure that occurs unconsciously to the soul itself. And in saying this, we are manufacturing no theory, but simply setting forth the simple actual facts of the case. There is no avoiding the conclusion, unless we are bold enough to affirm that only that portion of a sinner's life is responsible and guilty, during which he sins deliberately, and with the consciousness that he is sinning.

We have called attention to this fact, that the human Will can and does put forth its deepest action below the sphere of consciousness, to prepare the way for the investigation of the connection of original sin, as found in each individual, with the fall of Adam. If this hypothesis of the unconscious action of the Will has been established, the only serious objection will have been removed, that can be made to what we suppose is the Scriptural statement of the doctrine of the connection of the individual with Adam, contained in the Westminster Assembly's Catechism. According to the form of doctrine laid down by that body of profound and learned divines, each individual of the human race is supposed to have been in some way responsibly present in Adam, and responsibly sharing in his apostasy from God. The statement in the creed which they drew up, is as follows:—"The covenant being made with Adam, not only for himself but for his posterity, all mankind descending from him by ordinary generation *sinned in him and fell with him* in his first transgression." And the two strongest texts which they cite in proof of the truth of their creed, are these: "By one man's disobedience, many were made sinners." (Rom. 5: 19.) "In Adam all die." (1 Cor. 15: 22.)

Now it is to be remembered, that these men were making distinct and scientific statements, and their language, consequently, is not to be regarded as merely metaphorical. It must, therefore, be understood in the same way that scientific language is always to be understood — be taken in its literal meaning, unless a palpable contradiction or absurdity is involved in so doing. In this doctrinal and scientific statement, then, it is affirmed, that all men sinned in Adam, and fell with Adam in his first transgression. This implies and teaches that all men were, in some sense, co-existent in Adam, otherwise they could not have sinned *in* him. It teaches that all men were, in some sense, co-agent in Adam, otherwise they could not have fallen *with* him. The mode of this co-existence and co-agency of the whole human race in the first man, they do not, it is true, attempt to set forth; but their language distinctly implies that they believed there was such a co-existence and co-agency, whether it could be explained or not. They regarded Adam not merely as an individual, but as a common person; as having a generic as well as individual character. They taught that he was substantially the race of mankind, and that his whole posterity existed in him. Consequently, whatever befell Adam, befell the race. In Adam's fall, the race fell. And what is to be particularly noted is, that they did not regard the fall of Adam considered as an individual, as any more guilty than the fall of each and every one of his posterity, or that original sin was any the less guilt in his posterity than it was in him. So far as responsibility was concerned, Adam and his posterity were all *alike* guilty of apostasy. They were all involved in a common condemnation, because they were all *alike* concurrent in the fall. The *race* fell in Adam, and consequently each individual of the race was in some mysterious yet real manner, existent in this common parent of all.*

* This phraseology is not to be understood as implying that the individual is in the genus *as a distinct individual*. Adam, as the generic man, was not a mere receptacle containing millions of separate individuals. The genus is not an aggregation, but a single, simple, essence. *As such*, it is not yet characterized by individuality. It, however, *becomes* varied and manifold by being individualized *in its propagation, or development into a series*. The individual consequently (with the exception of the first man, who is immediately created, and is both individual and generic) is always the result of propagation, and not of creation. In the instance of man, the creation proper is the origination of the generic species, which species is individualized in its propagation under the preserving, and providential, (but not now creating,) agency of the Creator. The individual, *as such*, is consequently only a subsequent *modus existendi;* the first and antecedent mode being the generic humanity, of which this subsequent serial mode is only another *aspect* or manifestation. Had the members of the series of human generations existed *in their proper individuality* in the progenitor, there would have been no need of the subsequent process of *individualization*, or propagation.

The doctrine of *Traducianism* is unquestionably more accordant with that of original sin than that of *Creationism*, and the only reason why Augustine, and others after him, hesitated with regard to its *formal* adoption, was its supposed incompatibility with the doctrine of the soul's immateriality and immortality. If, however, the distinction between creation and development be clearly conceived and rigorously observed, it will be seen that there is no danger of materialism in the doctrine of the soul's propagation. For development cannot change the essence of that which is being developed. It must unfold that, and only that, which is given in creation. Now, granting the creation of the generic man *in his totality of soul and body*, it is plain that his mere individualization by propagation must leave both his physical and spiritual natures as it found them, so far as this distinction between mind and matter is concerned. For matter cannot be converted into mind by mere expansion, and neither can mind be changed into matter by it. Both parts of man will, therefore, preserve their original created qualities and characteristics in this process of propagation, or individualizing of the generic, which is conducted, moreover, beneath the preserving and providential agency of the Creator. That which is flesh will be propagated *as flesh*, and that which is spirit will be propagated *as spirit;* and this because mere propagation, or development, cannot *change the kind or essence*. If, therefore, it is conceded that the *creation* of man was com-

It is on this ground that they taught that original sin is real sin — is guilt. The sinful nature they held, could be properly charged upon every child of Adam, as a nature for which he, and not his Creator, was responsible, and which rendered him obnoxious to the eternal displeasure of God — even though, as in the case of infants dying before the dawn of self-consciousness, this nature should never have manifested itself in conscious transgression. Every child of Adam fell from God, in Adam, and together with Adam, and therefore is justly chargeable with all that Adam is chargeable with, and precisely on the same ground, viz., on the ground that his fall was not necessitated, but self-determined. For the Will of Adam was not the Will of a single isolated individual merely: it was also, and besides this, the Will of the human species — the human Will generically. If he fell freely, so did his posterity — yet not one after another, and each by himself, as the series of individuals, in which the one seminal human nature manifests itself, were born into the world, but all together and all at once, in that first transgression, which stands a most awful and awfully pregnant event at the beginning of human history.

The aim of the Westminster symbol accordingly, and, it may be added, of all the creeds on the Augustinian side of the controversy, was to combine two elements, each having truth in it — to teach the fall of the human race as a unity, and, at the same time, recognize the existence, freedom, and guilt of the individual in the fall. Accordingly they locate the individual in Adam, and

plete, involving the origination from non-entity of the *entire* humanity as a synthesis of matter and mind, flesh and spirit, then it follows that mere propagation, taking him up at this point, cannot change the essence upon either side of the complex being, but can only individualize it.

make him, in some mysterious but real manner, a responsible partaker in Adam's sin — a guilty sharer, and, in some solid sense of the word, *co-agent* in a common apostasy. As proof of this assertion, we shall quote from a few of the leading authors on this side of the great controversy.

Augustine, although the first to philosophize upon this difficult point, in order to bring it within the limits of a doctrinal system, has, nevertheless, as it seems to us, not been excelled by any of his successors in the profundity and comprehensiveness of his views. He is explicit in teaching the oneness of the human race in Adam, and of the fall of Adam and his posterity in the first transgression. In his work on the desert and remission of sin, he says: "All men at that time sinned in Adam, since, in his nature, all men were as yet that one man." * And the sentiment is repeated still more distinctly in that most elaborate of his treatises — De Civitate Dei; a work which was the fruit of mature reason, and ripe Christian experience, and which, notwithstanding the crudity of some of its speculations on subjects pertaining to the sensuous nature of man, and to the physical nature generally, is unrivalled for the depth and clearness of its insight into all that is distinctively and purely spiritual. "We were all *in* that one man, since we *were* all that one man, who lapsed into sin through that woman, who was made from him previous to transgression. *The form in which we were to live as individuals had not been created and assigned to us, man by man*, but that seminal nature was in existence, from which we were to be propagated." † In the words of Neander,

* In Adamo omnes tunc peccaverunt, quando in ejus natura adhuc omnes ille unus fuerunt. — De pec. mer. et rem. III. 7.

† Omnes enim fuimus in illo uno, quando omnes fuimus ille unus, qui

"Augustine, supposed not only that that bondage, under the principle of sin, by which sin is its own punishment, was transmitted by the progenitor of the human race to his posterity; but also that the first transgression, as an act, was to be imputed to the whole human race—that the guilt and the penalty were propagated from one to all. This participation of all in Adam's transgression, Augustine made clear to his own mind in this way: Adam was the representative of the whole race, and bore in himself the entire human nature and kind, in germ, since it was from him that it unfolded itself. And this theory would easily blend with Augustine's speculative form of thought, as he had appropriated to himself the Platonico-Aristotelian realism, in the doctrine of general conceptions, *and conceived of general conceptions as the original types of the kind realized in individual things*."*

Calvin, though not so explicit as his predecessor Augustine, or as some of his successors, in regard to the precise nature of the individual's connection with Adam, yet leaves no doubt in the mind of the reader that he believed in the original oneness of Adam and his posterity, in the act of apostasy. He says: "It is certain that Adam was not only the progenitor, but, as it were, the root of mankind, and therefore all the race were necessarily vitiated in his corruption." Again he says: "He who pronounces that we were all dead in Adam, does also, at the same time, plainly declare that we were implicated in the guilt of his sin. For no condemnation could

per feminam lapsus est in peccatum, quæ de illo facta est ante peccatum. Nondum erat nobis singillatim creata et distributa forma, in qua singuli viveremus; sed jam natura erat seminalis ex qua propagaremur.—De Civ Dei. XIII. 14.

* Torrey's Neander, II. 609.

each those who were perfectly clear from all charge of niquity," [as Adam's posterity would be, were each and very man merely a distinct and isolated individual, exsting entirely by himself.] Again he says: "No other xplanation, therefore, can be given of our being said to e in Adam, than that his transgression not only procurd misery and ruin for himself, but also precipitated our ature into similar destruction; and that not by his personal guilt as an individual, which pertains not to us, out because he infected all his descendants with the coruption into which he had fallen."*

John Owen is more explicit still, and he unquestionably reflects the views of the Westminster divines, to say nothing of his general profundity and clearness on all points of systematic theology. In his treatise, entitled "A Display of Arminianism,"† in connection with some other answers to the objection that original sin is not voluntary, and therefore cannot be sin in the sense of guilt, he expressly affirms that it *is* voluntary, in some sense of that word — that it has the element of free self-determination in it. "But, thirdly," he says, "in respect to our wills, we are not thus innocent neither, for we all sinned in Adam, as the apostle affirmeth. Now all sin is voluntary, say the remonstrants, [the party whom Owen was opposing, but whose statement in this case he was willing to grant,] and therefore Adam's transgression was our voluntary sin also, and that in divers respects; *first*, in that his voluntary act is imputed to us as ours, by reason of the covenant which was made with him in our behalf; but because this consisting in an imputation, must needs be extrinsical to us; therefore, *secondly*, we

* Institutes, Book II. Chapter 1. Allen's Trans.

† Works, V. 127. Russell's Ed.

say that Adam, being the root and head of all human kind, and we all branches from that root, all parts of that body whereof he was the head, his will may be said to be ours; we were then all that one man, (omnes eramus unus ille homo, Aug.,) we were all in him, and had no other will but his; so that though that (viz., Adam's will) be extrinsical unto us, considered as particular persons, yet it (viz., Adam's will) is intrinsical, as we are all parts of one common nature; as in him we sinned, so in him we had a will of sinning." In a passage in his "Vindiciæ Evangelicæ,"* he also says, "By Adam sin entered into the world, so that all sinned in him, and are made sinners thereby — so that also his sin is called the 'sin of the world;' in him all mankind sinned, and his sin is imputed to them."†

* Works, VIII. p. 222. Russell's Ed.

† This same reasoning, from the basis of realism, is seen in John Robinson, the pastor of the Plymouth Pilgrims. In his "Defence of the doctrine of the Synod of Dort," he answers the question, Did infants sin in Adam? — in the affirmative, on the ground that they "had being in Adam after a sort, namely, so far as they were in him. If they had being in Adam any way, they had life also in him; for nothing in Adam was dead, but all living; their being, therefore, so far as it was in him, was a living being." This 'being,' Robinson goes on to argue, was that of a rational existence composed of understanding and will. — Robinson's Works, I. 404 et seq. Congregational Board's Ed.

Leigh, a graduate of Magdalen Hall, Oxford, published a system of divinity in 1654, which has the *imprimatur* of Edmund Calamy. In it we find the following:

"The first Adam represented all mankind, and the second all the elect. *God might as well ground an imputation on a natural, as on a mystical, union Omnes eramus unus ille homo.* (Augustine); therefore the sin of that one man is the sin of us all.

"*Objection.* This sin of Adam, being but one, could not defile the universal nature. *Socinus.*

"*Answer.* Adam had in him the whole nature of mankind, 1 Cor. 15: 47; by one offence the whole nature of man was defiled, Rom. 5: 12, 17.

"*Objection.* Adam's sin was not voluntary in us, we never gave consent to it.

"*Answer.* There is a two-fold will. 1. *Voluntas naturae*, the whole nature

One more quotation shall suffice, in corroboration of the view presented of the oneness of Adam and his posterity, in respect both to the act and the guilt of apostasy, and this shall be from Jonathan Edwards. In his treatise upon original sin, after citing the passage, "By one man sin entered into the world," he adds, "this passage implies that sin became *universal* in the world, and not merely (which would be a trifling insignificant assertion) that one man, who was made first, sinned first, be-

of man was represented in Adam, therefore the will of nature was sufficient to convey the sin of nature. 2. *Voluntas personae*, by every actual sin we justify Adam's breach of covenant. Rom. 5 : 12, 19 seems clear for the imputation of Adam's sin. All were in Adam, and sinned in him, as, after Augustine, Beza doth interpret ἐφ' ᾧ in Rom. 5 : 12; and so our last translators in the margent. And though it be rendered, 'for that all have sinned,' by us, the Syriac, Erasmus, Vatablus, Calvin, and Piscatorius, *yet must it be so understood that all have sinned in Adam. For otherwise, it is not true that all upon whom death hath passed have sinned, as namely infants newly born.* It is not said *all are sinners*, but, all *have sinned*, which imports an imputation of Adam's *act* unto his posterity.

"Some divines do not differ so much *re* as *modo loquendi* about this point. They grant the imputation of Adam's sin to his posterity, in some sense, so as that there is a communication of it with them, and the guilt is charged upon them, yet they deny the imputation of it to posterity as it was Adams's personal sin. But it is not to be considered as Adam's personal sin, but as the sin of all mankind, whose person Adam did then represent. Adam's personal sin did infect the whole nature, and ever since the nature hath infected the personal actions."—Leigh's Body of Divinity, Book IV. Chap. 1.

"The whole history of the first man evinces, that he was not looked upon as an individual person, but that the whole human nature was considered in him. For it was not said to our first parents only, *Increase and multiply;* by virtue of which words the propagation of the human race is still continued; nor is it true of Adam only, *It is not good that man should be alone;* nor does that conjugal law concern him alone, *Therefore shall a man leave his father and his mother, and these two shall be one flesh;* which Christ still urges (Mt. 19 : 5); nor did the penalty, which God threatened to Adam in case of sin, affect him alone, *Dying thou shalt die;* but *death passed upon all men*, as the Apostle observes. All which loudly proclaim, that Adam was here considered as the head of mankind." — Witsius on the Covenants, II. 14.

fore other men sinned; or that it did not so happen that many men began to sin just together at the same moment." "The latter part of the verse" (he goes on to say) 'and death by sin, and so death passed upon all men, for that all have sinned,' shows that in the eye of the Judge of the world, in Adam's first sin *all* sinned; not only *in some sort*, but all sinned *so* as to be exposed to that *death* and final destruction, which is the proper *wages of sin*."* In another chapter of this treatise he combats the objection made against the imputation of Adam's sin to his posterity "that such imputation is unjust and unreasonable, inasmuch as Adam and his posterity are not one and the same," (one of the principal objections to the doctrine, and a fatal one, if it can maintained). He combats it by denying the truth of the affirmation, that Adam and his posterity are not one and the same, and by establishing the contrary position by as profound and truthful a course of speculation as ever emanated from his mind. "I think," (he says) "it would go far towards directing us to the more clear and distinct conceiving and right stating of this affair, (of original sin,) were we steadily to bear this in mind: that God, in each step of his proceeding with Adam, in relation to the covenant or constitution established with him, looked on his posterity as being *one with him*. * * * Therefore, I am humbly of opinion, that if any have supposed the children of Adam to come into the world with a *double guilt:* one, the guilt of Adam's sin; another, the guilt arising from their having a corrupt heart, they have not so well conceived of the matter. The *guilt* a man has on his soul at his first existence is one and simple, viz., the guilt of the original apostasy, the guilt of the sin by

* The italics are Edwards's, and the italics of Edwards are always significant.

which the species first rebelled from God. * * The *first existing* of a corrupt disposition in the hearts of Adam's posterity is not to be looked upon as sin belonging to them, *distinct* from their participation of Adam's first sin: it is, as it were, the *extended pollution* of that sin, through the whole tree, by virtue of the constituted *union* of the branches with the root; or the *inherence* of the sin of that head of the species in the members, in the consent and concurrence of the hearts of the members, with the head in that first act." Edwards also quotes with approbation the following from Stapfer: "It is objected against the imputation of Adam's sin, that we never committed the same sin with Adam, neither in number nor in kind. I answer, we should distinguish here between the physical act itself, which Adam committed, and the morality of the action and consent to it. If we have respect only to the external act, to be sure it must be confessed that Adam's posterity did not put forth their hands to the forbidden fruit: in which sense that act of transgression, and that fall of Adam, cannot be physically one with the sin of his posterity. But if we consider the morality of the action, [*i. e.* the voluntary ground of it,] and what consent there is to it, it is altogether to be maintained that his posterity committed the same sin both in number and in kind, inasmuch as they are to be looked upon as consenting to it; for where there is a consent to a sin, there the same sin is committed. Seeing, therefore, that Adam, with all his posterity, constitute but one moral person, and are united in the same covenant, and are transgressors of the same law, they are also to be looked upon as having, in a moral estimation, committed the same transgression of the law both in manner and in kind." Edwards finally remarks, that all the objections that can be brought against the doctrine of the imputation of Adam's sin to his posterity, are summed up in this assumption and assertion — viz., that Adam and his posterity are *not originally one*, but are from first to last entirely *distinct and individual agents:* this assumption he earnestly denies, and enters into a long and subtle investigation, well worthy any man's study, of what is meant by personal identity, to show that there is no absurdity or contradiction in the hypothesis, that, by the divine establishment and constitution, all of Adam's posterity were, in some real and important sense, in him and one with him.*

Any one who will take the pains to study the history of the doctrine of original sin, and to trace its development, will find that the more profound minds in the Christian church have ever sought to relieve the subject of those difficulties which encompass it, by this doctrine of the oneness of Adam with his posterity. A mystery overhangs, and, perhaps, ever must overhang the nature and possibility of this oneness; but this mystery being once waived, or put up with by the mind, the principal difficulties that beset the doctrine of a sinful nature originated antecedently to all consciousness, and beginning to manifest itself in the case of every individual with the first dawn of self-consciousness, disappear. Granting the possibility and the fact of the individual's fall in Adam and with Adam, then it is easy to see how this fall can be charged as guilt upon the individual, and the sinful nature be truly and really a self-determined and responsible nature, deserving and incurring the wrath of God. Original sin, by this hypothesis, is seen to be the work of the creature, and not the Creator, the chief peculiarity in this case being, that it was originated by the

* Edwards on Original Sin. Part IV. Chap. 3.

whole race, and for the whole race, *not as it exists in the historical series of its individual members, but as it existed a seminal and common nature in the first man.*

With regard to the possibility of such a co-existence of Adam and his posterity, little can be said, although the more the mind reflects upon the subject, the less surprising does it seem. One thing is certain, that the mysteriousness of the subject has not deterred the human mind from receiving the doctrine. We see the clearest and deepest minds of the church, men of unquestioned intellectual power, and of profound insight into their own hearts, drawn, as by a spell, to this hypothesis, as the best theory by which to free the doctrine of original sin from its principal difficulties: and this fact of itself constitutes a strong ground for the belief that the truth lies in this direction.

1. We would merely call attention, however, to the fact, that the doctrine of the oneness and co-existence of the race in the first man, by no means contradicts what we know from physiology, but rather finds a corroboration from it. When the first individuals of a new species are created out of nothing by the Creator of all things, the *species*, as well as these individuals, is created. The remaining individuals of the species — the posterity of the first pair — do not come into existence each by a new fiat, like that which called the first into being, but by a propagation. The primordial elements of all the individuals of the series are created, when the first pair of the species is created, and then are developed into a series of individuals. Any catastrophe, therefore, any radical change that befalls these first individuals, affects the whole species, and in precisely the same way. If that science, whose business it is to investigate the nature and mutual relations of the species and the individual,

and to give an account of the development of the creation of God, teaches anything, it teaches this.

2. The other principal objection — that the individual was never conscious of this fall in Adam — has been removed by what has been advanced in regard to the possibility of a voluntary action that is deeper than consciousness. If there can be, and actually is, action of the human Will, unaccompanied by self-consciousness, then it is not absurd or self-contradictory to affirm that the Will of the whole species, generically including the Will of every individual within it, fell in the first man.

The doctrine of original sin, then, as stated in the Westminster Catechism taken in its strict and literal acceptation, we deem to be in accordance with the teaching of Scripture on this subject. Only put up with the inexplicability of the oneness, and co-existence, of Adam and his posterity — only grant this assumption, which all the analogies in the world of physical nature, and all the investigations of physiology, yet seem to corroborate — and we can hold to a sinful nature, and a sinful nature that is guilt. We know of no other theory that does not in the end, either reduce sin to a minimum, by recognizing no sin but that of single volitions, or else, while asserting a sinful nature, does it at the expense of human freedom and responsibility. And surely a theory which removes the real and honest difficulties that cling to one of the most vexed questions in theology, ought not to be rejected merely on the ground of a mystery that attaches to one of its parts. Manifest absurdity and self-contradiction would be the only valid grounds for rejecting it; and these, we think, cannot be fixed upon it.

In conclusion, we would say, that we cannot think, with some, that such speculations into a difficult doctrine like that of original sin, are valueless — that they merely baffle the mind and harden the heart. We rise from this investigation with a more profound belief than ever, in the doctrine of the innate and total depravity of man — of his bondage to evil, and his guilt in this bondage. It is only when we turn away our eye from the particular exhibitions of sin to that evil nature that lies under them all, and lies under them all the while — it is only when we turn away from what we *do* to what we *are* — that we become filled with that deep sense of guilt, that profound self-abasement, before the infinite purity of God, and that utter self-despair, which alone fit us to be the subjects of renewing and sanctifying grace. If the church and the ministry of the present day need any one thing more than another, it is profound views of sin; and if the current theology of the day is lacking in any one thing, it is in that thorough-going, that truly philosophic, and, at the same time, truly edifying theory of sin, which runs like a strong muscular cord through all the soundest theology of the church.

THE ATONEMENT, A SATISFACTION FOR THE ETHICAL NATURE OF BOTH GOD AND MAN.*

It is a very important question whether, in the reconciliation of man with God, the change of feeling and relationship that confessedly occurs between the parties, is solely upon the side of man, or whether that method which proposes to bring about peace and harmony between the sinner and his Judge, contains a provision that refers immediately to the being and ethical nature of God. Is the Divine Essence absolutely passive, and entirely unaffected by the propitiatory death of Christ, and is all the movement and affection that occurs confined to human nature; or is there in the Godhead itself, by virtue of its essential nature and quality, something that requires a judicial satisfaction for sin, and which, when satisfied, produces the specific *sense* of satisfaction, or, to use a biblical term, of "propitiation," in the Deity himself? In short, is the reconciliation of man with God merely and wholly subjective, an occurrence in the human soul but no real event and fact in the Divine Mind? Is the sinner merely reconciled to God, God remaining precisely the same towards him that He is irrespective of the work of Christ, and antecedent to his appropriation of that work; or does God first, by and

* Reprinted from the Bibliotheca Sacra, Oct. 1859.

through a judicial infliction of his own providing, and his own enduring in the person of the Son, — Himself the judge, Himself the priest, Himself the sacrifice, — conciliate his own holy justice towards the guilty, and thereby lay the foundation for the *consciousness* of reconciliation in the penitent?*

The phraseology of scripture teaches, beyond a doubt, that the transaction of reconciliation is not confined exclusively to human nature. We are told, for example, by the apostle John, that "Jesus Christ the righteous is the *propitiation* for our sins."† Propitiation is the strong word employed to denote the real nature of Christ's work by that mild and loving apostle whose intuition of Christianity some biblical critics would array against that of Paul, and in whose writings they profess to find only the doctrine of spiritual life and sanctification, and not that of expiation and justification. But this term certainly implies two parties, — an offending and an

* That God, in the work of atonement, is both the first cause and last end, or, in other words, at once the propitiating and the offended party, is plainly taught in such texts as 2 Cor. v. 18, and Coloss. i. 20: "God hath reconciled us to *Himself*, by Jesus Christ. It pleased God . . . by Christ to reconcile all things to *Himself*, having made peace through the blood of his cross." *Augustine* notices this fact in the following manner: "How hast Thou loved us, for whom He that thought it no robbery to be equal with Thee, was made subject even to the death of the cross, He alone, free among the dead, having power to lay down His life, and power to take it again; for us, to Thee, *both victor and victim*, and therefore victor because the victim; for us, to Thee, *both priest and sacrifice*, and therefore priest because the sacrifice." — Confessions, X. xliii. 69. The same thought is expressed in a very dense and comprehensive form by *John Wessel*, one of the forerunners of the Reformation: "Ipse deus, ipse sacerdos, ipse hostia, pro se, de se, sibi satisfecit." — De causis incarnationis, c. 17. And *Pascal* makes a similar remark in his fragmentary reflections: "Agnus occisus est ab origine mundi. The judge himself is the sacrifice." — Thoughts, London Ed. by Pearce, p. 255.

† 1 John ii. 2.

offended one. "A mediator," argues Paul, in his Epistle to the Galatians, "is not a mediator of one;" that is, in order to mediation, there must be two persons between whom to mediate. In like manner, propitiation implies that one being has wakened the just displeasure of another being, and that the latter needs to be placated by some valid and satisfactory method. Propitiation, therefore, — an idea that weaves the warp and weaves the woof of the entire scriptures, — if it has any solid signification, looks Godward.* God, and not man, is the party primarily offended by sin. It is *his* nature which requires the propitiatory sacrifice, and he himself provides it. "Since, in his crucifixion," says John Howe, "Christ was a sacrifice, that is, was placatory and reconciling, and since reconciliations are always mutual, of both the contending parties to one another, it must have the proper influence of a sacrifice immediately upon *both*, and as well mollify men's hearts towards God, as *procure that he should express favorable inclinations towards them.*" †

Another very pointed scripture text, from which we

* This is very apparent when we analyze those words in different languages which bring to view the relation of sinful man to the Supreme Being. The primary meaning always implies that the *Deity* is displacent, and it is only the secondary signification that refers to the creature. The word *ἱλάσκομαι*, for example, in Homer, is always objective in its signification when applied to the gods. Ἱλάσκεσθαι θεόν primarily means to appease God, to produce a favorable feeling or affection in God, and then in a secondary sense to reconcile oneself to him, to attain a peaceful feeling subjectively. The Saxon *bot* (whence the modern boot) signifies a compensation paid to an *injured* party, a redressing, recompense, amends, satisfaction, offering; then a remedy or cure, effected by such compensation; and *lastly*, a *repentance, renewing, restoring*, wrought out by means of boot or satisfaction given. In this way repentance is inseparable from atonement; and its genuineness is evinced by the cordiality with which judicial satisfaction is rendered, if it can be, or appropriated as rendered by a substitute, in case it cannot be.

† Living Temple, Pt. II. c. 5. (Vol. I. p. 81. New York Ed.).

cannot deduce anything but the doctrine of a real satisfaction of the Divine Nature by the work of Christ, is the declaration of Paul, that "if while we were yet [impenitent] sinners Christ died for us, much more, then, being now justified by his blood we shall be *saved from wrath* through him."* *Whose* wrath is this, from which, the apostle teaches, we are saved by the propitiatory death of Christ? Is it the wrath of man, and not the wrath of God? Most certainly it is not from that selfish and wicked passion in the human heart, which we most commonly associate with the term *anger*, that we are delivered by the blood of redemption. But may it not be our own moral indignation *merely*, and not that of our Creator and Judge, to which the apostle refers? May not the appeasing effect of Christ's blood of expiation be confined to the human conscience solely, and there be no actual pacification of any attribute or feeling in the Deity? But this is only a part of the truth. We do, indeed, need to be saved from the terrible wrath and remorse of our own consciences, as they bite back (*remordere*) upon us after the commission of sin, — and of this we shall speak in its place, — but we need primarily to be saved from the judicial displeasure of that immaculate Spirit, in whose character and ethical feeling towards sin the human conscience itself has its eternal ground and authority, and of which it is the most sensitive index and measure.

The natural teaching, then, of these and similar passages of scripture is, that the atoning sacrifice of the God-man renders, "*propitious*" towards the transgressor, that particular side of the Divine Nature, and that one specific emotion of the living God, which other-

* Romans, v. 8, 9.

wise and without it is displacent and unappeased. This atonement is a satisfaction for the ethical nature of God as well as man. This propitiation sustains an immediate relation to an attribute and quality in the Divine Essence, and exerts a specific influence upon it. By it God's holy justice and moral anger against sin are conciliated to guilty man, that man's remorseful conscience may, as a consequence of this pacification in the Divine Essence, experience the peace that passeth all understanding. It will therefore be the purpose of this Essay to evince that the piacular work of the incarnate Deity sustains relations to *both* the nature of God and the nature of man; and more particularly to show that the pacification of the human conscience itself is possible only in case there has been an antecedent propitiation and satisfaction of that side of the Divine Nature which is the deep and eternal ground of conscience.

Before commencing the discussion, we would in the very outset guard against a misconception, which almost uniformly arises in a certain class of minds, and which is not only incompatible with any just understanding of the doctrine of atonement, but prevents even a dispassionate and candid attention to it. When it is asserted that "God requires to be propitiated," and that " his wrath needs to be averted by a judicial infliction upon the sinner's substitute," the image immediately arises before such minds of an enraged and ugly demon, whose wrath is *wrong*, and who must be pacified by some *other* being than himself. Such minds labor under a twofold error, of which they ought to be disabused. Their first fatal misconception is, that the Divine anger is selfish and vindictive, instead of just and vindicative of law. And their second consists in their assumption that the placation issues from some other source than the offended One himself. Assuming, as they do, that anger in God is illegitimate, the attribution of this emotion to him, of course undeifies him. And assuming, still further, that wrath against the sinner's *sin* cannot exist at the same instant with compassion towards the sinner's *soul*, they find no pity in the Deity as thus defined. His sole emotion must be that of wrath, because, as they imagine, He can have but one feeling at a time, and therefore the creature who has incurred God's displeasure must look elsewhere than to God for the source of hope and peace.

Now this whole view overlooks the complex nature, the infinite plenitude, of the Godhead. For at the very instant when the immaculate holiness of God is burning with intensity, and reacting by an organic recoil against sin,* the infinite pity of God is yearning with a fathomless desire to save the transgressor from *the effects of this very displeasure.* The emotion of anger against sin is constitutional to the Deity, and is irrepressible at the sight of sin. But this is entirely compatible with the existence and exercise of another and opposite feeling, at the very same moment, in reference, not indeed to the sin, but to the *soul* of the sinner.† Mercy and

* The inspired words that express the emotion of displacency in the Divine Being are startling from their energy and vividness. The primary sensuous meaning, or the visual image called up by them, illustrates this. The verb זָעַם, employed in Ps. vii. 11, signifies *to foam at the mouth*; the verb קָצַף means to *cut up*, or *break up, into pieces*; the verb אָנַף signifies *to breathe hard through the distended nostrils*; etc. Does not the application of such words as these to the emotions of the Deity imply an inspiration that includes phraseology as well as ideas? Would an uninspired writer venture upon such diction in such a connection?

† The two emotions of which we are speaking, are clearly discriminated from each other by the fact that one of them is constitutional, and the other

truth meet *together*, righteousness and peace kiss each other, in the Divine Essence; and it is a mutilated and meagre conception of the Godhead that can grasp but one of these opposites at once. Even within the narrow and imperfect sphere of human life there may be, and were man holier, there often would be, the most holy and unselfish indignation at wrong doing, united with the utmost readiness to suffer and die if need be for the eternal welfare of the wrong doer.

Such being the actual relation of indignation to com-

voluntary. The Divine wrath (ὀργὴ Θεοῦ, Rom. i. 18), issues from the necessary antagonism between the pure essence of the Godhead, and moral evil. It is, therefore, natural, organic, necessary, and eternal. The logical idea of the Holy implies it. But the love of benevolence, or the Divine compassion, issues from the voluntary disposition of God, — from his heart and affections. It is good-*will*. It is, consequently, easy to see that the existence of the constitutional emotion is perfectly compatible with that of the voluntary, in one and the same being, and at one and the same moment; and, in God, from all eternity, since he is unchangeable. Says *Augustine* (Tractatus in Joannem, 110): "It is written, 'God commendeth his love towards us, in that, while we were yet sinners, Christ died for us' (Rom. v. 8). He loved us, therefore, even when, in the exercise of enmity against him, we were working iniquity. And yet it is said with perfect truth: 'Thou hatest, O Lord, all workers of iniquity' (Ps. v. 5). Wherefore, in a wonderful and divine manner, *he both hated and loved us at the same time.* He hated us, as being different from what he had made us; but as our iniquity had not entirely destroyed his work in us, he could at the same time, in every one of us, hate what we had *done* and love what he had *created* In every instance it is truly said of God: 'Thou hatest nothing which thou hast made; for never wouldest thou have made anything, if thou hadst hated it' (Wisdom xi. 24)." *Calvin*, after quoting the above from Augustine, remarks (Institutes II. xvi. 3): "God, who is the perfection of righteousness, cannot love iniquity, which he beholds in us all. We all, therefore, have in us that which deserves God's hatred. Wherefore, in respect to our corrupt nature, and the succeeding depravity of our lives, we are all really offensive to God, guilty in his sight, and born to the damnation of hell. But because the Lord will not lose in us that which is his own, he yet discovers something that his goodness may love. For notwithstanding we are *sinners* through our own fault, yet we are still his *creatures;* notwithstanding we have brought death upon ourselves, yet he had created us for life."

passion in the Divine Essence, it is plain that it is God himself that propitiates himself to the transgressor. In the *incarnate* person of the Son, God voluntarily endures the weight of his own judicial displeasure, in order that the real criminal may be spared. The Divine compassion itself bears the inflictions of the Divine indignation, in the place of the transgressor.* That ethical emotion in the being of God, which from the nature and necessity of the case is incensed against sin, God himself placates by a personal self-sacrifice that inures to the benefit of the creature, The "propitiation" spoken of by the apostle John is, therefore, no oblation *ab extra*, no device of a third party, or even of man himself, to render God placable towards man. It is wholly *ab intra*, a *self*-oblation upon the part of Deity itself, by which to satisfy those immanent and eternal imperatives of the Divine Nature which without it must find their satisfaction in the punishment of the transgressor, or else be outraged. Neither does the purpose to employ this method of salvation, to provide this satisfaction of ethical and judicial claims, originate outside of the Divine Nature. God is inherently willing to forgive; and there is no proof of this so strong as the fact, that he does not shrink from this amazing *self*-sacrifice which forgiveness necessitates. The desire to save his transgressing and guilty creature wells up and overflows from the depths of his own compassionate

* In all these statements we would be understood as making them in harmony with, and subject to, all the limitations of the catholic doctrine of the two natures in the one Person of Christ. The Divine Nature, in itself, is impassible; but we have scriptural warrant in Acts xx. 28, for saying that God *incarnate*, or the *God-Man*, is passible, and suffers and dies. Hence, while there can be no transfer of predicates from one *nature* to the other, the predicates of both natures alike belong to the *Person*, and that Person is God as well as man.

heart, and needs no soliciting or prompting from without. Side by side in the Godhead, then, there dwell the impulse to punish and the desire to pardon ; but the desire to pardon is realized in act, by *carrying out* the impulse to punish, not indeed upon the person of the criminal, but upon that of his substitute. And the substitute is the Punisher Himself! Side by side in the Godhead there reside the emotion of moral wrath and the feeling of pity; but the feeling of pity is manifested, not by denying, but by asserting, the entire legitimacy of the emotion of moral wrath, and "propitiating" its holy intensity by a sufficient oblation. And that oblation is incarnate Deity Itself!

Viewed from this central point, and under this focal light, how impossible it is not to recognize *both* love and wrath in the Godhead,* and how impossible it is to conceive of a schism in the Divine Being, and separate his justice from his mercy. It is a real "propitiation" of the Divine anger against sin that is effected, but it is a propitiation that is effected by the Deity himself, out of his own self-sacrificing and principled compassion.

Turning now to the discussion of the theme proposed, the first step requires us to consider the relation which the ethical nature of man sustains to the ethical nature of God. For if both alike are to be satisfied by one and the same atoning work of one and the same

* The inspired assertion that "God is a consuming fire" (Heb. xi. 29), is just as categorical and unqualified as the inspired assertion that "God is love" (1 John iv. 8), or the inspired assertion that "God is light" (1 John i. 5). Hence it is as inaccurate to resolve all the Divine emotions into love, as it would be to resolve them all into wrath. The truth is, that it is the Divine *Essence* alone, and not any one particular attribute, that can be logically regarded as the unity in which all the characteristic qualities of the Deity centre and inhere.

Person, the Lord Jesus Christ, it is plain that there must be some common kindredness and sympathy between them. What then is the actual relation that exists between conscience in man and the attribute of justice in God? Do they give differing judgments with respect to the demerit of sin, and do they require different methods of satisfaction for it? Is the human conscience clamorous for an atonement, while the Divine Nature is wholly indifferent? Or, does the judicial sentiment in the Deity demand the infliction of penalty upon crime, while that of man is opposed to such an infliction? Is there, or is there not, an entire and perfect agreement between the finite faculty and the infinite attribute, upon these points, so that in reference to sin and guilt, what God requires, man's moral nature also insists upon, and what an awakened conscience craves, eternal Justice also demands?

The moral reason, as containing for its substance and inlay the moral law of God, and the conscience as the faculty that testifies with respect to the harmony or the hostility of the will with this law, — this side of human nature is a part of that "image and likeness of God," after which man was originally created. These faculties have to do with what is religious, ethical, eternal; and, notwithstanding the apostasy and corruption of man's heart and will, they still constitute a point of connection and communication between the being of man and the being of God. The moral reason and conscience are the intellectual media whereby, if we may so speak, man and his Maker are put *en rapport*. When the Eternal Judge addresses the creature upon the subject of religion, upon the duties which he owes, and the liabilities under which he stands, he speaks first of all, not to his imagination, or his taste, or his hostile heart, or his perverse will, but to his moral sense and sentiment. When God begins the work of conviction, and in order to this throws in an influence from his own holy and immaculate Essence, He first shoots a pang through this part of man's complex being. This, like Darien, is the isthmus of volcanic fire that both divides and joins the oceans.

Here, then, if anywhere in the being of man, we are to look for views of the Deity that correspond to his real nature and character. And here, in particular, we are to find the true index of his *judicial emotions* towards sin, and the clue to what his ethical nature and feeling demands in order to its remission. We must not ask the sinful heart, or the taste, or the mere understanding, what God thinks of sin, and what is his feeling respecting it. Upon these points we must take counsel of the conscience. For the God of the selfish heart is the deity of sentimentalism; the God of the imagination and the taste is the beautiful Grecian Apollo; the God of the understanding merely is the cold and unemotional abstraction of the deist and the pantheist; but the God of the conscience is the living and holy God of Israel, — the God of punishments and atonements. This ethical part of man's being, then, has a closer affinity than any other part with the Divine Essence, and consequently its phenomena, its pangs and its pacification, have a more intimate connection than those of any other of his powers, with the processes of the Eternal Mind. This is the finite contacting point in man that corresponds with the infinite surface in God. The moral reason and conscience, thus having their counterpart and antithesis in the Deity, must, therefore, be regarded as indexes of him, and particularly of what goes on in his being in relation to human sin and guilt. The calm condemnation of man's ethical nature, and the unselfish organic remorse of his conscience, which are consequent upon his transgression of law, are effluences from that Being whose eyes "devour all iniquity." The righteous indignation into which the judicial part of the human soul is stirred by sin, is the finite but *homogeneous* expression of that anger against moral evil which burns with an eternal intensity in the purity of the Divine Essence.

Hence it follows that a careful examination of what we find in the workings of this part of the human constitution, instead of deterring, will compel us to transfer in the same species to God, what exists in man in only a finite degree. In other words, the emotion of the human conscience towards sin will be found to be the same in *kind* with the emotion of God towards sin. The analysis must, indeed, be very careful. We must eliminate from the indignation of the moral sense all elements of selfish passion that have become mixed with it, owing to that corruption of human nature which prevents even as serious a power as conscience from working with a perfectly normal action.* We must clarify remorse until the residuum left is pure spiritual wrath against pure wickedness. We must do our utmost, under the illumination of divine truth and the actuation of the Holy Spirit, to have conscience do its

* *Trench* remarks upon Eph. iv. 26, that "St. Paul is not, as so many understand him, condescending to human infirmity, and saying: 'Your anger shall not be imputed to you as a sin, if you put it away before nightfall;' but rather, 'Be ye angry, yet in this anger of yours suffer no sinful element to mingle;' there is that which may cleave even to a righteous anger, the παροργισμός, the irritation, the exasperation, which must be dismissed at once; that so, being defecated of this impurer element which mingled with it, that only which ought to remain, may remain." — *Synonymes of N. T*, § 37.

perfect, unmixed work; and then we need not shrink from asserting, that this righteous displacency of the moral sense, against the voluntary wickedness, is precisely the same emotion *in specie* with the wrath of God.*

It will aid us if at this point we direct attention to the distinction between the human conscience and the human heart; and particularly to the difference between *emotion in conscience* and *emotion in the heart.*† The feelings and passions of the corrupt human heart we cannot, in any form, attribute to God. Envy, pride, malice, shame, selfish love, and selfish hatred, cannot possibly exist in that pure and blessed Nature. Hence it is that we are so apt to shrink from those portions of scripture which clothe the Deity with indignant and

* Hence the Divine injunction in Ps. xcvii. 18: "Ye that love the Lord, *hate evil;*" and in Rom. xii. 9: "*Abhor* that which is evil." This pure and spiritual displacency towards moral evil, unmixed with any elements of sinful and human passion, is one of the last accomplishments of the Christian life. Hear the following low and sad refrain from the spirit of the intensely earnest and ethical Master of Rugby, as he muses under the dark chestnut-trees, and beside the limpid waters, and beneath the cerulean sky of Lake Como: "It is almost awful to look at the overwhelming beauty around me, and then think of moral evil; it seems as if heaven and hell, instead of being separated by a great gulf from one another, were absolutely on each other's confines, and indeed not far from every one of us. Might the sense of moral evil be as strong in me as my delight in external beauty; *for in a deep sense of moral evil, more perhaps than in anything else, abides a saving knowledge of God!* It is not so much to admire moral good; that we may do, and yet not be ourselves conformed to it; but if we really do *abhor* that which is evil, not the persons in whom evil resides, but the evil that dwelleth in them, and much more manifestly and certainly to our own knowledge, in our own hearts, — this is to have the feeling of God and of Christ, and to have our spirit in sympathy with the spirit of God. Alas! how easy to see this and say it, — how hard to do it and to feel it!" — *Arnold's Life and Correspondence.* Appendix D.

† For some further explanation, and illustration, of the important distinction between the mental and the moral, the constitutional and the voluntary, etc., the writer would refer to his *Lectures upon the Philosophy of History*, pp. 65—69.

condemnatory feelings, because this class of emotions are those in and by which the depravity of the human heart is most wont to display itself. But the emotion of which we are speaking is not a passion of the human *heart*. The heart of man *loves* sin; but we are describing *remorse*, which is the wrath of the conscience *against* sin. We are delineating the operations and processes of a very different part of the human constitution from that which is the source and seat of earthly passions and sinful emotions. We have passed beyond the hot and passionate heart of man to the cool and silent *judicial* centre of his being; and here we find feelings and processes of an altogether different and higher order. Indignation in conscience is a totally different emotion from indignation in the heart. A man's moral displeasure at his own sin is an entirely different mental exercise from his selfish displeasure towards his neighbor. The former is an ethical and impartial emotion, totally independent of the will and affections, and called out involuntarily from the conscience by the mere sheer contact between it and the heart's iniquity. Hence a man never condemns himself for the existence of such a species of displeasure within his breast. He may be angry in this style and sin not.* The sun may go down upon this kind of wrath. And yet it is not a virtue for which he can take credit to himself; for it is no product of his. It is not an emotion of his heart or his will, but is simply an involuntary and irrepressible efflux from his rational nature. He may only give glory to his Creator for it, as the only relic left him, in his total

* "I further read: '*Be angry and sin not.*' And how was I moved, O my God, who had now learned to be angry at myself, for things past, that I might not sin in time to come! Yea to be *justly* angry." — *Augustine's Confessions*, IX. iv. 10.

alienation of heart and will from God, of his primitive and constitutional kindredness with the First Perfect and the First Fair.

Again, this judicial emotion, this *conscientious* wrath of which we are speaking, differs from the selfish and partial emotions of the human heart, in that it is not intrinsically an unhappy feeling. It does not, like the latter, of necessity render the being in whom it exists miserable. Envy, hatred, malice, shame, pride, are each and all of them unhappy exercises in themselves, as well as in their consequences. They cannot exist in any being without mental suffering. But it is not so with the moral displeasure of the moral sense. Whether this just and legitimate emotion be a torment or not, depends altogether upon the state of the heart and will, upon the moral character. It is indeed true that it causes unhappiness in a *sinful* being, because in this instance the emotions of the heart are in antagonism with the emotion of conscience; because the executive faculty is not in harmony with the judicial faculty. But where there is no personal sin, both the wrath of conscience and the wrath of God are as innocuous as fire upon asbestos. Hence this very same emotion of moral indignation and abhorrence exists in an intense degree in the angels and the seraphim, but is productive of no disquietude in them, because there is nothing evil in their *own* character upon which it can wreak its force. There is a perfect harmony within them, between the emotions of the heart and the judicial emotion, between the character and the conscience. And, in like manner, this same feeling of ethical displeasure exists in an infinite degree in the being of God, without disturbing, in the least, the ineffable peace and blessedness of that pure nature which is the paradise and elysium of all who are conformed to it. For this judicial sentiment is a *legitimate* one, and nothing that is legitimate can be intrinsically miserable. And therefore it is that the saints and the seraphim, as they look down from the crystal battlements with holy abhorrence and indignation upon the sorceries and murders and uncleanness of the fallen Babylon, are not distressed by their emotion, but, on the contrary, rejoice with a holy joy at the final triumph of justice in the universe of God, and say, Alleluia, as the smoke of that just torment rises up for ever and ever.* And therefore it is that God himself carries eternally, in his own blessed nature, a righteous indignation against moral evil, that is no source of disquietude to him, because there is no moral evil in him, nor to the angels and saints and seraphim, because there is none in them; but only to those rebellious and wicked spirits into whom it does fall like lightning from the sky.

For if the emotion of moral indignation were intrinsically one of unhappiness, then the existence of evil would be the destruction of the Divine blessedness; because God "cannot look upon evil with allowance,"†

* "And after these things, I heard a great voice of much people in heaven, saying, Alleluia: Salvation, and glory, and honor, and power unto the Lord our God: for *true and righteous are his judgments,* for he hath judged the great whore which did corrupt the earth with her fornication, and hath avenged the blood of his servants at her hand. And again they said, Alleluia: *and her smoke rose up forever and ever.* And the four and twenty elders, and the four beasts fell down, and worshipped God that sat on the throne, saying, *Amen, Alleluia.*" — Rev. xix. 1—4.

† "Thou art not a God that hath pleasure in wickedness. Thou hatest all workers of iniquity" (Ps. v. 5, 6). "God is angry with the wicked every day" (Ps. vii. 11). "Who may stand in thy sight when once thou art angry" (Ps. lxxvi. 7). "Who knoweth the power of thine anger? Even according to thy fear so is thy wrath" (Ps. xc. 11). "He that believeth not the Son, shall not see life; but the wrath of God abideth on him" (John iii. 36).

and yet he is constantly looking upon it. But it is not so. On the contrary, the Deity is *blessed* in his displacency at that which is vile and hateful. For pleasure is the coincidence between a feeling and its correlated object. It implies intrinsic congruity and fitness. It would therefore be unhappiness in any being to hate what is lovely, or to love what is hateful; to be pleased with what is wrong, and displeased with what is right; because the proper coincidence between the emotion and the object would not obtain. But when God, or any being, hates what is hateful, and is angry at that which *merits* wrath, the true nature and fitness of things is observed, and that inward harmony which is the substance of mental happiness is maintained. Anger and hatred are almost indissolubly connected in our minds with mental wretchedness, because we behold their exercise only in an abnormal and sinful sphere. In an apostate world, as such, there is no proper and fitting coincidence between emotions and their objects. A sinner hates holiness, which he ought to love; and loves sin, which he ought to hate. The anger of his heart is not legitimate, but passionate and selfish. The love of his heart is illicit; and therefore, as it is styled in the scripture, is mere lust or evil concupiscence (ἐπιθυμία). In a sinful world, as such, all the true relations and correlations are reversed. Love and hatred are expended upon exactly the wrong objects. But when these emotions are contemplated within the sphere of the Holy and the Eternal; when they are beheld in God, exercised only upon their appropriate and deserving objects; when the wrath falls only upon the sin and uncleanness of hell, and burns up nothing but filth in its pure celestial flame; the emotion is not merely legitimate, but beautiful with an august beauty, and is no source of pain either to the Divine Mind or to any minds in sympathy with it. It is only upon this principle that we can explain the blessedness of the Deity, in connection with his omniscience and omnipresence. We know that sin and the punishment of sin are ever before him. The smoke of torment is perpetually rolling up in the presence of the Omnipresent. And yet he is supremely blessed. But he can be so only because there is a just and proper correlationship between his wrath and the object upon which it falls; only because he condemns that which is intrinsically damnable.* The least disturbance of this coincidence, the slightest love for the hateful, or hatred for the lovely, would indeed render God a wretched being. But the perfect harmony of it makes him "God over *all*," hell as well as heaven, "blessed forever."† Were this ethical feeling once to be outraged by the final triumph of iniquity over righteousness; were the smoke of torment to ascend eter-

* It is at this point that the metaphysical necessity of endless punishment appears. For if sin be intrinsically damnable, it is intrinsically punishable. If then the question be asked: How *long* is it intrinsically damnable and punishable? there is but one answer. There is, in fact, no logical mean between no punishment at all of sin as an *intrinsic* evil, and an absolute, that is, an endless punishment of it.

† It is a standing objection of infidelity to the Biblical idea and representation of the Deity, that it conflicts with the natural intuitions of the human mind. It is asserted that the instinctive sentiments of the soul repel the doctrine of anger against sin. The ethics of nature, say these theorizers, are contrary to the ethics of scripture upon this point, and hence mankind must make a choice between the two. But a careful study of the most profound systems of natural religion does not corroborate this assertion. Probably no mind, outside of the pale of Christianity, has made a more discriminating and truthful representation of the natural sentiments of the human mind, than Aristotle. But this dispassionate thinker asserts that "He who feels anger on proper occasions, at proper persons, and in a proper manner, and for a proper length of time, is an object of praise." — *Nicomachean Ethics*, Book IV. c. 5.

nally from pure and innocent spirits, and were the revelry of joy to steam up everlastingly from the souls of the vile and the worthless; were the great relations of right and wrong, sin and penalty, happiness and misery, once to be reversed in the universe, and under the government of God, then indeed this quick sense of justice, and this holy indignation at sin, would be a grief and a sorrow to its possessor. And therefore it is, that, in all the Divine administration, and in the entire plan of redemption, the utmost possible pains is taken to justify, and legitimate, and satisfy this judicial sentiment, and to see that its demands are fully met.

There must be this correspondence between the judicial nature of man and the judicial nature of God, or religion is impossible. How can man even know what is meant by justice in the Deity, if there is absolutely nothing of the same species in his own rational constitution, which if realized in his own character as it is in that of God, would make him just as God is just? How can he know what is meant by moral perfection in God, if in his own rational spirit there is absolutely no ideal of moral excellence, which if realized in himself as it is in the Creator, would make him excellent as he is excellent? Without some mental correspondent, to which to appeal and commend themselves, the teachings of revelation could not be apprehended. A body of knowledge alone is not the whole; there must be an inlet for it, an organ of apprehension. But if there is no such particular part of the human constitution as has been described, and these calm judgments of the moral sense, and this righteous displeasure of the conscience, are to be put upon a level with the workings of the fancy and imagination, or the selfish passions of the human heart, then there is no point of contact and communication between the nature of man and the being of God. There is no part of his own complex being upon which man may fall back, with the certainty of not being mistaken in judgments of ethics and religion. Both anchor and anchoring-ground are gone, and he is afloat upon the boundless, starless ocean of ignorance and scepticism. Even if revelations are made, they cannot enter his mind. There is no contacting surface through which they can approach and take hold of his being. They cannot be seen to be what they really are, the absolute truth of God, because there is no eye with which to see them.

Assuming, then, that there is this correspondence and correlationship between the moral constitution of man and the Divine Nature, we proceed, in the light of the fact, to evince the doctrine, taught in the scripture texts which we have cited, that the atonement of Christ is a real satisfaction both on the part of God and man. The death of incarnate Deity has always been regarded, by those who have believed that the Deity became incarnate in Jesus Christ, as *expiatory*. As such, it relates immediately to the attribute of justice in the Creator, and to the faculty of conscience in the creature. And the position taken here, is that it sustains the *same* relation to both. It satisfies that which would be dissatisfied both in God and man if the penalty of sin were merely set aside and abolished by an act of will. It placates an ethical feeling which is manifesting itself in the form of remorse in the conscience of the transgressor, only because it has first existed in the nature of God in the form of a judicial displeasure towards moral evil.

A fundamental attribute of Deity is justice. This comes first into view, and continues in sight to the very last, in all inquiries into the Divine Nature. No attribute can be conceived of that is more ultimate and central than this one. This is proved by the fact that the operation of all the other Divine attributes, love itself not excepted, is *conditioned* and *limited* by justice. For whatever else God may be, or may not be, he must be just. It is not optional with him to exercise this attribute, or not to exercise it, as it is in the instance of that class of attributes which are antithetic to it. We can say: "God may be merciful or not, as he pleases;" but we cannot say: "God may be just or not, as he pleases." It cannot be asserted that God is inexorably obligated to show pity; but it can be categorically affirmed that God is inexorably obligated to do justly.* For the characteristic of justice is necessary exaction; while, if we may accommodate a Shaksperean phrase, "the quality of mercy is not *strained*." Hence the exercise of justice can be demonstrated upon *à priori* grounds, while that of mercy is known only by a declaration or *promise* upon the part of God. It is for this reason that man can have no *certainty* that the

* *Owen* (Dissertation on Divine Justice, Chap. II.), notices the self-contradiction there is, in conceding that justice is an essential attribute in God, and yet that it can be set aside by an act of arbitrary omnipotence, in the following terms: "To me, these arguments are altogether astonishing, viz.: 'That sin-punishing justice should be natural to God, and yet that God, sin being supposed to exist, *may either exercise it, or not exercise it.*' They may also say, and with as much propriety, that truth is natural to God, but upon a supposition that he were to converse with man, *he might either use it, or not;* or, that omnipotence is natural to God, but upon a supposition that he were inclined to do any work without (extra) himself, that *it were free to him to act omnipotently or not;* or, finally, that sin-punishing justice is among the primary causes of the death of Christ, and that Christ was set forth as a propitiation, to declare his righteousness, and yet that that justice required not the punishment of sin. For if it should require it, how is it possible that it should not *necessarily* require it, since God would be unjust, if he should not inflict punishment."

Deity is a merciful being, except as he obtains it from a special revelation. When the thoughtful pagan looked up into the pure heavens above him, or into the deep recesses within him, he had no doubt that the Infinite One is just, and a punisher of evil doing, because he *must* be such. Hence he trembled; and hence he offered a propitiatory sacrifice. But neither from the heavens, nor from anything in his own moral constitution, could he obtain certainty in regard to the attribute of mercy; because there is nothing of a *necessary* nature in the exercise of this attribute. God might or might not be merciful to him. Man may dare to hope that there is pity in the Deity; but whether there actually is, he cannot know with certainty until the heavens are opened, and a voice issues from the lips of the Supreme himself, saying: "I *will* show mercy, and this is my beloved Son in whom I am well pleased." The light of nature is sufficient for man's damnation; but it casts not a ray in the direction of his salvation. There is ample evidence from natural religion that the Deity is holy and impartial; but it is only from revealed religion that the human mind obtains its warrant for believing in the Divine clemency. From the position of natural ethics alone, man is merely condemned to retribution; and, as matter of fact, while standing only upon this position, his conscience accuses him, and fills him with fears and forebodings of judgment. Nothing but a *promise* of forgiveness, from the mouth of God, can remove these fears; but a promise to pardon is not *à priori*, and necessary, like a threatening to punish.

The absolute and indefeasible nature of justice is seen, again, by considering the nature of law. If we regard the moral law as the efflux of the Divine Nature, and not, as in the Grotian theory, a positive statute which may be relaxed in part, or wholly abrogated, by the law-making power,* we find this same stark necessity existing. The law is *obligated* to punish the transgressor, as much as the transgressor is obligated to obey the law. Human society, for instance, has claim upon law for penalty, as really as law has claim upon human society for obedience. Law has no option. Justice has but one function. The necessity of penalty is as great as the necessity of obligation. The law itself is under law; that is, it is under the necessity of its own nature; and therefore the only possible way whereby a transgressor can escape the penalty of law, is for a substitute to endure it for him. The language of Milton respecting the transgressor is metaphysically true:

* "All positive laws," says *Grotius* (Defensio Fidei, Caput. III. p. 310, Ed. Amstelaedemi, 1679), "are relaxable. Those who fear that if we concede this, we do an injury to God because we thereby represent him as mutable, are much deceived. For law is not something internal in God, or in the will itself of God, but it is *a particular effect or product* of his will (voluntatis quidam effectus). But that the effects, or products of the Divine will are mutable, is very certain. Moreover, in promulgating a positive law, which he might wish to relax at some future time, God does not exhibit any fickleness of will. For God seriously indicated that he desired that his law should be valid, and obligatory; *while yet he reserved the right of relaxing it, if he saw fit,* because this right pertains to a positive law, from the very nature of the case, and cannot be abdicated by the Deity. Nay more, the Deity does not abdicate the right of even abrogating law altogether, as is apparent from the instance of the ceremonial law." Grotius then proceeds to apply this principle to the moral law, and the penalty accompanying it, and though intending to counteract the Socinian theory, lays down positions which in the judgment of dogmatic historians logically lead to it. — See *Baumgarten — Crusius* (Dogmengeschichte, II. 274); *Münscher — Von Cölln — Neudecker* (Dogmengeschichte, III. 508); *Baur* (Versöhnungslehre, 414—435, — translated in Bibliotheca Sacra, IX. 259—272); *Hagenbach,* (Dogmengeschichte, 3 Aufl. § 268); *Ersch und Gruber's Encyclopädie* (Art. Acceptilatio); *Hengstenberg's Kirchen-Zeitung* for 1834.

"He, with all his posterity, must die:
Die he, or justice must; unless for him
Some other able, and as willing, pay
The rigid satisfaction, death for death."*

And *the mercy of God consists in substituting Himself incarnate for his creature, for purposes of atonement.* Analyzed to its ultimate elements, God's pity towards the soul of man is God's satisfying his own eternal attribute of justice for it. It does not consist in outraging his own law, and the guilt-smitten conscience itself, by simply snatching the criminal away from their retributions, in the exercise of an unprincipled and an unbridled almightiness, or in substituting a partial for a complete atonement; but in enduring the full and entire penal infliction by which both are satisfied.†

* *Paradise Lost,* III. 209—212.

† It was one of the objections of Socinus to the theory of plenary satisfaction, that if God has received a full equivalent for the punishment due to man, then he does not exercise any mercy in remitting his sin. But this objection overlooks the fact that the equivalent is not furnished by man, but by God. Were the atonement the *creature's* oblation to justice, Socinus's objection would have force. But it is *God,* and not man, who satisfies justice for the sinner. It is indeed a *self*-satisfaction upon the part of God, yet none the less a self-*sacrifice;* and self-sacrifice is confessedly the highest form of love. The truth is, that this objection of Socinus begs the question in dispute, by defining mercy in its own way. It assumes (as Socinus expressly argues, *Bib. Frat. Pol.* I. 566 sq.) that the ideas of satisfaction and mercy mutually exclude each other; that mercy consists in *relaxing* and *waiving* justice, and not in *vicariously satisfying* it. From this premiss it follows, of course, that where there is any satisfaction of justice there is no mercy, and where there is any waiving of justice there is mercy. A complete atonement, consequently, would exclude mercy altogether; a partial atonement would allow some room for mercy, in partially waiving legal claims; and no atonement at all would afford full play for the attribute, by the entire nullification of all judicial demands. According to the catholic view, on the contrary, the ideas of satisfaction and mercy are combined and harmonized in a *vicarious* atonement. or the *assumption* of penalty by a competent person. If the sinner himself should suffer the penalty, there

Still another proof of the primary nature of justice is found in the fact of human accountability. The most distinguishing characteristic of man is evidence of the most distinguishing characteristic of God; and thus the correspondence between the Divine and the human meets us again. Man is not a link in the necessary chain of material nature. He is by creation a free creature; capable of continuing holy as he was created, or of turning to sin. Now, over against this freedom and responsibility on the part of man, there stands justice on the part of God. This great divine attribute presupposes the hazardous human endowment of *will*, and holds the possessor of it accountable for its use or abuse. Without such a characteristic, man could not stand in any sort of relationship to such solemn realities as law and justice. There would be nothing in his constitution that could feel the tremendous swing and blow of penal infliction. For justice smites a transgressor as one who has illegitimately assumed a centre of his own, and who is wickedly standing upon that centre, in hostility to the being and government of God. In a certain sense, though not that which excludes the permissive decree and the preventive power of the Supreme Being, justice supposes the sinner to be sustaining something of the isolated and self-asserting relation to God that the principle of evil in the system of dualism sustains to the principle of good; and when the accountable self-will of a creature attempts to set itself up as an independent and hostile agent in the doing

would be no vicariousness in the suffering, and there would be the execution of justice merely, without any mercy. But when the incarnate Son of God, as the sinner's substitute, endures the penalty due to sin, justice is satisfied by the suffering which is undergone; and the Son of God, surely, shows the height of compassion in undergoing it.

of evil, it then feels the full force of the avenging, vindicating stroke of law, as if it were a single disconnected atom, all alone and by itself, in the middle of creation.

Any just view of sin as *guilt*, as the product of *will*, is, consequently, corroborative of the position that the attribute of which we are speaking is an immanent and necessary one in the Divine Nature. We might conceive of the same amount of evil consequences as those which flow from human transgression ; but if this latter were not the real work and agency of a responsible creature, Eternal Justice could take no cognizance of it. Unless sin is *crime*, penalty has no more relation to it than it has to the disease and corruption in the material world about us ; and the fall of man could no more be visited by the infliction of judicial suffering, than could that process of decay which is continually going on in the forests, by means of which a more luxuriant vegetation springs up, and a more glorious forest waves in the breeze.

It has been a query among those who have speculated upon the nature of the Deity : What is the base or substrate of His being ? The inquiry has too often been so answered as to bring in a subtle pantheïsm, because there was more reference to the natural than the ethical attributes of the Godhead. Whether the question in such a reference can be answered by the finite mind, we do not pretend to decide here ; but with reference to God's *moral* constitution, with reference to that congeries of *ethical* attributes which belongs to him as a personal being, it is as certain as anything can be, that the deep substrate and base of them all, is eternal law and impartial justice. This pervades all the rest, keeps them in equilibrium, and constitutes, as it were, the very divinity of the Deity. And this view of the primary nature of justice coincides with the convictions of men in all ages. In all time, justice has been the one particular divine attribute that has pressed most heavily upon the human race. This always comes first into man's mind, when the idea of the Deity overshadows him. He trembles when he remembers that God is just; and he remembers this when he remembers nothing else. Nor let it be objected that this is owing to the fact that man is sinful, and that this quality in the Supreme Being would not be so prominent in the mind of an unfallen creature who has nothing to fear from it. The utterance of the pure burning seraphim is: *Holy*, *Holy*, *Holy*. That which comes first into the minds of the spotless and unfearing worshippers in God's immediate presence,—they whose spirits, in the phrase of Jeremy Taylor, "are becalmed, and made even as the brow of Jesus, and smooth like the heart of God,"—is that particular characteristic in the Divine Being, by virtue of which he has a right to sit on the eternal throne; that specific attribute upon which the moral administration of the universe must be established.

Now, if this be a correct statement of the necessary nature and the capital position of Divine Justice, it is plain that any plan or method that has to do with sin and guilt, must have primary reference to it, and must give *plenary satisfaction* to it as it exists in God himself. Inasmuch as justice, and not mercy, is the *limiting* and *conditioning* attribute, its demands must be acknowledged and met in order that mercy may make even the first advances towards the transgressor. Compassion cannot, by mere arbitrary will and might, stride forward to reach its own private ends, and trample down justice by sheer force; but must come forth, as she does in the bleeding Lamb of God, as the voluntary servant and victim of Law, doing all its behests, and bearing all its burdens, and enduring its sharp, inexorable pains, *in the place of* (*vice*, *vicarie*) the helpless object whom vengeance suffereth not to live. The cup must be put to the lips of him who has volunteered to be the Atoner, and he must drink it to the bottom, for the guilty transgressor whose law-place he has taken. The God-man having, out of his own free will and affection, become the sinner's *Substitute*, must now receive a sinner's treatment, and be "numbered with the transgressors" (Isa. liii. 12). He cannot therefore escape the agony and passion, the hour and the power of darkness. He may give expression to his spontaneous shrinking from the awful self-oblation, as the hour darkens and draws on, in the utterance: "O my Father, if it be possible, let this cup pass from me;" but having taken the place of the *guilty*, it is not possible, and he must sweat the bloody sweat, he must cry: "My God, my God, why hast thou forsaken me?" that his voice may then ring through the universe and down the ages: "It is finished, — the atonement is made."*

For the Deity cannot, by an arbitrary and unprincipled procedure, release the transgressor's Substitute from the penal suffering, and inflict a wound upon that holy judicial nature, which is vital in every part with

* "The *justice* of God is exceedingly glorified in this work. God is so strictly and immutably just, that he would not spare his beloved Son when he took upon him the guilt of men's sins, and was substituted in the room of sinners. He would not abate him the least mite of that debt which justice demanded. Justice should take place, though it cost his infinitely dear Son his precious blood; and his enduring such extraordinary reproach, and pain, and death in its most dreadful form." — *Edwards's Works*, IV. 140.

the breath of law and the life of justice. By reason of an immanent necessity, he cannot disturb his own eternal sense of righteousness and ethical tranquillity, by doing damage to one whole side of his Godhead.

He has not. In the voluntary, the cordially offered, sacrifice of the incarnate Son, the judicial nature of God, which by a constitutional necessity requires the punishment of sin, finds its righteous requirement fully met. Plenary punishment is inflicted upon One who is infinite, and therefore competent; upon One who is finite, and therefore passible; upon One who is innocent, and therefore can suffer for others; upon One who is voluntary, and therefore uncompelled. By this theanthropic oblation, the ethical feeling, the organic emotion of displeasure in the Deity is, in the scripture phrase, made "propitious" towards the guilty, because it has been placated by it. Thus God is immutably just while he justifies (Rom. iii. 26), and his mercy is, in the last analysis, one with his truth and his law.

We turn, now, to the other half of the proposition derived from the scripture texts that have been cited, and proceed to show that the atonement of Christ effects a real satisfaction upon the part of man. We have seen that the propitiatory death of the God-man meets the immanent ethical necessities of the Divine Nature. We have now the easier task of evincing that it meets the moral wants of human nature.

In discussing the fact of a divinely-established correspondence between the judicial nature of man and that of God, we have already observed that the attribute of justice naturally selects this judicial part of man as the inlet of approach to him. Eternal law has, in all ages, poured itself down through the human *conscience*, like a fountain through the channel it has worn for itself, and in this instance like hot lava down a mountain gorge. Hence by watching its workings within this particular faculty, we are enabled to determine what man's judicial nature requires, and also incidentally to throw back some more light upon the relations of the atonement to the Divine Nature. It is indeed true that Divine Justice manifests itself in other modes than this. There are revelations of it in the written word, and in the course of providence and human history. But we are endeavoring to establish the position that the atonement has an *internal* necessity grounded in the very moral being of man. It is necessary, therefore, to look at the principle of law in its vital and felt manifestation within the soul of the criminal himself. By the analysis of the contents of a remorseful conscience, especially if it has been made unusually living and poignant by the truth and Spirit of God, we may discover much of the real quality of Eternal Justice. As this august attribute acts and reacts within the breast of man upon his violation of law, we may obtain some clear and *conscious* knowledge of its nature and operations; and also of what the human conscience itself demands, and with what it is satisfied.

The commission of sin is either attended or succeeded by the sensation of *guilt*, — one of the most distinct and unique of all the sensations that emerge within the horizon of self-consciousness. Provided conscience does its unmixed work, the transgressor is conscious, not merely of unhappiness, which is a very low form of feeling, but of *criminality*, which is a very high form. Nay, the more profound and thorough the operation of the moral faculty becomes, the more does the sense of mere wretchedness retreat into the background, and the sense of ill-desert come forth into the foreground of consciousness. It is possible for this latter element to drive out, for a time, the particular feeling of misery, and to absorb the mind in the sense of *horror* and *amazement* at the past transgression. The guilty, in the final day, are represented as calling upon the rocks and the mountains to fall upon them, as inviting new forms of suffering, in the vain hope that the awful consciousness of crime may be drowned thereby.

Now, seizing and holding the experience of the transgressor at this point, let us examine it more closely. Notice that this consciousness of guilt, pure and simple, is wholly *involuntary*. It comes in upon the criminal, not only without his will, but in spite of it. He would keep it out, if he could. He would drive it out, if he could. His experience at this stage, then, is the result of no voluntary effort upon his part, but of the simple *reaction of law*, the most dispassionate and unselfish of all realities, against its violator. In the conscience, that part of the human constitution which we have seen to be the proper seat and organ for such an operation, the commandment is making itself felt again, not as at first in the form of command, but of condemnation. The free agent has responsibly disobeyed the holy, just, and good statute, and is now feeling the tremendous reaction of it in his own moral being. This remorse, or damnatory emotion, therefore, is the work of God's law, and not of man's will. There is, consequently, very little of the selfish and the earthly, but much of the unearthly and the eternal, in the transgressor's experience held at this point. He can take no merit to himself, because it is of such an intensely ethical and spiritual character, since the entire process, so far as he is concerned, is involuntary and organic. It is provided for in his judicial constitution, and as an operation within himself it is to be regarded, not as the working of his corrupt heart, but as the *infliction* of Divine retribution and justice, in and through the judicial faculty. Man can take no merit to himself because he possesses a power that condemns evil, and distresses therefor. For this is the workmanship of the Creator, and it exists in hell as well as heaven. The workings of conscience are as much beyond the control of the will, are as truly organic, as those of the sympathetic nerve, and therefore are worthy of neither praise nor blame. Given conscience and sin, within one and the same soul, and remorse must follow as a matter of necessity. Hence remorse is never made the subject of a command. Man is commanded to melt down in godly sorrow, but never to be filled with remorse; for this is provided for in the moral constitution given by Him who makes it the fiery chariot by which he himself rides into man's being, in majesty, to judgment.

Hence this sense of ill-desert, though its sensorium is the human conscience, must be traced back for its first cause, to a yet deeper ground, and a yet higher origin. For if it were a fact, that remorse had nothing but a human source, though that source were the highest and most venerable of the human faculties, and the transgressor should know it, he could overcome and suppress it. Nothing that has a merely finite origin can be a permanent source of misery; and if the victim of remorse could but be certain that the just and holy God has had nothing to do with the origin of the distress within him, he could ultimately expel it from his breast. If he could be assured that the terrible emotion which follows the commission of evil, though welling up from the lowest springs of his own nature, yet has no connection with the nether fountains of the Divine Essence, he could put an end to his torment. For no man is afraid of himself alone, and irrespective of his Maker and Judge. That which renders a portion of our common and finite humanity terrible to us, is the fact, that it is grounded in and supported by that which is more than human. In the instance before us, the highest part of the human constitution supports itself by striking its deep roots into the holiness and justice of the Godhead; and therefore it is that conscience makes cowards of us all, and its remorse is a feeling that is invincible by the strongest finite will, and requires, in order to its extinction, the blood of atonement.

We are, therefore, compelled back into the being and character of God, for the ultimate origin of this sense of guilt, and this "fearful looking-for of judgment and fiery indignation." And why should we not be? If Justice is living and sensitive anywhere, it must be so in its eternal seat and home. If law is jealous for its own authority and maintenance anywhere, it must be in that Being to whom all eyes in the universe are turned with the inquiry: "Shall not the Judge of all the earth do right?" What, therefore, conscience affirms, in the transgressor's case, God affirms, and is the first to affirm. What, therefore, conscience feels in respect to the sinner's transgression, God feels, and is the first to feel. What, therefore, conscience requires in order that it may cease to punish the guilty spirit, God requires and is the first to require. In fine, all that is requisite in order to the satisfaction and pacification of conscience towards the sinful soul in which it dwells, is also requisite in order to the satisfaction and "propitiation" of God the Just; and it is requisite in the former case only because it is first requisite in the latter. The subjective in man is shaped by the objective in God, and not the objective in God by the subjective in man. The consciousness of the conscience is the reflex of the consciousness of God.

But what, now, does conscience require, in order that it may become pacified with respect to past transgression? We answer, simply and solely an *atonement* for that past transgression; simply and solely that just *infliction* which is due to guilt. That is a powerful, because profoundly truthful, passage in Coleridge's play of "Remorse," in which the guilty and guilt-smitten Ordonio is stabbed by Alhadra, the wife of the murdered Isidore. As the steel drinks his own heart's blood, he utters the one single word "*Atonement!*" His self-accusing spirit, which is wrung with its remorseful recollections, and which the warm and hearty forgiveness of his injured brother has not been able to soothe in the least, actually feels its first gush of relief only as the avenging knife enters, and crime meets penalty.* And how often, in the annals of guilt, is this principle illustrated! The criminal has wandered up and down the earth, vainly seeking repose of conscience, but finds none until he surrenders himself to the penalty of law. Those are the only hopeful executions, in which the guilty goes to his death *justifying* the judicial sentence that condemns him, and, as a completing act of the solemn mental process, appropriating that yet more august and transcendent expiation which has been made for man by a higher Being than man. A guilty conscience, when it

* *Remorse*, Act V. Scene 1. *Coleridge's Works*, VII. p. 401.—The psychology of crime, or the analysis of the consciousness of guilt (Schuldbewusztseyn), is a portion of mental philosophy that has been generally neglected. The only treatise specifically devoted to it, that we have met with, is the *Criminal-Psychologie* of Heinroth.

has come to a clear consciousness, *wants* its guilt expiated by the infliction of punishment. It feels that strange unearthly thirst of which Christ speaks, and for which he asserts that his blood of atonement is "drink *indeed.*" It cannot be made peaceful except through the medium of a judicial infliction; that is to say, of a particular species of suffering that will *expiate* its guilt. The mere offer of kindness, or good-humor, to remit the sin without any regard to that eternal law of retribution which is now distressing the soul by its righteous claim, does not meet the ethical wants. The moral sense, when in normal action, feels the *necessity* that crime be punished. Hence the human conscience is a faculty that is unappeased, and gnaws like a blind worm, until it hears of the Lamb, the *Atonement*, of God, that taketh away the *guilt* of the world. Hence, however much the selfish heart may desire to escape at the expense of right and justice, the impartial conscience can do no such thing. Before this judicial faculty can be pacified, crime must incur penalty, transgression must receive an exact recompense of reward. When this is done, there is entire pacification; there is great peace, such as death, and Satan the accuser, and the day of judgment, and the bar of justice, and the final doom, cannot disturb with a single ripple.

For the correlate to guilt is punishment; and nothing but the correlate itself can perform the function of a correlate. A liquid, for example, is the correlative to thirst, and nothing that is not liquid, however nutritious, and necessary to human life in other relations, it may be, can be a substitute for it. There may be the "fat kidneys of wheat," in superabundance, but if there be not also the "brook in the way," the human body must die of thirst. In like manner, a judicial infliction, or *suffering for purposes of justice*, is the only means by which culpability can be extinguished. Sanctification, or holiness, in this reference, is powerless, because there is nothing penal, nothing correlated to guilt, in it. The Tridentine method of justification by sanctification, is not an adaptation of means to ends. So far as the guilt of an act, — in other words, its obligation to punishment, — is concerned, if the transgressor, or his *accepted* substitute,* has endured the infliction that is set

* Accepted by the law and lawgiver. The primal source of law has no power to abolish penalty any more than to abolish law, but it has full power to *substitute* penalty. In case of a substitution, however, it must be a *strict* equivalent, and not a fictitious or nominal one. It would contravene the attribute of justice, instead of satisfying it, should God, for instance, by an arbitrary act of will, substitute the sacrifice of bulls and goats for the penalty due to man; or if he should offset any *finite* oblation against the infinite demerit of moral evil. The inquiry whether the satisfaction of justice by Christ's atonement was a strict and literal one, has a practical and not merely theoretical importance. A guilt-smitten conscience is exceedingly timorous, and hence, if there be room for doubting the strict adequacy of the judicial provision that has been made for satisfying the claims of law, a perfect peace, the "peace of God," is impossible. Hence the doctrine of a plenary satisfaction by an infinite substitute is the only one that ministers to evangelical repose. The dispute upon this point has sometimes, at least, resulted from a confusion of ideas and terms. Strict equivalency has been confounded with *identity*. The assertion that Christ's death is a literal equivalent for the punishment due to mankind, has been supposed to be the same as the assertion, that it is identical with it; and a punishment identical with that due to man would involve remorse, and endless duration. But identity of punishment is ruled out by the principle of *substitution* or *vicariousness*, — a principle that is conceded by all who hold the doctrine of atonement. The penalty endured by Christ, therefore, must be a *substituted*, and not an identical one. And the only question that remains is, whether that which is to be substituted shall be of a *strictly equal value* with that, the place of which it takes, or whether it may be of an inferior value, — and it must be one or the other. When a loan of one hundred dollars in silver is repaid by one hundred dollars in gold, there is a substitution of one metal for another. It is not an identical payment; for this would require the return of the very identical hundred pieces of silver, the *ipsissima pecunia*, that had been loaned. But it is a *strictly* and *literally*

over against it, the law is satisfied, and the obligation to punishment is discharged. And so far as guilt, or obligation to punishment is concerned, until the affixed penalty has been endured, by himself or his accepted substitute, he is a guilty man, do what else he may. Even if he should be renewed and sanctified by the Spirit of God, this sanctification has in it nothing *expiatory*, or correlative to guilt, and therefore could not remove his remorse. Food is good and necessary, but it cannot slake thirst. Personal holiness is excellent and indispensable, but it cannot perform the function of atonement. Hence sanctification is wrought by spiritual influences, but justification by expiating blood. The former is the work of the third Person in the Trinity; the latter is that of the second. Hence, when the convicted man is distressed because of what the Psalmist denominates the "*iniquity* of sin," its intrinsic guilty quality, in distinction from its miserable consequences, he craves expiation sometimes with a hunger like that of famine. And hence his desperate endeavor to atone for the past, until he discovers that it is impossible. Then he cries with David: "Thou desirest not sacrifice"—such atonement as I can render is inadequate—"*else would I give it.*"* Taking him at this

equivalent payment. *All* claims are cancelled by it. In like manner, when the suffering and death of God incarnate is substituted for that of the creature, the satisfaction rendered to law is strictly plenary, though not identical with that which is exacted from the transgressor. It contains the element of infinitude, which is the element of value in the case, with even greater precision than the satisfaction of the creature does; because it is the suffering of a strictly infinite Person in a finite time, while the latter is only the suffering of a finite person in an endless but not strictly infinite time. A strictly infinite duration would be without beginning, as well as without end.

* The true and accurate rendering of Psalm li. 7, is not "*purge* me with hyssop," but "*atone* me (תְּחַטְּאֵנִי) with hyssop." David, in the poignancy

point in his experience, his desire is for *justification.* He wants, first of all, to be *pardoned;* and, be it observed, *to be pardoned upon those just and eternal principles that will not give way in the great judicial emergencies of this life and the life to come.* Then he will commence the good fight of faith. Then he will run in the way of obedience with an exulting heart, because he is no longer under condemnation. "Whom he justifies, them he glorifies."

Such, it is conceived, is the general doctrine of atonement, to be deduced from the sharp and pointed texts of scripture cited in the outset of this discussion. The Christian atonement possesses both an objective and a subjective validity; it is a satisfaction for the ethical nature of both God and man.

Having thus contemplated the inward and metaphysical nature of that atoning work of incarnate Deity, which is the most stupendous fact in the history of the world, and one upon which all its religious hopes and welfare hang, we naturally turn, in conclusion, to the more external and practical aspects of the great theme. And the application of the doctrine will be found to be all the more acceptable to the Christian heart, and profitable for Christian edification, if the principles and theory from which it flows are profound and thorough. The cup of cold water is all the more grateful to the thirsty soul, if it has been drawn up from the deep wells; and it is certain that divine truth gains, rather than loses, in popular and practical efficiency, upon both the mind and heart, if it be sought for in its purest and most central sources. That view of the work of Christ which represents it as meeting all the ethical

of his consciousness of guilt, prays, not for a cleansing merely but, for an *expiatory* cleansing.

necessities of both the divine and the human natures, is well fitted to inspire belief and trust in it, and to draw out the heart towards its Blessed Author.

1. One of the first and obvious inferences, then, from the subject as it has been unfolded, is, that an atonement for sin is no arbitrary requirement on the part of God. If the positions taken in this discussion are correct, the doctrine of expiation contains a *metaphysique*, and is defensible at the bar of philosophic reason.

One great obstacle to the reception of the evangelical system lies in the fact, that very many are of opinion that the scripture method of forgiving sin is needlessly embarrassed by a sacrificial expiation. "Why should not God," they ask, "forgive the creature of his footstool in the same manner that an earthly father does his child? Why does he not, at once, and without any of this apparatus of atonement, bid the erring one go his way, with the assurance that the past is forgotten? Is not this expiation, even though made by the Deity himself, after all, a hinderance rather than an encouragement to an approach to the eternal throne? Is it not, at least, something that is not *strictly* necessary, and might have been dispensed with?" This lurking or open doubt, with regard to the rationality and intrinsic necessity of an atonement for sin, cuts the root of all evangelical faith in a large class of men.

Indeed, it may be a question whether the preacher in Christian lands has not a more difficult task to perform for a certain class of minds, in reference to the doctrine of Christ crucified, than the missionary in pagan lands has; and whether Christian theology itself would not have an easier labor than it now has, to vindicate the ways of God to man, in the respect of which we are speaking, if the Old-Ethnic, or what is far better, the

Old-Jewish ideas respecting guilt and retribution were more current than they are in a certain class in nominal Christendom. Taking a portion of men in the modern civilized world as a sample, it would seem as if the unregenerate Christian world does not possess such a spontaneous and irrepressible conviction that guilt must be punished, as did the old unsophisticated Pagan world.* The system of bloody sacrifices, an emphatic acknowledgment of this great truth, was almost universal among them; and the doctrine that mere sorrow for transgression is a sufficient ground for its forgiveness, had little force. The Grecian Nemesis, or personification of vindicative justice, was a divinity to whom even Jove himself was subject. The ancient religious institutions and ceremonials, fanciful and irrational as they were in most of their elements, yet distinctly recognized, through their sacrificial cultus, the amenability of man to law, and his culpability. Add to this, the workings of natural conscience, and we have, even in the midst of polytheism, quite a strong influence at work to keep the pagan mind healthy and sound upon the relations of guilt to justice. Men could not well deny the need

* The barbarians of Melita, when they saw the venomous beast hanging upon the hand of Paul, said among themselves: "No doubt this man is a murderer, whom though he hath escaped the sea, *yet vengeance* (Δίκη) *suffereth not to live.*" Their ethical instinct was sound and healthy, though their knowledge of the facts in the case was inaccurate. But when, in the middle of the nineteenth century, and upon a spot where the edifices and emblems of government cast their solemn shadows, a human being, in the heat and fury of his heart, slays his foe to mutilation in the illegal redress of his own wrongs, and the public conscience is found to be so debauched that only one in one hundred of the resident population condemns the deed, the comparison between Christendom and Paganism is humiliating. Such occurrences illustrate the difference between private revenge and public justice, and prove that the only security which society has against the former, is in the rigid and impartial execution of the latter.

of sin-expiation before whose eyes the blood of the piacular victim was constantly smoking, in accordance with a custom that had come down from their ancestors, and which fell in so accordantly with the workings of a remorseful conscience.

But a portion of the modern world have made use of Christianity itself to undermine the very foundations of Christianity. The Christian religion, by *furnishing* that one great sacrifice and real atonement, to which all other sacrifices look and point, has of course abolished the system of external sacrifices, and now that class of minds who live under its outward and civilizing influences without appropriating its inward and spiritual blessings, reject the legal and judicial elements which it contains, and deny the necessity of satisfying justice in the plan of redemption. There is nothing in the religious rites and customs under which they live to elicit the sense of guilt; and hence, from an inadequate knowledge of their own consciences and a defective apprehension of Christianity, they strenuously combat that fundamental truth, "without the shedding of blood there is no remission," upon which Christianity itself is founded, and in reference to which alone it has any worth or preciousness for a guilt-smitten soul.

The same tendency to underestimate the fact of human criminality, and the value of the piacular provision for it in the gospel, is seen also in the individual. How difficult it is to bring the person, for whose spiritual interests we are anxious, to see himself in the light of law and condemnation! How we ourselves shrink from the clear, solemn assertion of his culpability, and turn aside to enlarge upon the unworthiness or the unhappiness of his sin! When we make the attempt to charge home guilt upon him, how lacking we are in that tender solemnity, and earnest truthfulness of tone, which make the impression! And, even if we have succeeded in wakening his conscience to a somewhat normal action in this respect, how swiftly does he elude the terrible but righteous feeling, which alone can prepare him for the sprinkling of the blood of Jesus!

When we pass up into the Christian experience, we discover the same fact in a different form and degree. How difficult does the believer find it to obtain such a clear and transparent conception of his own guiltiness, that the atoning work of his Redeemer becomes all luminous before his eyes, and he knows instantaneously that he needs it, and that it is all he needs! Usually, this crystal clearness of vision is reserved for certain critical moments in his religious history, when he must have it or die. Usually it is the hour of affliction, or sickness, or death, that affords this rare and unutterably tranquillizing view of the guilty self and the dying Lord. "We have the *blood* of Christ," said the dying Schleiermacher, as, in his last moments, he began to count up the grounds of his confidence on the brink of the invisible world. Here was a mind uncommonly contemplative and profound; that had made the spiritual world its home, as it were, for many long years of theological study and reflection; that, in its tone and temper, seemed to be prepared to pass over into the supernatural realm without any misgivings or apprehensions; that had mused long and speculated subtly upon the nature of moral evil; that had sounded the depths of reason and revelation with no short plummet-line, — here was a man who, now that death had actually come, and the responsible human will must now encounter Holy Justice face to face, found that nothing but the *blood*, the *atonement*, of Jesus Christ could calm the perturbations of his planet-like spirit. The errors and inadequate statements of his theological system, which cluster mostly about this very doctrine of expiation, are tacitly renounced in the implied confession of guiltiness and need of atonement, contained these few simple words: "We have the BLOOD of Christ."

It is related that bishop Butler, in his last days drawing nearer to that dread tribunal where the highest and the lowest must alike stand in judgment, trembled in spirit, and turned this way and that for tranquillity of conscience. One of his clergy, among other texts, quoted to him the words: "The *blood* of Jesus Christ cleanseth from all sin." A flush of peace and joy passed, like the bland west wind, through his fevered conscience, as he made answer: "I have read those words a thousand times, but I never felt their meaning as now." And who does not remember that the final hours of the remarkably earnest, but too legal, life of the great English Moralist were lighted up with a peace that he had never been able to attain in the days of his health, by the evangelism of a humble curate?

Such facts and phenomena as these, evince that it is difficult for man to know sin as guilt, and thoroughly to apprehend Christ as a Priest and a Sacrifice. But one of the best correctives of this tendency to underestimate both guilt and expiation, is found in the clear perception that the two are *necessarily* related to each other, and that consequently the death of the Redeemer has nothing arbitrary in it. When one is convinced that Christ "*must needs* have suffered," he is relieved from the doubts respecting the meaning and efficacy of the atonement, and surrenders his conscience directly to its pacifying influence and power. He that *doubteth* is damned, in this respect also. The least shaking of belief that this great gospel provision is absolutely necessary, if sinners are to be saved; the faintest querying whether it may not, in the nature of things, have been a superfluity; so far as it tends at all, tends to dull the edge of man's contrition, and destroy the keenness of his sense of the Divine pity.

It has often been remarked, that the Passion of the Redeemer performs two functions. It not merely removes the sense of guilt, but it also elicits it. The experience of the Moravian missionaries is frequently cited to prove that a contemplation of the sufferings and death of Christ sometimes accomplishes what the naked exhibition of the law fails to accomplish, in bringing men to a sense of their sinfulness. The stern commandment had been applied to the hardened conscience of the savage, and iron met iron. The pity of a dying, atoning High Priest was shown, and the rock gushed out water. And such, undoubtedly, is often the case in the history of conversions. But shall we not find in this instance, also, that the force and energy of the impression made, results from a perception, more or less clear, that this death of the Substitute was *inexorably necessary*, in order to the criminal's release? The operations of the human mind are wonderfully swift, and difficult to follow or trace. Though the Esquimaux passed through no long process of reasoning, he *felt in his conscience* the unavoidableness of that mysterious Passion of that mysterious Person, in case his own wicked soul was to be spared the just inflictions of the future. By a very rapid but perfectly legitimate conclusion, he inferred the magnitude of his guilt from the greatness and necessity of the expiation. For suppose the lurking query, to which we have alluded, had sprung up in his mind just at this moment, and instead of the felt necessity of an atoning sacrifice, the faint querying had arisen whether his sin were not venial without the satisfaction of justice, would he have *instantaneously* melted down in contrition? So long as men are possessed with the feeling that the New Testament method of salvation is an abitrary one, containing elements and provisions that might have been different, or that are superfluous, they will receive little or no moral impression from it. But when they see plainly, that in all its parts and particles it refers directly to what is ethical in both themselves and the Eternal Judge, and is necessitated by the best portion of their own constitution, and by the perfect nature of the Godhead, they will then draw a very quick and accurate inference with respect to the intrinsic nature of that transgression which has introduced such a dire and stark necessity. When a man realizes that the great and eternal God cannot pardon his individual sins except through a passion that wrings great drops of blood from every pore of incarnate Deity, he realizes what is involved in the transgression of moral law.

2. A second obvious inference from the doctrine, that the sacrifice of Christ is a satisfaction for both the Divine and the human nature, is, that such an atonement is thorough and complete. It leaves nothing unsatisfied, or dissatisfied, either in God's holy nature or in man's moral sense. The work is ample and reliable.

This is a feature of the utmost value and importance in a scheme of Redemption. For no method will be put to a more fiery trial, ultimately, than the gospel method of salvation. It undergoes some severe tests here in time. The dying-bed draped with the recollection of past sins and transgressions, the pangs of remorse shooting through the conscience, and the fears for the future undulating through the whole being,—all this solemn experience before the soul shoots the gulf between time and eternity, calls for a most "*sovereign* remedy." And we may be certain that the disclosures and revelations that are to be made in the other world, and particularly upon the day of judgment, will subject the atoning work of the Redeemer to tests and trials such as no other work, and especially no "dead work" of a moralist, can endure for an instant. The energy of justice, and the energy of conscience, and the power of memory, and the searchings of God the Holy Ghost, will at that bar reach their height and combination; and any provision that shall legitimately countervail that energy, and enable the human soul to stand tranquil under such revelations, and beneath such claims, will be infinite and omnipotent indeed. But the believer need never fear lest the work of the Eternal Word, who was made flesh, the co-equal Son of the Eternal Father, prove inadequate under even such crucial tests. He needs only fear lest his feeble, wavering faith grasp it too insecurely. If he does but set his feet upon it, he will find it the Rock of Ages. *All* judicial claims are cancelled, because the oblation to justice is an infinite one. "There is *no* condemnation to them which are in Christ Jesus."*

For we have seen that the very mercy of God, in the last analysis, consists in the entire satisfaction of God's justice by God himself, for the helpless criminal. What method of Redemption can be conceived of, more perfectly sure and trustworthy than this? "What com-

* Michael Angelo, that loftiest and most religious of artists, gives expression, in the following sonnet, to this natural shrinking of the soul in

passion," says Anselm, "can equal the words of God the Father addressed to the sinner condemned to eternal punishment, and having no means of redeeming himself: 'Take my only-begotten Son, and make him an offering for thyself;' or the words of the Son: 'Take me and ransom thy soul?' For this is what both say, when they invite and draw us to faith in the gospel. And can anything be more just than for God to remit all debt, when in this way he receives a satisfaction greater than all the debt, provided only it be offered with the right feeling?"* "The pardon of sin," says an old English divine, "is not merely an act of mercy, but also an act of justice in God." By this he means that mercy and justice are concurrent in the gospel method of Redemption,—mercy satisfies justice, and justice acknowledges the satisfaction. "What abundant cause of comfort," he adds, "may this be to all believers, that God's justice as well as his mercy shall acquit them! that that attribute of God, at the apprehension of which they are wont to tremble, should interpose on their

view of the fiery judicial trial that awaits it, and also to the cheerful reassurance induced by the recollection of Christ's Passion:

> "Despite thy promises, O Lord, 't would seem
> Too much to hope that even love like Thine
> Can overlook my countless wanderings:
> And yet Thy *blood* helps us to comprehend
> That if Thy pangs for us were measureless,
> No less beyond all measure is thy grace."
> *Harford's Life of Angelo*, II. 166.

How immensely deeper is the intuition of divine things, how immensely clearer is the insight into the nature and mutual relations of God and man, which is indicated by such a sonnet from the soul of him who poised the dome of St. Peter's. and crowded the frescoes of the Sistine chapel with grandeur and beauty, than that of the modern brood of *dilettanti*, as expressed in much of the current literature, and the current art.

* *Cur Deus homo?* II. 20.

behalf, and plead for them! And yet through the all-sufficient expiation and atonement that Christ hath made for our sins, this mystery is effected, and justice itself brought over, from being a formidable adversary, to be our party, and to plead for us. Therefore the apostle tells us that God is faithful and *just* to forgive us our sins."*

Consonant with this is the well-known language of the elder Edwards: "It is," he says, "so ordered now, that the glory of the attribute of Divine justice requires the salvation of those that believe. The justice of God that [irrespective of the atonement] required man's damnation, and seemed inconsistent with his salvation, now [having respect to the atonement] as much requires the salvation of those that believe in Christ [and thereby appropriate the atonement], as ever before it required their damnation. Salvation is an absolute debt to the believer from God, so that he may in justice demand it on the ground of what his Surety has done."† Do these last words sound rash? But scruti-

* *Bp. Ezekiel Hopkins's Exposition of the Lord's Prayer.* Works, I. 124.

† Works, IV. 150. New York Ed. For the soteriology of this eminent writer, see his discourses on "Justification by Faith alone," "The wisdom of God displayed in the way of salvation," and "Satisfaction for sin." Among his positions are the following: Justification frees from all obligation to eternal punishment (IV. 78, 104, 150). Christ's suffering is equivalent to the eternal suffering of a finite creature (IV. 101, 551). Christ experienced the wrath of God (IV. 182, 195). God's wrath is appeased by the atonement (IV. 142). God cannot accept an atonement that falls short of the full claims of justice (IV. 94). The voluntary substitute is, in this capacity, under obligation to suffer the punishment due to the sinner (IV. 96, 137). Justice does not abate any of its claims in the plan of redemption (IV. 140, 552). Christ satisfied "revenging," or distributive, justice (IV. 150, 189).

Samuel Hopkins is equally explicit in maintaining the theory of a strict satisfaction, as is evident from the following: "One important and necessary part of the work of the Redeemer of man was to make atonement

nize them. "Salvation is an absolute debt to the believer *on the ground of what his Surety has done;*" not on the ground, therefore, of anything that the believer has done. It is merely saying, that the soul which feels its own desert of damnation, may plead the merit of Christ with entire confidence that it cancels *all* legal claims, and that there is nothing outstanding and un-

for their sins, by *suffering in his own person the penalty or curse of the law,* under which, by transgression, they had fallen . . . . The sufferings of Christ were, therefore, for sin, and consequently must be *the evil which sin deserves,* and that to which the sinner was exposed, and which he must have suffered had not Christ suffered it in his stead, or that which is equivalent. . . . . The Mediator did not suffer precisely the same kind of pain, in all respects, which the sinner suffers when the curse is executed on him. He did not suffer that particular kind of pain which is the necessary attendant, or natural consequence, of being a sinner, and which none but the sinner can suffer. But this is only a circumstance of the punishment of sin, and not of the essence of it. *The whole penalty of the law may be suffered, and the evil suffered may be as much, and as great, without suffering that particular sort of pain.* Therefore, Christ, though without sin, might suffer the *whole penalty,* — that is, *as much and as great evil* as the law denounces against transgression. The evil which sinners may suffer, on whom the penalty of the law is inflicted, may, and doubtless will, differ in many circumstances, and not be precisely of the same kind in all respects, and yet each one of them suffer the penalty of the same law . . . . The evil of the sufferings of Christ, being, in the magnitude of it, commensurate with the dignity and worth of his person, *is equal to, is as great as, the evil which is threatened to the transgressors of the law, and as great as the sinner deserves;* yea, it is as great as the endless sufferings of mankind . . . . The curse of the law consists in the infinite evil, pain, and suffering which sin deserves. He who suffers this for sin, suffers the curse of the law, is accursed, or made a curse. *Jesus Christ suffered this curse, the infinite natural evil in which the penalty or the curse of the law consists;* and in suffering it for sinners, and in their stead, was made a curse. This might be consistent with his having the approbation of the Father, and his favor and love to the highest degree. The displeasure of God, which was the cause of his sufferings when he voluntarily took, and stood in, the place of sinners, was displeasure with sin and the sinner, and not with him who suffered, the state of the case being fully understood by the spectators . . . . It is evident from scripture, that the law of God does admit of a substitute, both in obeying the precepts, and suffering the penalty of it." — *Hopkins's Works,* I. pp. 321—341. Doctrinal Tract Society's Ed.

covered by that Divine atonement upon which it relies for justification. It is simply asserting that God incarnate, the redeeming Deity, can demand, upon principles of justice, the release of a soul that trusts solely in his atoning death; because by that death he has *completely*, and not partially, satisfied eternal justice for it, and in its stead.* They are the bold words of a very cautious

* It is needless to remark, that Edwards does not concede that the mere atonement itself gives any and every man *a claim upon God for the benefits of the atonement*, — as is sometimes argued by the advocates of universal salvation. God is under no obligation to make an atonement for the sin of the world; and, *after he has made one, he is at perfect liberty to apply it to whom he pleases, or not to apply it at all.* The atonement is *his*, and not man's, and he may do what he will with his own. Hence, according to Edwards, two distinct acts of sovereignty on the part of God are necessary in order to a soul's salvation. The providing of an atonement in the first place, is a sovereign act; and then the application, or giving over, of the atonement, when provided, to any particular elected sinner, is a second act of sovereignty. The sufferings and death of Christ constitute the atonement; and even if not a single soul should appropriate it by the act of faith, it would be the same expiatory oblation still, though unapplied. Hence, the second of these sovereign acts is as necessary as the first, in order to salvation. But when *both* of these acts of sovereignty *have taken place*, — when the atonement has been made, and has actually been given over to and accepted by an individual, — *then*, says Edwards, it is a matter of strict justice that the penal claims of the law be not exacted from the believer, because this would be to exact them twice; once from Christ, and once from one to whom, by the supposition, Christ's satisfaction has actually been made over by a sovereign act of God. For God to do this, would be to pour contempt upon his own atonement. It would be a confession that his own provision is *insufficient* to satisfy the claims of law, and needs to be supplemented by an additional infliction upon the believer. It would be an acknowledgment that the atonement, when it comes to be actually tested in an individual instance, fails to satisfy the claims of justice, and therefore is an entire failure. The sum of money which was given to the poor debtor, with the expectation that it was large enough completely to liquidate his debt, is found to fall short, and leaves him still in the debtor's prison, from which he cannot come out "until he has paid the uttermost farthing."

That this is a correct representation of the views of Edwards is evident from the following answer which he gives to the question: What does God's sovereignty in the salvation of man imply? — "God's sovereignty

and accurate thinker; but are they any bolder than that challenging jubilant shout of St. Paul: "Who is he that condemeth? It is CHRIST that died." As if, flinging his voice out into all worlds, and all universes, he asked: "What claims are those which the blood of the Eternal Son of God has not been able to satisfy? Is the atonement of the great God Himself not equal to the demands of his law? Is the Deity feebler upon the side of his expiation, than upon the side of his retribution?"

It is a false humility, and not unmingled with a legal spirit, that would prevent the believer from joining in these bold and confident statements respecting the amplitude and completeness of the work of his atoning Lord and God. He need be under no concern lest he underestimate the attribute of justice, if he make this hearty and salient evangelical feeling his own. He disparages no attribute of God, when he magnifies and makes his boast in the atonement of God. Christ was equal to all he undertook; and he undertook to satisfy the claims of the Divine law for the sin of the world, down to the *least jot and tittle*; to pay the immense debt

in the salvation of men implies that God can either bestow salvation on any of the children of men, or refuse it, without any prejudice to the glory of any of his attributes, *except where he has been pleased to declare that he will or will not bestow it.* It cannot be said absolutely, as the case *now* stands, that God can, without any prejudice to the honor of *any* of his attributes, bestow salvation on any of the children of men, or refuse it, because concerning some, God has been pleased to declare either that he will or that he will not bestow salvation on them; and thus *to bind himself* by his own promise. And concerning some he has been pleased to declare that he never will bestow salvation upon them; viz., those who have committed the sin against the Holy Ghost. Hence, as the case *now* stands, he is obliged; he cannot bestow salvation in one case, or refuse it in the other, without prejudice to the honor of his *truth.* But God exercised his sovereignty *in making these declarations.* God was not obliged to promise that he would save all who believe in Christ; nor was he obliged to declare that he who committed the sin against the Holy Ghost should never be forgiven. But *it pleased him so to declare.*" — *Edwards's Works*, IV. 530. N. Y. Ed.

to the *uttermost farthing*. "Think not," he says, "that I am come to destroy the law or the prophets. I am not come to destroy, but to *fulfil.* For verily I say unto you, Till heaven and earth pass, one jot or one tittle shall in no wise pass from the law till *all* be fulfilled." And the incarnate Deity did what he undertook. He had a view of the extent and spirituality of law, and of the demerit of sin, such as no finite mind is capable of entertaining, and he knew whereof he affirmed when, at the close of his life of sorrow and his death of passion and agony, he bowed his head and gave up the ghost, with the words, significant beyond all conception: "*It is finished,*— the oblation is complete." Jesus Christ, the God-Man, in the garden of Gethsemane and on the middle cross of Calvary, had a conception of the rigor of justice and the exaction of law, such as no human or angelic mind can ever have in equal degree; and the believer may be certain that when HE invites him to rest his complete justification, and the entire satisfaction of all judicial claims, before that law, upon what HE has wrought in reference to it, he is not invited to a procedure that will be a disparagement, or dishonor, either to law or to justice.

Man is not straitened in the atoning work of incarnate Deity. He is straitened in his own blind and unbelieving soul. He only needs to take a profound view of justice, a profound view of sin, and a profound view of God's atonement for it, to come out into a region of peace, liberty, and joy unspeakable. Feeble views upon any one of these subjects debilitate his Christianity. He should distinctly see how sacred is the nature of justice, and how indefeasible are its claims. He should distinctly feel the full impression and energy of this attribute. Then he should as distinctly see how complete and perfect is the liquidation of these holy claims, by the death of the incarnate Son of God, — that august Personage denominated by the prophet as "the Wonderful, the Counsellor, the Mighty God, the Everlasting Father, the Prince of Peace."

That very interesting mystic of the Middle Ages, Henry Von Suso, enlarging in his poetic manner upon the compassion of God towards a sinful world, tells us that the "blood of Christ is full of love and red as a rose."* This roseate conception of the atonement is not the one that will meet the necessities of man's conscience, in the solemn hour of his mental anguish and his moral fear. There is love unutterable in that blood, but it was wrung from a heart to which all merely *sentimental* affection was as alien as it is to the vengeance of eternal fire. He only can appreciate and understand that love of principle, that love of self-immolation, who sympathizes thoroughly with that regard for the holiness and justice of God, united with compassion for lost souls, that led the Redeemer to undertake the full expiation of human guilt.

Whoever is granted this clear crystalline vision of the atonement, will die in peace, and pass through all the unknown transport and terror of the day of doom with serenity and joy. It ought to be the toil and study of the believer to render his conceptions of the work of Christ more vivid, simple, and vital. For whatever may be the extent of his religious knowledge in other directions; whatever may be the worth of his religious experience in other phases; there is no knowledge and no experience that will stand him in such stead, in those moments that try the soul, as the experience of the pure sense of guilt quenched by the pure blood of Christ.

* "Minnerichen, rosenfarbenen Blute."

ELLICOTT'S COMMENTARY, CRITICAL AND GRAMMATICAL, on St. Paul's Epistle to the Galatians. With an Introductory Notice by C. E. STOWE, Professor in Andover Theological Seminary. 8vo. pp. 183. $1 75.

The Commentaries of Prof. Ellicott supply an urgent want in their sphere of criticism. Prof. Stowe says of them, in his Notice: "It is the crowning excellence of these Commentaries that they are exactly what they profess to be, *critical* and *grammatical*, and therefore, in the best sense of the term, *exegetical*. . . . . . His results are worthy of all confidence. He is more careful than Tischendorf, slower and more steadily deliberate than Alford, and more patiently laborious than any other living New Testament critic, with the exception, perhaps, of Tregelles."

"They [Ellicott's Commentaries] have set the first example, in this country, [England] of a thorough and fearless examination of the grammatical and philological requirements of every word of the sacred text. I do not know of anything superior to them, in their own particular line, in Germany; and they add, what, alas! is so seldom found in that country, profound reverence for the matter and subjects on which the author is laboring; nor is their value lessened by Mr. Ellicott's having confined himself for the most part to one department of a commentator's work — the grammatical and philological." — *Dean Alford.*

"The *critical* part is devoted to the settling of the text, and this is admirably done, with a labor, skill, and conscientiousness unsurpassed." — *Bib. Sacra.*

"We have never met with a learned commentary on any book of the New Testament so nearly perfect in every respect as the 'Commentary on the Epistle to the Galatians,' by Prof. Ellicott, of King's College, London, — learned, devout, and orthodox." — *Independent.*

"We would recommend all scholars of the original Scriptures who seek directness, luminous brevity, the absence of everything irrelevant to strict grammatical inquiry, with a concise and yet very complete view of the opinions of others, to possess themselves of Ellicott's Commentaries." — *American Presbyterian.*

COMMENTARY ON EPHESIANS. 8vo. pp. 190. $1.75.

COMMENTARY ON THESSALONIANS. 8vo. pp. 171. $1.75.

COMMENTARY ON THE PASTORAL EPISTLES. 8vo. $2.50.

COMMENTARY ON PHILIPPIANS, COLOSSIANS, AND PHILEMON. $2.50.

THE SET in five vols., on fine paper, extra cloth, bevelled, gilt tops. $12.00.
THE SET in two vols., black cloth $ 8.00.

HENDERSON ON THE MINOR PROPHETS. THE BOOK OF THE TWELVE MINOR PROPHETS. Translated from the Original Hebrew. With a Commentary, Critical, Philological, and Exegetical. By E. HENDERSON, D.D. With a Biographical Sketch of the Author, by E. P. BARROWS, Hitchcock Professor in Andover Theological Seminary. 8vo. pp. 490. $4.00.

"This Commentary on the Minor Prophets, like that on the Prophecy of Isaiah, has been highly and deservedly esteemed by professional scholars, and has been of great service to the working ministry. We are happy to welcome it in an American edition, very neatly printed." — *Bib. Sacra.*

"Clergymen and other students of the Bible will be glad to see this handsome American edition of a work which has a standard reputation in its department, and which fills a place that is filled, so far as we know, by no other single volume in the English language. Dr. Henderson was a good Hebrew and Biblical scholar, and in his Commentaries he is intelligent, brief, and to the point." — *Boston Recorder.*

"The American publisher issues this valuable work with the consent and approbation of the author, obtained from himself before his death. It is published in substantial and elegant style, clear white paper and beautiful type. The work is invaluable for its philological research and critical acumen. The notes are learned, reliable, and practical, and the volume deserves a place in every theological student's library." — *American Presbyterian, etc.*

"Of all his Commentaries none are more popular than his Book of the Minor Prophets." — *Christian Observer.*

"This is probably the best Commentary extant on the Minor Prophets. The work is worthy of a place in the library of every scholar and every diligent and earnest reader of the Bible." — *Christian Chronicle.*

COMMENTARY ON THE EPISTLE TO THE ROMANS. By MOSES STUART, late Professor of Sacred Literature in the Theological Seminary at Andover. Third Edition. Edited and revised by PROF. R. D. C. ROBBINS. 12mo. pp. 544. $2.25.

"His Commentary on the Romans is the most elaborate of all his works. It has elicited more discussion than any of his other exegetical volumes. It is the result of long continued, patient thought. It expresses, in clear style, his maturest conclusions. It has the animating influence of an original treatise, written on a novel plan, and under a sense of personal responsibility. Regarding it in all its relations, its antecedents and consequents, we pronounce it the most important Commentary which has appeared in this country on this Epistle."— *Bib. Sacra.*

"We heartily commend this work to all students of the Bible. The production of one of the first Biblical scholars of our age, on the most important of all the doctrinal books of the New Testament, it deserves the careful study, not only of those who agree with Prof. Stuart in his theological and exegetical principles, but of those who earnestly dissent from some of his views in both respects." — *Watchman and Reflector.*

"This contribution by Prof. Stuart has justly taken a high place among the Commentaries on the Epistle to the Romans, and, with his other works, will always be held in high estimation by the student of the Sacred Scriptures." — *New York Observer.*

COMMENTARY ON THE EPISTLE TO THE HEBREWS. By PROF. M. STUART. Third Edition. Edited and revised by PROF. R. D. C. ROBBINS. 12mo. pp. 575. $2.25.

"It is a rich treasure for the student of the original. As a commentator, Prof. Stuart was especially arduous and faithful in following up the thought and displaying the connection of a passage, and his work as a scholar will bear comparison with any that have since appeared on either side of the Atlantic." — *American Presbyterian.*

"This Commentary is classical, both as to its literary and its theological merits. The edition before us is very skilfully edited, by Professor Robbins, and gives in full Dr. Stuart's text, with additions bringing it down to the present day." — *Episcopal Recorder.*

"We have always regarded this excellent Commentary as the happiest effort of the late Andover Professor. It seems to us well-nigh to exhaust the subjects which the author comprehended in his plan." — *Boston Recorder.*

"It is from the mind and heart of an eminent Biblical scholar, whose labors in the cause of sacred learning will not soon be forgotten." — *Christian Observer.*

COMMENTARY ON THE BOOK OF PROVERBS. By PROF. M. STUART. 12mo. pp. 432. $1.75.

"This is the last work from the pen of Prof. Stuart. Both this Commentary and the one preceding it, on Ecclesiastes, exhibit a mellowness of spirit which savors of the good man ripening for heaven; and the style is more condensed, and, in that respect, more agreeable, than in some of the works which were written in the unabated freshness and exuberant vigor of his mind. In learning and critical acumen they are equal to his former works. No English reader, we venture to say, can elsewhere find so complete a philological exposition of these two important books of the Old Testament." — *Bib. Sacra.*

COMMENTARY ON ECCLESIASTES. By MOSES STUART, late Professor of Sacred Literature in the Theological Seminary at Andover. Second Edition. Edited and revised by R. D. C. ROBBINS, Professor in Middlebury College. 12mo. $1.50.

The Introduction discusses the general nature of the book; its special design and method, diction, authority, credit, and general history; ancient and modern versions, and commentaries. The Commentary is strictly and minutely exegetical.

STUART'S MISCELLANIES. pp. 369. 12mo. $1.00.

CONTENTS. — I. Letters to Dr. Channing on the Trinity. — II. Two Sermons on the Atonement. — III. Sacramental Sermon on the Lamb of God. — IV. Dedication Sermon. — Real Christianity. — V. Letter to Dr. Channing on Religious Liberty. — VI. Supplementary Notes and Postscripts.

COMMENTARY ON THE APOCALYPSE. 2 vols. 8vo. pp. 504, 504. $5.00.

CRITICAL HISTORY AND DEFENCE OF THE OLD TESTAMENT CANON. 12mo. pp. 450. $1.50.

GUERICKE'S CHURCH HISTORY. Translated by W. G. T. Shedd, Brown Professor in Andover Theological Seminary. 449 pp. 8vo. $3.00.

This volume includes the period of the Ancient Church (the first six centuries, A. C.) or the Apostolic and Patristic Church.

We regard Professor Shedd's version, now under notice, as a happy specimen of the transfusion rather than a translation, which many of the German treatises should receive. The style of his version is far superior to that of the original.— [Bib. Sacra, Jan. 1858.

The established credit of Guericke's labors in the department of Ecclesiastical History, and the use made of his works by many English writers will make this volume acceptable to a very large class of students and readers. — *London Journal of Sacred Literature.*

Guericke's History is characterized by research, devoutness, firm grasp of evangelical truth, and careful exhibition of the practical as well as the intellectual aspects of Christianity. — *North British Review.*

DISCOURSES AND ESSAYS. By Prof. W. G. T. Shedd. 271 pp. 12mo. $1.50.

Few clearer and more penetrating minds can be found in our country than that of Prof. Shedd. And besides, he writes with a chaste and sturdy eloquence, transparent as crystal; so that if he goes deep, we love to follow him. If the mind gets dull, or dry, or ungovernable, put it to grappling with these masterly productions. — [Congregational Herald, Chicago.

The striking sincerity, vigor, and learning of this volume will be admired even by those readers who cannot go with the author in all his opinions. Whatever debate the philosophical tendencies of the book may challenge, its literary ability and moral spirit will be commended every where. — *New Englander.*

These discourses are all marked by profound thought and perspicuity of sentiment. — *Princeton Review.*

LECTURES UPON THE PHILOSOPHY OF HISTORY. By Prof. W. G. T. Shedd. 128 pp. 12mo. 75 cents.

Contents. — The abstract Idea of History. — The Nature and Definition of Secular History. — The Nature and Definition of Church History. — The Verifying Test in Church History.

The style of these Lectures has striking merits. The author chooses his words with rare skill and taste, from an ample vocabulary, and writes with strength and refreshing simplicity. The Philosophy of Realism, in application to history and historical theology, is advocated by vigorous reasoning, and made intelligible by original and felicitous illustrations. — *New Englander.*

Professor Shedd has already achieved a high reputation for the union of philosophic insight with genuine scholarship, of depth and clearness of thought with force and elegance of style, and for profound views of sin and grace, cherished not merely on theoretical, but still more on moral and experimental grounds. — *Princeton Review.*

OUTLINES OF A SYSTEMATIC RHETORIC. From the German of Dr. Francis Theremin, by William G. T. Shedd. Third and Revised Edition, with an Introductory Essay by the translator. pp. 216. 12mo. $1.00.

This is a work of much solid value. It is adapted to advanced students, and can be read and reread with advantage by professed public speakers, however accomplished they may be in the important art of persuasion. This edition is an improvement upon the other, containing a new introductory essay, illustrating the leading position of the work, and a series of questions adapting it to the use of the student. — *Boston Recorder.*

It is not a work of surface suggestions, but of thorough and philosophic analysis, and, as such, is of great value to the student, and especially to him who habitually addresses men on the most important themes. — *Congregational Quarterly.*

The Introductory Essay which Professor Shedd has prefixed to this valuable Treatise, is elaborate, vigorous, impressive. It excites the mind not only to thought, but also to the expression of thought, to inward and outward activity. The whole volume is characterized by freshness and originality of remark, a purity and earnestness of moral feeling. — *Bib. Sacra,* 1859.

THEOLOGIA GERMANICA. Which setteth forth many fair lineaments of Divine Truth, and saith very lofty and lovely things touching a Perfect Life. Edited by DR. PFEIFFER, from the only complete manuscript yet known. Translated from the German by SUSANNA WINKWORTH. With a Preface by the REV. CHARLES KINGSLEY, Rector of Eversley; and a Letter to the Translator, by the CHEVALIER BUNSEN, D. D., D. C. L., etc.; and an Introduction by PROF. CALVIN E. STOWE, D. D. 275 pp. 16mo. Cloth, $1.50.

This treatise was discovered by Luther, who first brought it into notice by an edition which he published in 1516, of which he says: "And I will say, though it be boasting of myself, and 'I speak as a fool,' that, next to the Bible and St. Augustine, no book hath ever come into my hands whence I have learnt, or would wish to learn, more of what God and Christ, and man, and all things, are."

"The times and the circumstances in which this most rich, thoughtful, and spiritually quickening little treatise was produced, — the national and ecclesiastical tendencies and influences which invested its author, and which gave tone, direction, and pressure to his thoughts, — are amply and well set forth in the preface by Miss Winkworth, and the letter of Bunsen. The treatise itself is richly deserving of the eulogies upon it so emphatically and affectionately uttered by Prof. Stowe and Mr. Kingsley, and, long before them, by Luther, who said that it had profited him 'more than any other book, save only the Bible and the works of Augustine.' Sin, as a universal disease and defilement of the nature of man; Christ, as an indwelling life, light, and heavenly power; Holiness, as the utmost good for the soul; and Heaven, as the state or place of the consummation of this holiness, with the consequent vision of God, and the ineffable joy and peace, — these are the theme of the book. And it has the grand, and in this day the so rare and almost singular merit, of having been prompted by a real and deep religious experience, and of having been written, not with outward assistance, but with the enthusiasm, the spiritual wisdom, and the immense inward freedom and energy, of a soul itself conscious of union with Christ, and exulting in the sense of being made, through him, 'a partaker of the Divine nature.'

"Those who have known the most of Christ will value most this "golden treatise." Those whose experience of the divine truth has been deepest and most central will find the most in it to instruct and to quicken them. To such it will be an invaluable volume worth thousands upon thousands of modern scientific or hortatory essays upon "Religion made easy."

"It is printed by Mr. Draper, at the Andover press, in the old English style, with beautiful carefulness and skill, and is sent, post paid, to all who remit him one dollar."— *Independent.*

"The work is at once a literary curiosity and a theological gem." — *Puritan Recorder.*

"This little volume, which is brought out in antique type, is, apart from its intrinsic value, a curiosity of literature. It may be regarded as the harbinger of the Protestant Reformation." — *Evening Traveller.*

THE CONFESSIONS OF ST. AUGUSTINE. Edited, with an Introduction, by Prof. W. G. T. SHEDD. $1.50.

"In this beautiful edition of Augustine's Confessions, published in the antique style, the translation has been carefully revised by Prof. Shedd, of Andover, from a comparison with the Latin text. His Introduction presents a fine analysis of Augustine's religious experience in its bearing upon his theological system. Both the intellect and the heart of the modern preacher may be refreshed and stimulated by the frequent perusal of these confessions." — *Independent.*

"Prof. Shedd has earned our heartfelt thanks for this elegant edition of Augustine's Confessions. The book is profitable for the Christian to study, and we would commend it as a daily companion in the closet of the intelligent believer who desires to be taught the way to holiness through communion of the Spirit. Prof. Shedd's Introduction is a masterly essay, which itself is a volume for attentive reading. It ought to be read before the book is begun. Thorough, searching, and discriminating beyond the facts it communicates, its instructions and hints are suggestive and invaluable." — *N. Y. Observer.*

"This is a beautiful edition of a precious work. The Confessions of Augustine are so honest, that we easily become enthusiastic in their praise. The depth of his piety, the boldness of his imagination, the profoundness of his genius, his extravagant conceptions, his very straining and stretching of philosophical and biblical statements, have all a certain charm which ensures for his works an enduring popularity."—*Bib. Sacra*, 1860, p. 671.

"We have long wanted to see just such an edition of Augustine's Confessions. The editor has done a public service in introducing it; and its typographical beauty is no small recommendation of it." — *Presbyterian,* June 23, 1860.

WORKS OF LEONARD WOODS, D. D. 5 vols. 8vo. $12.00.

Vols. I., II. and III., Lectures. — Vol. IV., Letters and Essays. — Vol. V. Essays and Sermons. A new Edition, on superior paper.

WORKS OF JESSE APPLETON, D. D., late President of Bowdoin College, embracing his Course of Theological Lectures, his Academic Addresses, and a selection from his Sermons, with a Memoir of his Life and Character. 2 Vols. 8vo. $3.00.

"They will ever form standard volumes in American Theological Literature." — *Biblical Repository*, 1837, p. 249.

AUGUSTINISM AND PELAGIANISM By G. F. WIGGERS, D. D. Translated from the German, by PROFESSOR R. EMERSON, D. D. pp. 383. 8vo. $1.50.

CODEX VATICANUS. Η ΚΑΙΝΗ ΔΙΑΘΗΚΗ. Novum Testamentum Graece, ex antiquissimo Codice Vaticano edidit Angelus Maius, S. R. E. Card. 8vo. $3.00.

Professor Tischendorf and Dr. Tregelles ascribe its date as early as to the middle of the fourth century. It has generally been held to be the most venerable manuscript of the New Testament. It has been guarded with great vigilance by the authorities of the Vatican. A thorough collation, even, has never before been permitted, though often sought. The present work is an exact reprint.

WRITINGS OF PROFESSOR B. B. EDWARDS. With a Memoir by PROF. EDWARDS A. PARK. 2 vols. 12mo. $3.00.

These works consist of seven Sermons, sixteen Essays, Addresses and Lectures, and a Memoir by Professor Park.

ERSKINE ON THE INTERNAL EVIDENCE FOR THE TRUTH OF REVEALED RELIGION. Third American, from the Fifth Edinburgh Edition. pp. 139. 16mo. 75 cts.

"The entire treatise cannot fail to commend the positions which it advocates to intelligent and considerate minds. It is one of the best, perhaps THE best, of all the discussions of this momentous subject." — *Congregationalist.*

"This argument of Erskine for the Internal Evidence of the Truth of Revealed Religion, is the most compact, natural, and convincing we have ever read from any author." — *Chris. Chron.*

"No man ought to consider himself as having studied theology unless he has read, and pondered, and read again, 'Erskine on the Internal Evidence.'" — *Independent.*

PLUTARCHUS DE SERA NUMINIS VINDICTA. Plutarch on the Delay of the Deity in the Punishment of the Wicked. With Notes by H. B. HACKETT, Professor of Biblical Literature in Newton Theological Institution. pp. 172. 12mo. 60 cents.

[See a review of this work in Bib. Sacra, p. 609, 1856.]

PUNCHARD'S VIEW OF CONGREGATIONALISM, its Principles and Doctrines, the Testimony of Ecclesiastical History in its favor, its Practice and its advantages. With an Introductory Essay by R. S. STORRS, D. D. Second edition. 16mo. pp. 331. 60 cents.

HISTORICAL DEVELOPMENT OF SPECULATIVE PHI-LOSOPHY FROM KANT TO HEGEL. From the German of DR. H. M. CHALYBAEUS. With an Introductory Note by SIR WILLIAM HAMILTON. pp. 413. 12mo. $1.50.

"One of the best of the many Introductions which have been prepared to lead the inquirer to a knowledge of the recent speculative philosophy." — *Bib. Sacra.*

"Those who are in search of knowledge on this perplexed subject, without having time to investigate the original sources for information, will receive great assistance from this careful, thorough, and perspicuous analysis." — *Biblical Repertory, and Princeton Review.*

MESSIANIC PROPHECY AND THE LIFE OF CHRIST. By Rev. W. S. KENNEDY. 12mo. pp. 484. $1.25.

"The plan of the author is to collect all the prophecies of the Old Testament referring to the Messiah, with appropriate comments and reflections, and then to pursue the subject through the New Testament in the life of Christ as he appeared among men. The reader will find the results of Hengstenberg and Neander here gathered up, and presented in a readable shape."—*The Presbyterian.*

"This is a work of great comprehensiveness. Here, in the compass of less than five hundred duodecimo pages, we have the Christology of the Old and New Testament Scriptures, something like a combination of the Christology of Hengstenberg and Neander's Life of Christ. Of course the fulness of these great works is not imitated, but the reader will find the results of these and similar investigations carefully gathered up, and presented in a clear, readable shape. The Life of Christ is based upon Robinson's Harmony of the Gospels."—*American Presbyterian.*

SCHAUFFLER'S MEDITATIONS ON THE LAST DAYS OF CHRIST. 12mo. pp. 439. $1.25.

The first sixteen chapters of the book consist of Meditations on the last days of Christ, preached in the midst of plague and death, by Rev. Mr. Schauffler, at Constantinople; the second part, of eight sermons on the 17th chapter of John, and is a practical exposition of that chapter.

BIBLE HISTORY OF PRAYER. By C. A. GOODRICH. 12mo. pp. 384. $1.25.

The aim of this little volume is to embody an account of the delightful and successful intercourse of believers with heaven for some four thousand years. The author has indulged a good deal in narrative, opening and explaining the circumstances which gave birth to the several prayers.

MONOD'S DISCOURSES ON THE LIFE OF ST. PAUL. Translated from the French, by Rev. J. H. MYERS, D.D. 12mo. pp. 191. 90cts.

"The aim of the author is to present an estimate of the character, labors, and writings of the apostle Paul in the light of an example, and to apply the principles which actuated him, and which he maintained, to Christians of the present day."—*Boston Journal.*

"These Discourses are distinguished for genuine eloquence, thorough research. and profound thought, accompanied with a glowing, earnest spirit, adapting the lessons of the great Apostle to the spiritual wants of men."—*Christian Observer.*

HYMNS AND CHOIRS: OR, THE MATTER AND THE MANNER OF THE SERVICE OF SONG IN THE HOUSE OF THE LORD. By AUSTIN PHELPS, and EDWARDS A. PARK, Professors at Andover, and DANIEL L. FURBER, Pastor at Newton. 12mo. pp. 425. $1 50.

This volume describes the true design and character of Hymns; it comments on their rhetorical structure and style; points out the proper method of uttering them in public worship; and the most important principles and rules for congregational singing.

SELECT SERMONS OF REV. WORTHINGTON SMITH. D. D. With a Memoir of his Life, by REV. JOSEPH TORREY, D. D., Professor in Burlington College. 12mo. pp. 380. $1.25.

"This is a memorial volume of Dr. Smith, late President of the Vermont University, and was prepared at the request of many of his friends. An interesting Memoir of his Life, edited by Rev. Joseph Torrey, D. D., Professor of Intellectual and Moral Philosophy, introduces the Sermons. Dr. Smith was a native of Hadley, Mass., and was for many years pastor over a religious society in St. Albans, Vermont. For six years he officiated as President of the Vermont University at Burlington, which office he resigned in consequence of ill health, and died a few months afterward. The Memoir is followed by sixteen Sermons on various subjects."—*Boston Daily Advertiser.*

THE DEBATE BETWEEN THE CHURCH AND SCIENCE; or, The Ancient Hebraic Idea of the Six Days of Creation. With an Essay on the Literary Character of TAYLER LEWIS. 12mo. pp. 437. $1.25.

DÖDERLEIN'S HAND-BOOK OF LATIN SYNONYMES. Translated by REV. H. H. ARNOLD, B. A., with an Introduction by S. H. TAYLOR, LL. D. New Edition, with an Index of Greek words. 16mo. pp. 267. 1.25.

"The present hand-book of Doderlein is remarkable for the brevity, distinctness, perspicuity, and appositeness of its definitions. It will richly reward not merely the classical, but the general student, for the labor he may devote to it. It is difficult to open the volume, even at random, without discovering some hint which may be useful to a theologian. . . . . From the preceding extracts, it will be seen that this hand-book is useful in elucidating many Greek as well as Latin synonymes." — *Bib. Sacra.*

"The little volume mentioned above, introduced to the American public by an eminent Scholar and Teacher, Samuel H. Taylor, LL. D., is one of the best helps to the thorough appreciation of the nice shades of meaning in Latin words that have met my eye. It deserves the attention of teachers and learners, and will amply reward patient study." — *E. D. Sanborn, late Professor of Latin in Dartmouth College.*

"The study of it will conduce much to thorough and accurate knowledge of the old Roman tongue. To the present edition is appended an 'Index of Greek words,' which embraces all the Greek words contained in the Latin Synonymes, and affords valuable aid in the elucidation of Greek Synonymes." — *Boston Recorder.*

POLITICAL ECONOMY. Designed as a Text-Book for Colleges. By JOHN BASCOM, A. M., Professor in Williams College. 12mo. pp. 366. $1.50.

"It goes over the whole ground in a logical order. The matter is perspicuously arranged under distinct chapters and sections; it is a compendious exhibition of the principles of the science without prolonged disquisitions on particular points, and it is printed in the style for which the Andover Press has long been deservedly celebrated." — *Princeton Review.*

"This work is one of value to the student. It treats of the relations and character of political economy, its advantages as a study, and its history. Almost every subject in the range of the science is here touched upon and examined in a manner calculated to interest and instruct the reader." — *Amherst Express.*

"The book is worthy a careful study, both for the views it contains and as a mental training. The author understands himself, and has evidently studied his subject well. The style in which it is put forth also commends it to the reading community." — *Evening Express.*

"This is a valuable work upon a subject of much interest. Professor Bascom writes well, and his book makes an excellent manual. His stand-point in the middle of the 19th century gives it a character quite unlike that of the older works upon the subject." — *Boston Recorder.*

RUSSELL'S PULPIT ELOCUTION. Comprising Remarks on the Effect of Manner in public Discourse; the Elements of Elocution applied to the Reading of the Scriptures, Hymns and Sermons; with Observations on the Principles of Gesture; and a Selection of Exercises in Reading and Speaking. With an Introduction by PROF. E. A. PARK and REV. E. N. KIRK. 413 pp. 12mo. Second Edition. $1.50.

"Mr. Russell is known as one of the masters of elocutionary science in the United States. He has labored long, skilfully, and successfully in that most interesting field, and has acquired an honored name among the teachers and writers upon rhetoric. It is one of the most thorough publications upon the subject, and is admirably addressed to the correction of the various defects which diminish the influence of pulpit discourses. It is already an established authority in many places." — *Literary World.*

HISTORICAL MANUAL OF THE SOUTH CHURCH IN ANDOVER, MASS. Compiled by REV. GEORGE MOOAR; with a portrait of REV. SAMUEL PHILLIPS, first Pastor of the Church. 12mo. pp 200. $1.25.

"This manual has a value far beyond the promise made in its title-page. Henceforth, whatever may befall the records of the South Church in Andover, or even the Church itself, — though both were blotted from the earth, — its history for a hundred and fifty years is safe. And in that history is embraced an amount of instruction rarely condensed into so small a space. The catalogue of members, numbering 2,177, indicates the date and manner of admission — whether by profession or letter; the date and manner of removal — whether by death, dismission, or excommunication: generally the age of the deceased, and, if females who married during their membership, the names of their husbands." — *Congregational Quarterly.*

www.ingramcontent.com/pod-product-compliance
Lightning Source LLC
LaVergne TN
LVHW020217110826
845151LV00003B/749

* 9 7 8 1 4 2 5 5 3 3 6 1 8 *